J

Life Incidents

Adventist Pioneer Library

37457 Jasper Lowell Rd
Jasper, OR, 97438, USA
+1 (877) 585-1111
www.APLib.org

Originally published in 1868 by Steam Press of the Seventh-day Adventist Publishing Association.

Published in the USA

April, 2017

ISBN: 978-1-61455-051-8

LIFE INCIDENTS,

IN CONNECTION WITH THE

GREAT ADVENT MOVEMENT,

AS ILLUSTRATED BY

THE THREE ANGELS

— OF —

REVELATION 14.

By ELDER JAMES WHITE.

"And he said unto me, Unto two thousand and three hundred days, then shall the sanctuary be cleansed." — DANIEL.

"And the angel which I saw stand upon the sea and upon the earth, lifted up his hand to heaven, and sware by Him that liveth forever and ever, who created Heaven, and the things that therein are, and the earth, and the things that therein are, and the sea, and the things which are therein, that there should be time no longer..... And he said unto me, Thou must prophesy again before many peoples, and nations, and tongues, and kings." — JOHN.

VOLUME ONE.

STEAM PRESS

OF THE SEVENTH-DAY ADVENTIST PUBLISHING ASSOCIATION,

BATTLE CREEK, MICH.

1868.

JAMES SPRINGER WHITE (1821-1881)

Contents

Preface

The writer of these pages does not entertain the idea that he has done justice to the subject upon which they treat. The field is a wide one, and to do the subject full justice, would require much time, and many volumes the size of this. And it has been while laboring with the churches in Michigan that these thoughts have been hastily gathered from personal knowledge and experience, and from the writings of those who were deeply imbued with the sweet spirit of revealed truth. More time, undivided attention to the subject, and more pages, would greatly improve the work. But even such as it is, it is commended to the prayerful consideration of the reader, in confidence that it is calculated to revive the Advent hope and faith in the hearts of the fainting, and to cheer way-worn pilgrims to Mount Zion, and lead them to take fresh courage in the Lord. And may it not also be hoped that this historical sketch of the great Advent movement will lead some to see the subject clearly in the light of the sacred Scripture and Christian experience, and embrace the truth of God.

The writer has passed rapidly over the incidents in his early life, and has given only those of later years, which were connected with the Advent cause. His object has been to give those facts only which would serve to honor and magnify the name and power of God in the exhibition of divine truth. The fact, however, that he has been connected with the Advent cause since 1842, may [6] serve as an apology for introducing some incidents of personal Second-Advent experience into this work.

It has been with great pleasure that the great Advent movement has been revived in the preparation of these pages. It has been an intellectual and spiritual feast. The fundamental principles of the glorious doctrine of the soon coming of Christ, never appeared more firmly established. And the facts in Second-Advent history, fulfilling prophecy, never seemed so important to the people of God, as an anchor in the perilous storms of these last days, as since examining anew this whole question. May God make this work as great a blessing to the reader as it has been made to the writer in its preparation.

J.W.

Ancestry and Early Life

I was born in Palmyra, Somerset County, Maine, August 4th, 1821. Bloomfield, Me., which now forms a part of Skowhegan, was the birthplace of my father, Deacon John White. At the age of twenty-one he commenced life in the new township of Palmyra. At that time there were but twenty acres of trees felled on his land. The old farm is situated on the west side of a body of water which is called, as seen upon the large map of Somerset County, White's Pond. On this farm he lived and labored fifty-one years. He has since spent one year and a half in Ohio, and seven years at Battle Creek, Michigan, where he now resides.

My father descended from one of the Pilgrims who came to America in the ship May Flower, and landed upon Plymouth Rock, December, 1620. On board that ship was the father of Peregrine White, who wore a pair of silver knee-buckles, such as may be seen in the picture of the venerable signers of the Declaration of Independence.

The knee-buckles worn by this man were afterward given to his son, Peregrine White, who was born on the passage to this country, with the request that they [10] should be handed down in this line of the White family to the eldest son of each successive generation, whose name should be called John. My father had those buckles thirty years. They were as familiar to me in my boyhood days as the buttons upon my coat. He gave them to my brother John, who has passed them down to his son John, a young man of eighteen years.

My father possessed from his youth great physical strength, and activity of body and mind. With his own hands he cleared the heavy timber from his land. This revealed stones in the soil, which his own hands removed and placed into stone fence, to prepare the way for the plow. He toiled on for more than half a century, till the rock-bound soil was literally worn out, and much of the old farm lost its power to produce crops.

At the age of seventy-four he left it and sought rest in the more congenial climate of the West.

His religious experience, of more than sixty years, has been marked with firmness and zeal, and yet with freedom from that bigotry which prevents investigation and advancement, and shuts out love for all who seek to worship God in spirit and in truth.

At the age of twenty-one he was sprinkled, and joined the Congregational church, but never felt satisfied that in being sprinkled he had received Christian baptism. Several years later, a Baptist minister came into that new part of the State and taught immersion. My father was immersed and became a Baptist deacon. Still later he embraced the views held by the Christian denomination, which were more liberal and scriptural than those of the Calvinistic Baptists of those days, and communed with that people. The Baptists called a special meeting. The minister and many of the church members were present. The minister invited several to [11] open the meeting with prayer, but each in his turn wished to be excused. He waited. Finally, my father opened the meeting. They then excluded him for communing with the Christians. The minister made an effort to have someone close the meeting. No one moved. My father closed their meeting with prayer, and left them with feelings of love and tenderness. He soon joined the Christian church, and served them as deacon nearly forty years. During this entire period he was present at every conference meeting held by the church, excepting one, which, according to their custom, was held on Saturday afternoon of every fourth week.

As early as 1842 my father read with deep interest the lectures of William Miller upon the second coming of Christ. He has ever since that time cherished faith in the leading points of the advent doctrine. In 1860, with my good mother, he embraced the Sabbath, and dwells upon the evidences of the Bible Sabbath with clearness and much pleasure.

My mother is a granddaughter of Dr. Samuel Shephard, one of the first and most eminent Baptist ministers of New England. She possessed great firmness of constitution, a good mind, and a most amiable disposition. Her entire religious experience, for more than sixty years, has been marked with a meek and quiet spirit, devotion to the cause of Christ, and a consistent walk and godly conversation.

My venerable parents have reached the good old age of more than fourscore years. They keep house alone, and enjoy as much of life as their advanced age will allow. Yet each year visibly brings them nearer the grave. God grant that as they are being gently lowered to its embrace, they may sweetly ripen for immortality, to be given at the soon coming of Christ. [12]

In my father's family I stood in the center of nine children, four above me and four below me. But this family chain is now much worn, and nearly half its links are broken. The four above me in years, all live. All below me sleep. Time, toil and care have made their unmistakable impress on the remaining five.

My remaining brothers are both ministers, one of the M.E. Church, of Ohio, the other of the regular Baptist, of Vermont. Two sisters live in Maine. One brother is supposed to have lost his life by the Indians, in returning from California. Another sleeps beside a sister in Mount Hope Cemetery, Rochester, N.Y., while another brother, who died at the age of three years, rests in the old burying-ground in Palmyra, Maine.

My parents say I was an extremely feeble child. And, what added greatly to my difficulties, and cut off their hopes of my life, when less than three years old, I had what the doctors called worm fever, resulting in fits, which turned my eyes and nearly destroyed my sight. I am reported to have been extremely cross-eyed — not naturally, but from affection of the nerves, — a feeble, nervous, partially-blind boy. These are sufficient reasons why I could not enjoy the common advantages of school. And not until I was sixteen years old, when my health and strength greatly improved, and my eyes became quite natural, could I read a single verse in the Testament without resting my eyes. I felt keenly the fact that I was behind my school-mates in education. And with the poor advantages of those times I could do but little toward making up the almost total loss of ten years. I grew rapidly, and at eighteen was ahead of my years in size and strength. This added to my embarrassment as I entered the Academy at St. Albans, Me., at the age of nineteen. I could not then work a [13] simple problem in single rule of three, and I could not tell a verb from an adverb or an adjective, and was deficient in the other common branches. My friends advised me to turn my attention to farming, and not think of seeking for an education. But I could not take their advice.

At the close of the term of twelve weeks, I received from the preceptor, C.F. Allen, a certificate of my qualifications to teach the common branches, and the winter following taught school. This required close study eighteen hours of each twenty-four. A victory was gained. Much of my time previous to this I had viewed myself as nearly worthless in the world, and regretted my existence. But now I was beginning to hope that I had powers to become a man. No privation nor hardship formed an obstacle in my way. My father gave me my time at nineteen, and a suit of clothes. All I asked of my parents in addition to this was three dollars to pay my tuition, and six days' rations of bread to take with me each Monday morning for three months, as I should walk five miles to the school.

At the close of my first term of school-teaching I again attended school at St. Albans five weeks, then shouldered my pack and walked to the Penobscot river, forty miles, to offer myself as a raw hand in a saw mill. In the mill I cut my ankle, which resulted in permanent weakness and occasional painful lameness in my left foot. For twenty-six years I have been unable to bear my weight upon my left heel.

At the end of four months I returned home. I had lost much time in consequence of the severe wound in my ankle joint, and after paying my board during the time lost, I had but thirty dollars and a scanty amount of worn clothing. In order to be qualified to teach a [14] school where I could get first-class wages, it was necessary for me to attend school. I therefore immediately packed up my books and humble apparel for the school at Reedfield, Me., then favorably known as being under the control and support of the Episcopal Methodists. During that term my object was to thoroughly qualify myself to teach the common branches. Besides these, I took up Natural Philosophy, Algebra, and Latin. At the close of that term I had conquered all the Arithmetics within my reach, was regarded as a good grammarian, was prepared to teach penmanship, and was told by my preceptor that I could fit for college in one year.

My thirst for education increased, and my plans were laid to take a college course and pay my way, if labor, economy, and study would accomplish it. I had but little else to thank but God and my own energies for what advancement I had made. At Reedfield I wore old clothes, while my class-mates wore new, and lived three months on corn-meal pudding prepared by myself, and a few raw apples, while they enjoyed the conveniences and luxuries of the boarding house.

With the close of this term, also closed my school studies. I have attended high school, in all, twenty-nine weeks, and the entire cost of tuition, books, and board, has not exceeded fifty dollars. My apology for being so definite in this part of my narrative, is a desire to help those young men who wish to obtain an education while suffering under the unfriendly influences of poverty and pride. A poor boy may obtain an education by calling to his aid industry, economy, and application to his books. Such an one will prize his education, and be likely to make a good use of it. While the young man who looks to his father's purse, puts on fine clothes, spends much of his time in fashionable calls, [15] and acts the part of the spendthrift, will not get a thorough education, and will probably make a poor use of what he does obtain.

The following winter, covering a part of 1840 and 1841, I taught a large school, and also gave lessons in penmanship in two districts. And with my winter's earnings in my pocket, I returned home with a firm purpose to pursue my studies.

Christian Experience

At the age of fifteen I was baptized, and united with the Christian church. But at the age of twenty I had buried myself in the spirit of study and school teaching, and had lain down the cross. I had never descended to the common sin of profanity, and had not used tobacco, tea and coffee, nor had I ever raised a glass of spirituous liquor to my lips. Yet I loved this world more than I loved Christ and the next, and was worshiping education instead of the God of Heaven. In this state of mind I returned home from my second and last school, when my mother said to me: "James, Bro. Oakes, of Boston, has been lecturing at our meeting-house on the second coming of Christ about the year 1843, and many believe the doctrine, and there has followed these lectures a good reformation, in which most of your mates have experienced religion."

I had regarded what was commonly called Millerism as wild fanaticism, and this impression was confirmed by hearing one James Hall, of Maine, speak upon the subject at the house of worship at Palmyra. But now that my mother, in whose judgement and piety I had reason to confide, spoke to me upon the subject in words of earnestness, candor and solemnity, I was shocked and [16] distressed. In spite of me, conviction would fasten upon my mind that these things might be so. But, then, how could I have it so? I was unprepared, and my plans for this life were made. The conversation continued:

"But, Mother, this preacher Oakes, of whom you speak, professes to know more than the Lord and his angels, in teaching the time of the second advent. Christ himself has said, 'But of that day and that hour knoweth no man, no, not the angels which are in Heaven; neither the Son, but the Father.' This man Oakes is certainly wise above that which is written."

"'As the days of Noe were, so shall also the coming of the Son of Man be.' God gave the time to Noah. The Bible says, 'My Spirit shall not always strive with man, for that he also is flesh; yet his days shall be an hundred and twenty years.' Genesis 6:3. Noah had this time given him in which to build the ark and warn the world. And his message, based upon the word of the Lord that a flood of water would destroy man and beast from off the face of the earth at the close of the one hundred and twenty years, condemned the world.

"Jesus also says in this connection, that there shall be signs in the sun, moon, and stars, and adds, 'When ye shall see all these things, *know* that it is near, even at the doors.'

"But Paul has said, 'For yourselves know perfectly that the day of the Lord so cometh as a thief in the night.' 1 Thessalonians 5:2. This language is very plain, and shows that as the thief in the stillness of night quietly seeks his plunder, without giving notice, so Christ will come when least expected, hence this idea of warning the world of his soon coming is a mistake."

"But, James, of whom is the apostle in this verse [17] speaking? Not of Christians, but of the ungodly. They will not receive the warning. They will not be looking for Christ. They will be buried up in the spirit of this world. They will be saying, Peace and safety, and they will be suddenly and unexpectedly destroyed. Not so with those who love Jesus and his appearing. They will receive the warning. They will be looking for, waiting for, and loving the appearance of the dear Saviour, and that day will not come upon them as a thief. Notice with care the two classes mentioned in the two following verses. One is the ungodly. The other is the brethren. The day of the Lord will come on one class as a thief; but not so with the other. 'For when they shall say, Peace and safety, then sudden destruction cometh upon them, as travail upon a woman with child, and they shall not escape. But ye, brethren, are not in darkness, that that day should overtake you as a thief.'"

My good mother was ready to meet, calmly and pleasantly, all my objections, and I was now disposed to view the subject as worthy of my attention. And when in the house of God I heard my schoolmates speak of the love of Christ, and the glory of his appearing, I was deeply impressed that the hand of God was in the Advent doctrine.

Impressions of Duty

As I returned to the Lord, it was with strong convictions that I should renounce my worldly plans and give myself to the work of warning the people to prepare for the day of God. I had loved books generally, but, in my backslidden state, had neither time nor taste for the study of the sacred Scriptures, hence was ignorant [18] of the prophecies. I had, however, some knowledge of the Bible history of man, and had the idea that the race in six thousand years had depreciated physically, and, consequently, mentally. The subject came before my mind in this form: Man once lived nearly one thousand years. In length of days he has dwindled to seventy. In a few centuries, should time continue, with the same results upon the lifetime of man, the race would cease to exist. I had renounced the doctrine of the conversion of the world, and the temporal millennium, in which the soil and man were to be gradually restored to their Eden state, as taught me by my father. I therefore saw the necessity, in the very nature of things, for some great change, and the second coming of Christ seemed to be the event which would most probably bring about the change in man, and in the earth, to remove the curse and its results, and restore all to its Eden perfection and glory.

My mind turned to the young people of the school I had just left. In that school of fifty scholars, twenty were near my own age, several were older. My school was a happy one. I loved my scholars, and this love was mutual. As we parted, at the close of the last day of school, I said to them, "I am engaged to teach this school next winter, and should I fulfill this engagement, I will not ask one of you to obey my orders better than you have this term." As I found comfort in prayer, I began to pray for my scholars, and would sometimes wake myself in the night praying vocally for them. A strong impression came upon me, as if a voice said, Visit your scholars from house to house and pray with them. I could not conceive of a heavier cross than this. I prayed to be excused, that I might pursue my studies; but no relief came. I prayed for clearer evidence, [19] and the same impression seemed to say, Visit your scholars.

In this state of mind I went into my father's field, hoping that I could work off the feelings under which I suffered. But they followed me, and increased. I went to the grove to pray for relief. None came. But the impression, Visit your scholars, was still more distinct. My spirit rose in rebellion against God, and I recklessly said, I will not go. These words were accompanied with a firm stamp of the foot upon the ground, and in five minutes I was at the house, packing my books and clothes for Newport Academy. That afternoon I rode to the place with Eld. Bridges, who talked to me all the way upon the subject of preaching, greatly to my discomfort.

The next morning I secured a boarding place, and took my position in several classes in the school, and commenced study with a *will* to drive off my convictions. But in this I did not succeed. I became distressed and agitated. After spending several hours over my books, I tried to call to mind what I had been studying. This I could not do. My mental confusion was complete. The Spirit of God had followed me into the school-room in mercy, notwithstanding my rebellion, and I could find no rest there. Finally I resolved that I would do my duty, and immediately took my cap and went directly from the door of that school-room, on foot, to the town of Troy, the place of my last school. I had gone but a few rods on my way, when sweet peace from God flowed into my mind, and Heaven seemed to shine around me. I raised my hands and praised God with the voice of triumph.

With a light heart and cheerful step I walked on till sundown, when I came to a humble cottage which attracted [20] my special attention. I was strongly impressed to call, but had no reason for so doing, as it was but a few miles to the school district, where I should find a hearty welcome. I decided to go past this house, as I did not wish to find myself in the awkward position of calling upon strangers without some good reason. But the impression to call increased, and the excuse to ask for a drink of water occurred to me, and I stepped to the door and called for water. A man in the noon of life waited upon me, then kindly said, "Walk in." I saw that he had been weeping. In one hand he held the Bible. When I had taken the chair he offered me, this sad stranger addressed me in a most mournful manner, as follows: "I am in trouble. I am in deep affliction. To-day I have buried my dear son, and I have not the grace of God to sustain me. I am not a Christian, and my burden seems greater that I can bear. Will you please stop all night with me?"

He wept bitterly. Why he should so directly open his afflicted mind to a young stranger, has ever been to me a mystery. I could not refuse his invitation, and concluded to stop for the night. I told him my brief experience, and pointed him to Christ, who says, "Come unto me all ye that labor and are heavy laden, and I will give you rest. Take my yoke upon you, and learn of me; for I am meek and lowly in heart, and ye shall find rest unto your souls. For my yoke is easy, and my burden is light." We bowed in prayer, and my new friend seemed relieved. Then we sought rest in sleep. In the morning I assisted him in erecting the family altar, and went on my way. I have neither seen nor heard from him since.

But I had walked only two miles on that delightful spring morning, when all nature, animate and inanimate, [21] seemed to join my glad heart in the praise of God, before the same impression came upon me, as I was passing a neat log cottage. Something said to me, Go into the house. I stepped to the door, and called for a drink of water. And who should bring it to me but a young lady who had attended my school the past winter. As she recognized me, she exclaimed, "Why, schoolmaster, walk in." This family had just moved from the district, three miles, to a new settlement surrounded by forests. The father was absent. The mother and children greeted me with more than usual cordiality, each calling me, Master. There was the place for my work to commence. I told my errand, and asked the privilege to pray.

"Oh, yes!" said the already weeping woman. "But let me send out the children and call in my neighbors." Some half-dozen little boys and girls received dispatches from their mother, and cheerfully ran to as many log cottages with the word, "Our schoolmaster is at our house, and wishes to pray, and mother wants you to come as soon as you can." In less than half an hour I had before me a congregation of about twenty-five. In conversing with them, I learned that not one of that company professed Christianity. Lectures on the second advent had been given near them, and a general conviction that the doctrine might be true rested upon the people.

And as I related my experience of the few weeks in the past, stating my convictions relative to the soon coming of Christ, all were interested. I then bowed to pray, and was astonished to find that these twenty-five sinners all bowed with me. I could but weep. They all wept with me. And after pointing them to Christ, as best I could with my limited experience and knowledge of the Scriptures, I shook their [22] hands, said farewell, and joyfully pursued my journey.

As I entered the district I had so recently left, all seemed changed, yet no changes worthy of note had taken place but in me. The school-house, where I had spent happy hours in teaching willing minds, was closed, and my scholars were pursuing their daily tasks in the field and kitchen. I had left them, a proud, prayerless backslider, but now had come to pray with them. It seemed to me that the Lord could not have selected a duty more humbling to my pride. The district was made up of Universalists, formal professors, respectable sinners, and infidels. My employer, who had also engaged me to teach their school the next winter, was an infidel. I lost no time in making known the object of my visit, and in visiting and praying from house to house. No one opposed me. Some were deeply affected and bowed with me. My infidel friend said to me as I asked permission to pray in his house,

"I am very sorry, Mr. White, to find you in this state of mind. You are a good teacher, and a gentleman. I shall not forbid you."

This reception was decidedly cold when compared with what I had met from others. This infidel was evidently much disgusted and disappointed, but tried to conceal his feelings out of respect to mine. I tried to pray, and passed to the next house. In a few days my work in this direction was finished for that time, and I returned home with the sweet assurance that I had done my duty. A few weeks afterward, however, I visited the place again. A general reformation was in progress, under the labors of a Christian minister. On Sunday, the meeting was held in a barn. The interest was general, and the congregation large. After the minister closed his remarks, I improved a few moments. I felt [23] deeply, and my testimony reached the people, especially my scholars and their parents. The following summer, lectures were given in the town-house, and the next winter most of the people of that town embraced religion.

Much of the summer I was unsettled as to duty. I had visited my scholars, and sometimes hoped to be excused from anything further of the kind, and feel free to pursue my studies. But the definite idea of proclaiming the soon coming of Christ, and warning the people to prepare for the day of the Lord, was impressed upon my mind. I did not dare attend school. The Spirit of the Lord had driven me from the school-room once, and in following a sense of duty I had been greatly blessed. How could I resist present convictions, and again try to shut myself away from the Lord, over my books? But how could I renounce all my fondly-cherished hopes of the future? My brother in Ohio said to me by letter: "Come out into the sunny West, James, and I will help you." "Well," said I, "when I become a scholar." How could I give up my school books, and with my small stock of education think of becoming a preacher?

A school-mate, Elbridge Smith, who had also been a room-mate at St. Albans and at Reedfield, was a special friend of mine. He was a fine young man, of good habits, yet not a Christian. I loved him for what he was, and we mutually in confidence freely stated to each other all our plans, hopes and difficulties. To this young man I first opened my mind freely upon the subject of the second advent, and my convictions of duty to preach the doctrine. He treated the matter with candor, and seemed troubled as he learned from my own lips that I was inclined to believe that Christ would come about the year 1843. He had given the subject [24] no study, but evidently feared it might be so. He replied as follows:

"You know I am not a Christian, and therefore am poorly prepared to give you advice in relation to religious duty. I think of these things more than many suppose, though I publicly take no personal interest in them. I, however, think it well for me, and safe for you, to say at this time, Follow the convictions of your own mind."

I highly esteem this friend of my youth for his candor and good counsel. Who could have done better? We have met but a few times since, as I soon left that part of the State to proclaim the coming of the Lord, and he for Bowdoin College. He graduated in two years from that time, studied law, and now Elbridge Smith is a judge somewhere in the West.

The struggle with duty was a severe one. But I finally gave out an appointment, and had some freedom. I soon sent an appointment to speak at the Troy town-house. The congregation was large. Had rather a lean time, and felt embarrassed. And what seemed to well-nigh finish me, a good, honest, simple-hearted woman came up to me at the close of the meeting and said:

"Elder White, please come to our house and take dinner."

The word Elder cut me to the heart. I was confused and almost paralyzed. I will not attempt to narrate anything further that occurred on that day. The remaining portion of the day has ever seemed like a blank. I can only remember my confusion and anguish of spirit as I heard the unexpected word, Elder. I was unreconciled at the prospect before me, yet dared not refuse what seemed to be duty, and turn to my books. I was urged to speak in the presence of two young preachers, [25] and attempted to preach. In twenty minutes became confused and embarrassed, and sat down. I lacked resignation and humility, therefore was not sustained. I finally gave all for Christ and his gospel, and found peace and freedom.

Soon my mind was especially called to the second advent by hearing Elders J.V. Himes and A. Hale speak several times upon the subject, in the city of Bangor, Me. I then saw that it was a subject that required study, and felt the importance of commencing in earnest to prepare myself to teach others. I purchased Advent publications, read them closely, studied my Bible, and spoke a few times during the summer on the second coming of Christ with freedom, and felt encouraged.

William Miller

In September, Elders Himes, Miller, and others, held a meeting in the mammoth tent in Eastern Maine. In company with one Moses Polly, a Christian minister of my acquaintance, I attended that meeting. I there for the first time saw that great and good man, William Miller. His form and features showed great physical and mental strength. The benevolent, affable, and kind spirit manifested by him in conversation with numerous strangers who called on him to ask questions, proved him a humble, Christian gentleman. Infidels, Universalists, and some others came to him with opposing questions. He was quick to perceive their designs, and with becoming firmness and dignity promptly met their objections and sent them away in silence. So long had he, even then, been in the field, meeting opposition from every quarter, that he was prepared for any emergency. [26]

In his public labors his arguments were clear, and his appeals and exhortations most powerful. The tent in which he spoke was a circle whose diameter was one hundred and twenty feet. On one occasion, when this tent was full, and thousands stood around, he was unfortunate in the use of language, which the baser sort in the crowd turned against him by a general burst of laughter. He left his subject with ease, and in a moment his spirit rose above the mob-like spirit that prevailed, and in language the most scorching he spoke of the corruption of the hearts of those who chose to understand him to be as vile as they were. In a moment all was quiet. And the speaker continued to describe the terrible end of the ungodly in a solemn and impressive manner. He then affectionately exhorted them to repent of their sins, come to Christ, and be ready for his appearing. Many in that vast crowd wept. He then resumed his subject, and spoke with clearness and spirit, as though nothing had happened. In fact, it seemed that nothing could have occurred to fully give him the ears of the thousands before him, and to make his subject so impressive as this circumstance.

God raised up Paul to do a great work in his time. In order that the Gentiles might be clearly taught the great plan of redemption through Jesus, and that the infidelity of the Jews might be met, a great man was selected.

Martin Luther was the man for his time. He was daring and sometimes rash, yet was a great and good man. The little horn had prevailed, and millions of the saints of the Most High had been put to death. To fearlessly expose the vileness of the papal monks, and to meet their learning and their rage, and also to win the hearts of the common people with all the tenderness [27] and affection of the gospel, called for just such a man as Martin Luther. He could battle with the lion, or feed and tenderly nurse the lambs of Christ's fold.

So William Miller, in the hands of God, was the man for his time. True, he was a farmer, and had been in the service of his country, and had not the benefits of an early classical education. And it was not till he had passed the noon of life that God called him to search his word and open the prophecies to the people. He was, however, a historian from his love of history, and had a good practical knowledge of men and things. He had been an infidel. But on receiving the Bible as a revelation from God, he did not also receive the popular, contradictory ideas that many of its prophecies were clad in impenetrable mystery. Said William Miller: "The Bible, it is what it purports to be, will explain itself."

He sought for the harmony of Scripture and found it. And in the benevolence of his great and good heart and head, he spent the balance of his life in teaching it to the people in his written and oral lectures, and in warning and exhorting them to prepare for the second coming of Christ.

Much of the fruits of his labors are now seen. Much more will be seen hereafter. Heaven will be hung with the fruits of the labors of this truly great and good man. He sleeps. But if it can be said of any who have toiled and worn and suffered amid vile persecutions, "Blessed are the dead which die in the Lord from henceforth, that they may rest from their labors, and their works do follow them," it can be said of Wm. Miller. He nobly and faithfully did his duty, and the popular church, united with the world, paid him in persecutions and reproaches. [28] The very name of

Wm. Miller was despised everywhere, and Millerism was the jeer of the people from the pulpit to the brothel.

But, dear reader, if your deed of real estate be registered at the office of the county clerk, rough hands may tear the paper you hold in your hand which you call a deed, and your title is no less secure. And however roughly and wickedly men may have handled the name of Wm. Miller here, when the final triumphant deliverance of all who are written in the Book of Life comes, his will be found among the worthies, safe from the wrath of men and the rage of demons, securing to him the reward of immortality according to his works.

As I have introduced to the reader the man whom God raised up to lead off in the great advent movement, it may be expected that something of his life, experience and labors should here be given. I have room for only a very few sketches from his memoir. He was born in Pittsfield, Mass., February, 1782. His biographer says:

"In his early childhood, marks of more than ordinary intellectual strength and activity were manifested. A few years made these marks more and more noticeable to all who fell into his society. But where were the powers of the inner man to find the nutriment to satisfy their cravings, and the field for their exercise?

"Besides the natural elements of education, the objects, the scenes, and the changes of the natural world, which have ever furnished to all truly great minds their noblest aliment, the inspiring historical recollections associated with well-known localities of the neighboring country, and the society of domestic life, there was nothing within William's reach but the Bible, the psalter [29] and prayer-book, till he had resided at Low Hampton several years.

"His mother had taught him to read, so that he soon mastered the few books belonging to the family; and this prepared him to enter the senior class when the district school opened. But if the terms were short, the winter nights were long. Pine knots could be made to supply the want of candles, lamps, or gas. And the spacious fireplace in the log house was ample enough as a substitute for the school-house and lecture-room.

"He possessed a strong physical constitution, an active and naturally well-developed intellect, and an irreproachable moral character. He had appropriated to his use and amusement the small stock of literature afforded by the family while a child. He had enjoyed the limited advantages of the district school but a few years before it was generally admitted that his attainments exceeded those of the teachers usually employed. He drank in the inspiration of the natural world around him, and of the most exciting events of his country's history. His imagination had been quickened, and his heart warmed, by the adventures and gallantries of fiction, and his intellect enriched by history. And some of his earliest efforts with the pen, as well as the testimony of his associates, show that his mind and heart were ennobled by the lessons, if not by the spirit and power of religion. What, now, would have been the effect of what is called a regular course of education? Would it have perverted him, as it has thousands? or would it have made him instrumental of greater good in the cause of God?

"Whatever might have been the result of any established course of education in the case of Wm. Miller, such a course was beyond his reach: he was deprived [30] of the benefit, he has escaped the perversion. Let us be satisfied."

William Miller was married in 1802, and settled in Poultney, Vt. His biographer continues:

"But the men with whom he associated from the time of his removal to Poultney, and to whom he was considerably indebted for his worldly favors, were deeply affected with skeptical principles and deistical theories. They were not immoral men; but, as a class, were good citizens, and generally of serious deportment, humane, and benevolent. However, they rejected the Bible as the standard of religious truth, and endeavored to make its rejection plausible by such aid as could be obtained from the writings of Voltaire, Hume, Volney, Paine, Ethan Allen, and others. Mr. Miller studied these works closely, and at length avowed himself a deist. As he has stated the period must have begun in 1804; for he embraced or returned to the Christian faith in 1816. It may fairly be doubted, however, notwithstanding his known thoroughness and consistency, whether Mr. Miller ever was fully settled in that form of deism which reduces man to a level with the brutes, as to the supposed duration of their existence. And the question is worthy of a little inquiry, to what extent was he a deist?"

He received a captain's commission, and entered the army in 1810. He returned from the army, and moved his family to Low Hampton, N.Y., to begin there the occupation of farming, in 1812.

"As a farmer, he had more leisure for reading; and he was at an age when the future of man's existence *will* demand a portion of his thoughts. He found that his former views gave him no assurance of happiness [31] beyond the present life. Beyond the grave all was dark and gloomy. To use his own words: 'Annihilation was a cold and chilling thought, and accountability was sure destruction to all. The heavens were as brass over my head, and the earth as iron under my feet. *Eternity! — what was it? And death! — why was it?* The more I reasoned, the further I was from demonstration. The more I thought, the more scattered were my conclusions. I tried to stop thinking, but my thoughts would not understand *the cause.* I murmured and complained, but knew not of whom. I knew that there was a wrong, but knew not how or where to find the right. I mourned, but without hope.' He continued in this state of mind for some months, feeling that eternal consequences *might* hang on the nature and object of his belief.

"It devolved on Captain Miller, as usual in the minister's absence, to read a discourse of the deacons' selection. They had chosen one on the Importance of Parental Duties. Soon after commencing, he was overpowered by the inward struggle of emotion, with which the entire congregation sympathized, and took his seat. His deistical principles seemed an almost insurmountable difficulty with him. 'Soon after, suddenly,' he says, 'the character of the Saviour was vividly impressed upon my mind. It seemed that there might be a being so good and compassionate as to himself atone for our transgressions, and thereby save us from suffering the penalty of sin. I immediately felt how lovely such a being must be; and imagined that I could cast myself into the arms of, and trust in the mercy of, such an one. But the question arose, How can it be proved that such a being does exist? Aside from the Bible, I found [32] that I could get no evidence of the existence of such a Saviour, or even of a future state. I felt that to believe in such a Saviour, without evidence, would be visionary in the extreme.

"'I saw that the Bible did bring to view just such a Saviour as I needed; and I was perplexed to find how an uninspired book should develop principles so perfectly adapted to the wants of a fallen world. I was constrained to admit that the Scriptures must be a revelation from God. They became my delight; and in Jesus I found a friend. The Saviour became to me the chiefest among ten thousand; and the Scriptures, which before were dark and contradictory, now became the lamp to my feet and light to my path. My mind became settled and satisfied. I found the Lord God to be a rock in the midst of the ocean of life. The Bible now became my chief study, and I can truly say, I searched it with great delight. I found the half was never told me. I wondered why I had not seen its beauty and glory before, and marveled that I could have ever rejected it. I found everything revealed that my heart could desire, and a remedy for every disease of the soul. I lost all taste for other reading, and applied my heart to get wisdom from God.'

"Mr. Miller immediately erected the family altar; publicly professed his faith in that religion which had been food for his mirth, by connecting himself with the little church that he had despised; opened his house for meetings of prayer; and became an ornament and pillar in the church, and an aid to both pastor and people. The die was cast, and he had taken his stand for life as a soldier of the cross, as all who knew him felt assured; and henceforth the badge of discipleship, [33] in the church or world, in his family or closet, indicated whose he was, and whom he served.

"His pious relations had witnessed with pain his former irreligious opinions; how great were their rejoicings now! The church, favored with his liberality, and edified by his reading, but pained by his attacks on their faith, could now rejoice with the rejoicing. His infidel friends regarded his departure from them as the loss of a standard-bearer. And the new convert felt that henceforth, wherever he was, he must deport himself as a Christian, and perform his whole duty. His subsequent history must show how well this was done.

"Soon after his renunciation of deism, in conversing with a friend respecting the hope of a glorious eternity through the merits and intercessions of Christ, he was asked how he knew there was such a Saviour. He replied, "It is revealed in the Bible." "How do you know the Bible is true?" was the response, with a reiteration of his former arguments on the contradictions and mysticisms in which he had claimed it was shrouded.

"Mr. Miller felt such taunts in their full force. He was at first perplexed; but, on reflection, he considered that if the Bible is a revelation of God, it must be consistent with itself; all its parts must harmonize, must have been given for man's instruction, and, consequently, must be adapted to his understanding. He therefore said, 'Give me time, and I will harmonize all those apparent contradictions to my own satisfaction, or I will be a deist still.'

"He then devoted himself to a prayerful reading of the word. He laid aside all commentaries, and used the marginal references and his Concordance as his only helps. He saw that he must distinguish between the Bible and all the peculiar partisan interpretations of it. [34] The Bible was older than them all, must be above them all; and he placed it there. He saw that it must correct all interpretations; and in correcting them, its own pure light would shine without the mists which traditionary belief had involved it in. He resolved to lay aside all preconceived opinions, and to receive with child-like simplicity the natural and obvious meaning of the Scripture. He pursued the study of the Bible with the most intense interest — whole nights as well as days being devoted to that object. At times delighted with truth, which shone forth from the sacred volume, making clear to his understanding the great plan of God for the redemption of fallen man; and at times puzzled and almost distracted by seemingly inexplicable or contradictory passages, he persevered until the application of his great principle of interpretation was triumphant. He became puzzled only to be delighted, and delighted only to persevere the more in penetrating its beauties and mysteries.

"His manner of studying the Bible is thus described by himself: 'I determined to lay aside all my prepossessions, to thoroughly compare Scripture with Scripture, and to pursue its study in a regular, methodical manner. I commenced with Genesis, and read verse by verse, proceeding no faster than the meaning of the several passages should be so unfolded as to leave me free from embarrassment respecting any mysticisms or contradictions. Whenever I found anything obscure, my practice was to compare it will all collateral passages; and, by the help of Cruden, I examined all the texts of Scripture in which were found any of the prominent words contained in any obscure portion. Then, by letting every word have its proper bearing on the subject of the text, if my view of it harmonized with [35] every collateral passage in the Bible, it ceased to be a difficulty. In this way I pursued the study of the Bible, in my first perusal of it, for about two years, and was fully satisfied that it is its own interpreter. I found that by a comparison of Scripture with history, all the prophecies, as far as they have been fulfilled, had been fulfilled literally; that all the various figures, metaphors, parables, similitudes, etc., of the Bible, were either explained in their immediate connection, or the terms in which they were expressed were defined in other portions of the word; and when thus explained, are to be literally understood in accordance with such explanation. I was thus satisfied that the Bible is a system of revealed truths, so clearly and simply given, that the wayfaring man, though a fool, need not err therein.' In pursuing his study of the Holy Scriptures, Mr. Miller adopted the following rules of interpretation:

"1. Every word must have its proper bearing on the subject presented in the Bible. Proof, Matthew 5:18.

"2. All Scripture is necessary, and may be understood by a diligent application and study. Proof, 2 Timothy 3:15-17.

"3. Nothing revealed in the Scriptures can or will be hid from those who ask in faith, not wavering. Proof, Deuteronomy 29:29; Matthew 10:26, 27; 1 Corinthians 2:10; Philippians 3:15; Isaiah 45:11; Matthew 21:22; John 14:13, 14; 15:7; James 1:5, 6; 1 John 5:13-15.

"4. To understand doctrine, bring all the scriptures together on the subject you wish to know; then let every word have its proper influence; and if you can form your theory without a contradiction, you cannot be in error. Proof, Isaiah 28:7-29; 35:8; Proverbs 29:27; Luke 24:27, 44, 45; Romans 16:26; James 5:19; 2 Peter 1:19, 20. [36]

"5. Scripture must be its own expositor, since it is a rule of itself. If I depend on a teacher to expound to me, and he should guess at its meaning, or desire to have it so on account of his sectarian creed, or to be thought wise, then his guessing, desire, creed, or wisdom, is my rule, and not the Bible. Proof, Psalm 19:7-11; 119:97-105; Matthew 23:8-10; 1 Corinthians 2:12-16; Ezekiel 34:18, 19; Luke 11:52; Matthew 2:7, 8.

"6. God has revealed things to come, by visions, in figures and parables; and in this way the same things are oftentime revealed again and again, by different visions, or in different figures and parables. If you wish to understand them, you must combine them all in one. Proof, Psalm 89:19; Hosea 12:10; Habakkuk 2:2; Acts 2:17; 1 Corinthians 10:6; Hebrews 9:9, 24; Psalm 78:2; Matthew 13:13, 34; Genesis 41:1-32; Daniel 2:7 and 8; Acts 10:9-16.

"7. Visions are always mentioned as such. 2 Corinthians 12:1.

"8. Figures always have a figurative meaning, and are used much in prophecy to represent future things, times and events — such as mountains, meaning governments, Daniel 2:35, 44; beasts, meaning kingdoms, Daniel 7:8, 17; waters, meaning people, Revelation 17:1, 15; day meaning year, etc. Ezekiel 4:6.

"9. Parables are used as comparisons, to illustrate subjects, and must be explained in the same way as figures, by the subject and Bible. Mark 4:13.

"10. Figures sometimes have two or more different significations, as day is used in a figurative sense to represent three different periods of time, namely: first, indefinite, Ecclesiastes 7:14; and second, definite, a day for a year, Ezekiel 4:6; and third, a day for a thousand years, 2 Peter 3:8. [37]

"The right construction will harmonize with the Bible, and make good sense; other constructions will not.

"11. If a word makes good sense as it stands, and does no violence to the simple laws of nature, it is to be understood literally; if not, figuratively. Revelation 12:1, 2; 17:3-7.

"12. To learn the meaning of a figure, trace the word through your Bible, and when you find it explained, substitute the explanation for the word used; and if it make good sense, you need not look further; if not, look again.

"13. To know whether we have the true historical event for the fulfillment of prophecy: If you find every word of the prophecy (after the figures are understood) is literally fulfilled, then you may know that your history is the true event; but if one word lacks a fulfillment, then you must look for another event, or wait its future development; for God takes care that history and prophecy shall agree, so that the true believing children of God may never be ashamed. Psalm 22:5; Isaiah 45:17-19; 1 Peter 2:6; Revelation 17:17; Acts 3:18.

"14. The most important rule of all is, that you must have *faith.* It must be a faith that requires a sacrifice, and, if tried, would give up the dearest object on earth, the world and all its desires — character, living, occupation, friends, home, comforts, and worldly honors. If any of these should hinder our believing any part of God's word, it would show our faith to be vain. Nor can we ever believe so long as one of these motives lies lurking in our hearts. We must believe that God will never forfeit his word; and we can have confidence that He who takes notice of the sparrow's fall, and numbers the hairs of our head, will guard the translation. [38] of his own word, and throw a barrier around it, and prevent those who sincerely trust in God, and put implicit confidence in his word, from erring far from the truth.

"While thus studying the Scriptures," continuing the words of his own narrative, "I became satisfied if the prophecies which have fulfilled in the past are any criterion by which to judge of the manner of the fulfillment of those which are future, that the popular views of the spiritual reign of Christ — a temporal millennium before the end of the world, and the Jews' return — are not sustained by the word of God; for I found that all the scriptures on which those favorite theories are based, are as clearly expressed as are those that were *literally* fulfilled at the first advent, or at any other period in the past. I found it plainly taught in the Scriptures that Jesus Christ will again descend to this earth, coming in the clouds of heaven, in all the glory of his Father.

"I need not speak of the joy that filled my heart in view of the delightful prospect, nor of the ardent longings of my soul for a participation in the joys of the redeemed. The Bible was now to me a new book. It was indeed a feast of reason; all that was dark, mystical or obscure, to me, in its teachings, had been dissipated from my mind before the clear light that now dawned from its sacred pages; and oh, how bright and glorious the truth appeared! All the contradictions and inconsistencies I had before found in the word were gone; and, although there were many portions of which I was not satisfied I had a full understanding, yet so much light had emanated from it to the illumination of my before darkened mind, that I felt a delight in studying the Scriptures which I had not before supposed could be derived from its teachings. I commenced their [39] study with no expectation of finding the time of the Saviour's coming, and I could at first hardly believe the result to which I had arrived; but the evidence struck me with such force that I could not resist my convictions. I became nearly settled in my conclusions, and began to wait, and watch, and pray, for my Saviour's coming."

"From the time that Mr. Miller became established in his religious faith, till he commenced his public labors — a period of twelve or fourteen years — there were few prominent incidents in his life to distinguish him from other men. He was a good citizen, a kind neighbor, an affectionate husband and parent, and a devoted Christian; good to the poor, and benevolent, as objects of charity were presented; in the Sunday school was teacher and superintendent; in the church he performed important service as reader and exhorter, and, in the support of religious worship, no other member, perhaps, did as much as he. He was very exemplary in his life and conversation, endeavored at all times to perform the duties, whether public or private, which devolved on him, and whatever he did was done cheerfully, as for the glory of God. His leisure hours were devoted to reading and meditation; he kept himself well informed respecting the current events of the time; occasionally communicated his thoughts through the press, and often for his own private amusement, or for the entertainment of friends, indulged in various poetical effusions, which, for unstudied productions, are possessed of some merit; but his principal enjoyment was derived from the study of the Bible." [40]

His Views of Prophecy

What can be more natural than for man, as he looks forth upon the world where evil is everywhere present, and the marks of disorder and decay everywhere visible, to inquire whether or not this state of things shall always continue? And what inquiry can be of more interest and importance to the race than that which has respect to the age of the world in which we live? It would therefore be reasonable to conclude that God would give to man a revelation informing him in respect to subjects of such absorbing interest. And the declaration of the scripture is in strict accordance with enlightened reason, when it says, "Surely the Lord God will do nothing, but he revealeth his secret unto his servants, the prophets." Amos 3:7.

The object of prophecy is to forewarn the world of things to come, in time for the requisite preparation, and to inspire the people of God with fresh courage as they see the time for the full fruition of their hopes drawing nigh. No judgment has ever come upon the world unheralded; and none have ever fallen therein unwarned. And if, from the uniform dealings of God with our world in the past, we may judge of the future, then may we conclude that of the events yet to transpire, and above all, the great event in which earth's drama shall close — the ushering in of the great day of the Lord, and the coming of the Son of man — something will be known, and the world be faithfully warned thereof, ere they shall take place.

In calling attention to these things, William Miller and his associates were accused of prying into the secrets of the Almighty. From this charge, however, they needed no better vindication than the language of [41] Moses, in Deuteronomy 29:29: "The secret things belong unto the Lord our God, but those things *which are revealed* belong unto us and to our children forever." Prophecy belongs to that portion of the Bible which may properly be denominated a revelation. It is designed to reveal to us things of which we could not in any other way gain information.

Again, they were met with the plea that the prophecies could not be understood. But says the Saviour, referring directly to the prophecy of Daniel, "Whoso readeth *let him understand.*" Matthew 24:15. That many of the prophecies, such as those portions of Daniel which reach to the close of earthly governments, have not been understood, is very true. But to assert that they cannot at any time be understood, is a virtual denial that they are a portion of God's revelation to man.

The prophecy of Daniel, reaching far into the future, could not be understood by the prophet himself. Neither could it be understood by any until the time of the end, when much of it should be fulfilled. Hence the answer of the angel to the anxious inquiry of the prophet. "And I heard, but I understood not: then said I, O my Lord, what shall be the end of these things? And he said, Go thy way, Daniel, for the words are closed up and sealed till the time of the end. Many shall be purified and made white, and tried; but the wicked shall do wickedly, and none of the wicked shall understand; but the wise shall understand." Chap. 12:8-10. Again says the angel to the prophet: "But thou, O Daniel, shut up the words and seal the book, even to the time of the end. Many shall run to and fro, and knowledge shall be increased." Verse 4.

From the very nature of the prophecy of Daniel, it [42] was closed up and sealed till the time of the end, when, most of its prophetic history being past, it was to be unsealed, understood, and many were to run to and fro with the knowledge of the great subject upon which it treats. The result of the increase and spread of knowledge in relation to the approaching Judgement, which is the great theme of the prophecy, is also given. The wicked shall do wickedly, and none of the wicked shall understand. But the wise shall understand. With these remarks the attention of the reader is called to

Daniel, Chapter II

The scene opens with the kingdom of Babylon, or Chaldea, at the summit of its greatness and glory, B.C. 603. Nebuchadnezzar, the Chaldean monarch, as it is natural for man to do, had been anxiously looking into the future, and pondering what should come to pass thereafter. Verse 29. Instead of rebuking or discouraging this spirit of inquiry in man, God takes occasion to grant to the king, and through him to the world, the information which he sought. Under the symbol of a great image he presents before him the most impressive history of the world, from that time on, that can anywhere be found. This image's head was of fine gold, symbolizing the kingdom of Babylon, then existing. In his interpretation, the prophet addressed himself to the king in the following words: "Thou art this head of gold." Verse 38. The breast and arms of silver represented Media and Persia, which shortly supplanted Babylon in the empire of the world. The belly and sides of brass prefigured Grecia, which, conquering its predecessors, enjoyed its period of universal dominion. And finally Rome, the legs of the image, bore its iron [43] sway over all the earth. In development of the ten toes, said the prophet: "The kingdom shall be divided" [verse 41]: and so was Rome divided into ten kingdoms between the years A.D. 356 and 483. What next? The monarch beheld till a stone cut out of the mountain without hands smote the image upon its feet, ground its metallic parts to powder, became a great mountain, and filled the whole earth. The inspired interpretation of this impressive scene is given thus: "In the days of these kings shall the God of Heaven set up a kingdom which shall never be destroyed, ... but it shall break in pieces and consume all these kingdoms, and it shall stand forever." Verse 44.

The prophetic history of Babylon, Media and Persia, and Grecia, has long since been completed, and that of Rome also has been fulfilled, excepting the dashing in pieces to give place to the immortal kingdom of God. And mark: The stone smote the image upon the feet. And it was in the days of the kings, or kingdoms, represented by the ten toes of the image, that the God of Heaven was to set up an eternal kingdom purely his. This kingdom is not yet established. It is evident that it was not set up at the time of Christ's first advent, from the fact that Rome was not then divided into the ten kingdoms, represented by the ten toes of the image.

Paul looked forward to this kingdom in his solemn charge to Timothy in view of the Judgment at the appearing and kingdom of Christ. 2 Timothy 4:1. For this kingdom all Christians were to pray, "Thy kingdom come." Matthew 6:10. James speaks of this kingdom as a matter of promise to the poor of this world, rich in faith. Chap. 2:5.

Adventists never believed, however, that all that is said in the New Testament relative to the kingdom of [44] Heaven relates to the future kingdom of glory. Especially in some of the parables of our Lord does the term refer to the work of grace with the people of God in this mortal state. But if we may be allowed to express the relation between believers and their Lord in this mortal state by the term kingdom of grace, and the future relation of immortal beings with the King of kings by the kingdom of glory, the position that the kingdom was set up at the first advent is not relieved of any of its difficulties. For certainly the kingdom of grace was established immediately after the fall. Adam, Abel, Enoch, Abraham, and Moses, were as truly the subjects of the kingdom of grace as the apostles of Jesus. With this view of the subject every text relative to the kingdom can be harmonized.

It is true that both John and Jesus proclaimed the kingdom of Heaven at hand. The immortal kingdom of glory was then at hand in the sense that it was the next universal kingdom to come. In the time of the Babylonian kingdom, the kingdom of Persia was at hand. The kingdom of Greece was at hand in the period occupied by Media and Persia. And in the days of that kingdom, Rome was at hand, for it was the next kingdom to succeed. In this sense was the kingdom of Heaven at hand in the days of the ministry of John and of Christ.

Daniel, Chapter VII

In this chapter we have the same great outline of this world's history as symbolized by the image of chapter 2, again brought to view, but in a different form. The prophet here saw four great beasts, explained in verse 17 to be four great kingdoms, corresponding respectively [45] to the gold, silver, brass, and iron, of the great image.

The first was like a lion, and had eagles' wings. Verse 4. The Chaldean empire, as advanced to its summit of prosperity under Nebuchadnezzar, was intended by this beast. — *Scott.*

The second like to a bear, and it raised itself up on one side, and had three ribs in its mouth. Verse 5. A fit emblem of the character and conquest of the Persian nation which succeeded Babylon B.C. 538. — *Prideaux,* Vol. I, p. 139.

And lo, another like a leopard, which had four wings and four heads. Verse 6. This was the emblem of the Grecian or Macedonian empire, which for the time was the most renowned in the world. It was erected by Alexander the Great on the ruins of the Persian monarchy, and it continued in four divisions under his successors. The leopard being exceedingly fierce and swift, represented the kingdom, and especially under Alexander, its founder, but the swiftness of the quadruped was not an adequate emblem of the rapidity with which he made his conquests; the leopard had therefore four wings of a fowl upon his back. — *Scott. Prideaux,* Vol. I, p. 380. *Rollin's Hist. of Alexander.*

And behold a fourth beast, dreadful and terrible, and strong exceedingly. Verse 7. The kingdom that succeeded Greece was Rome, the invincible fortitude, hardiness and force of which, perhaps were never equaled. This beast had ten horns. These are declared in verse 24 to be ten kingdoms. The ten kingdoms are enumerated by Marchiaval, Bishop Lloyd, and Dr. Hales, as follows: 1. The Huns, A.D. 356. 2. The Ostrogoths, A.D. 377. 3. The Visgoths, A.D. 378. 4. The Franks, A.D. 407. 5. The Vandals,

A.D. 407. 6. The Suevi, [46] A.D. 407. 7. The Burgundians, A.D. 407. 8. The Heruli and Rugii, or Thuringi, A.D. 476. 9. The Anglo-Saxons, A.D. 476. 10. The Lombards, A.D. 483. It is certain that the Roman Empire was divided into ten kingdoms; and though they might be sometimes more and sometimes fewer, yet they were still known by the name of the ten kingdoms of the western empire. — *Scott.*

I considered the horns, and behold there came up among them another little horn, before whom there were three of the first horns plucked up by the roots. In this horn were eyes like the eyes of man, and a mouth speaking great things. Verse 8. This little horn is by all Protestants acknowledged to be a symbol of the Papacy. Said the angel, speaking of this horn, "He shall subdue three kings." Verse 24. The three kingdoms that were plucked up to make way for the Papacy were, 1. The Heruli, in 493. 2. The Vandals, in 534. And 3, The Ostrogoths in 538. *Gibbon's Decline and Fall.* Into the hands of this power the saints, times, and laws, were to be given for a time, times and the dividing of time, (1260 years; see Revelation 12:6, 14). From 538, when the Papacy was set up, 1260 years extend to 1798; and it is a notable fact of history, that on the 10th of February, 1798, Berthier, a general of Bonaparte's at the head of the Republican army of France, entered Rome and took it. The papal government was abolished, and the Pope died in exile in 1799. (See *Croley* on the Apocalypse, *Thier's History of the French Revolution, Clarke* on Daniel 7:25.) The Papacy has never been restored to its former power. We are by this chain of prophecy brought down to the eighteenth century. And the prophet does not see this beast gradually changing his wild and ferocious [47] nature to the innocence and gentleness of the lamb, to make way for a temporal millennium; but he looks only a step further, and says,

"I beheld even till the beast was slain, and his body destroyed, and given to the burning flame." Daniel 7:11.

Daniel, Chapter VIII

It is characteristic of the different chains of prophecy, that each succeeding one introduces particulars not furnished in any previously given. The seventh of Daniel, after covering the general field symbolized by the image of chapter 2, instructs us more particularly concerning the development of the little horn, or man of sin. In the eighth chapter we are again conducted over a portion of the world's great highway, with additional particulars concerning the mighty kingdoms that stand as waymarks along our journey. On the symbols of this chapter, the ram, he-goat, and horn which waxed exceeding great, the prophet received the following instruction:

The ram which thou sawest having two horns are the kings of Media and Persia. Verse 20. The Persian division of the empire was the highest and came up last. The ram with the two horns was the well-known emblem of the Medes and Persians. It was usual for the Persian kings to wear a diadem made like a ram's head of gold. — *Scott.*

And the rough goat is the king of Grecia; and the great horn that is between his eyes, is the first king. Verse 21. This was Alexander, who was born B.C. 356, decided the fate of Persia at the battle of Arbela, B.C. 331, and died eight years thereafter in a drunken fit, at the age of 33, B.C. 323. [48]

And whereas the great horn being broken, four came up in its stead, four kingdoms, said the angel, shall stand up out of the nation. Verse 22. These were Macedonia, Thrace, Syria, and Egypt, into which the empire was divided shortly after Alexander's death, governed respectively by Cassander, Lysimachus, Seleucus, and Ptolemy.

And out of one of them came forth a little horn. Verses 9, 23-27. Rome was not connected with the people of God, and hence is not introduced into prophecy, till after its conquest of Macedonia, one of the horns of the goat; hence it is represented as coming forth from one of those horns. That this little horn which waxed exceeding great was Rome, the following considerations prove:

1. It was to rise in the latter part of their kingdom, that is, of the four kingdoms. So did Rome, so far as its place in the prophecy is concerned. Its connection with the Jews commenced B.C. 161. — 1Mac. 8. *Josephus' Antiq.*, B. 12,100,10, sec.6. *Prideaux,* Vol. II., p. 166.

2. It was little at first. So was Rome.

3. It waxed "exceeding great, towards the east and towards the south." So did Rome. It conquered Macedonia, B.C. 168; Syria etc. to the river Tigris, B.C. 65; Egypt, B.C. 30. From this horn's increasing toward the *south* and *east* particularly, Sir Isaac Newton infers that it arose in the north-west corner of the goat's dominion, *i.e.,* in Italy; which points directly to the Romans.

4. It cast down some of the host and of the stars to the ground. So did Rome; persecuting the disciples and ministers of Jesus as no other power ever did.

5. He magnified himself even to the Prince of the [49] host. Thus did Rome, when both Herod and Pontius Pilate conspired against Jesus.

6. He shall destroy, wonderfully, the mighty and the holy people. Let from 50 to 100 millions of martyrs make good this charge against persecuting Rome. See *Religious Encyclopedia.*

7. It was the only power that succeeded the four kingdoms which waxed EXCEEDING GREAT.

8. In this vision Grecia succeeds Medo-Persia, just as it had been seen *twice before*; and it is absurd to suppose that the power which follows them in this vision is a *different* power from the one which *twice before* had been seen *succeeding them*, in chapters 2 and 7; and that power was Rome.

9. He shall be broken without hand. How clear a reference to the stone cut out without hand, which smites the image upon its feet. Chap. 2:34.

The 2300 Days

Besides the symbols of governments contained in Daniel 8, there is a definite period of time brought to view, which claims attention. As recorded in verse 13, Daniel heard one saint ask another the question, how long the vision should be concerning the daily [sacrifice] and the transgression of desolation to give both the sanctuary and the host to be trodden under foot. The angel then addressed himself to Daniel and said, "Unto two thousand and three hundred days, then shall the sanctuary be cleansed." Waiving for the present the question as to what may constitute the sanctuary, we wish to ascertain if possible the nature, the commencement, and termination of this period of time. There are two kinds of time to be met with in the Bible; literal and symbolic [50] In symbolic time, a day signifies a year. Numbers 10:34; Ezekiel 4:6. To which class do the 2300 days belong? Being brought in connection with acknowledged symbols, it would be both easy and natural to infer that they partook of the nature of the rest of the vision and were symbolic, presenting us with a period of 2300 years. And that such is the case is further evident from the fact, as is shown in the investigation of Daniel 8, that the field of the prophet's vision, was the empires of Persia, Greece and Rome. The 2300 days there given cannot therefore be literal days; for literal days (scarcely six years and a half) would by no means cover the duration of any one of these empires singly, much less embrace so nearly the whole of their existence put together, as they evidently do. They must consequently denote 2300 years. Can we now ascertain the commencement of this period? We answer, Yes; the key to the matter being in the *ninth* chapter of Daniel, between which and the eighth there is an unmistakable connection, as we shall now endeavor to show.

After their mention in verse 14, the 2300 days are not again spoken of in chapter 8. All the other parts of the vision are there fully explained; it must have been, therefore, this point concerning the time, that troubled the mind of the prophet, and in reference to which, solely, that he exclaims at the end of the chapter, I was astonished at the vision, but none understood it.

It was in the third year of Belshazzar, B.C., 553, that Daniel had this vision of chapter 8. Fifty-three years previous to this time, Jerusalem had been taken by Nebuchadnezzar, and the seventy years' captivity commenced; and thirty-five years before this, the Chaldeans had utterly demolished the city, broken down its [51] walls and burnt the house of God with fire. 2 Chronicles 36:19. Daniel had learned from the prophecy of Jeremiah, [chapter 25], that the seventy years of captivity were drawing near their close, in the first year of Darius, B.C., 538, as we read in the first verses of Daniel 9; and it is evident that he so far misunderstood the period of the 2300 days as to suppose that they ended with the seventy years of Israel's servitude; therefore, turning his face toward the prostrate city and the ruined temple of his fathers, he prays God to cause his face to shine upon his sanctuary which is desolate. Verse 17.

"While I was speaking in prayer," says he, [chapter 9:20-23], "even the man Gabriel, whom I had seen in the vision at the beginning, being caused to fly swiftly, touched me about the time of the evening oblation. And he informed me and talked with me, and said, O, Daniel, I am now come forth to give thee skill and understanding. At the beginning of thy supplications the commandment came forth, and I am come to show thee; for thou art greatly beloved; therefore understand the matter, and consider the vision. *Seventy weeks* are determined upon thy people and upon thy holy city," etc.

That this is a continuation of the explanation of the vision of chapter 8, would seem sufficiently evident without the aid of any special argument to prove it so. But as there is a vital point that hinges upon this fact, we will offer a few reasons which place it beyond the limits of contradiction.

1. Gabriel had received a charge [chapter 8:16], to make Daniel understand the vision; but at the end of the chapter, Daniel says he was astonished at the vision, but none understood it. Gabriel therefore did not complete his mission in chapter 8; the charge [52] still rested upon him, Make this man to understand the vision.

2. The being who came to Daniel at the time of the supplication, was the very same who had appeared to him in the vision at the beginning; namely, Gabriel. And that he had now come to undeceive him concerning his application of the time, is evident in that he says, I am *now* come forth to give thee skill and understanding. Why did he not give him a full understanding of the vision at first? We answer, because he revealed to him all that he was then able to bear. He fainted and was sick certain days.

3. Direct reference is made to *the* vision at the beginning. And if that is not the vision of chapter 8, it is impossible to find it. And again, if Gabriel does not explain in chapter 9, what he omitted in chapter 8, it is impossible for any man to show wherein Gabriel fulfilled his commission to make this man understand the vision.

4. When Gabriel commenced his further explanation, he did not explain the symbol of the ram; for that he had already explained. He did not explain the goat; for he had likewise explained that. Neither did he commence about the little horn; for he had made that plain also in chapter 8. What then did he explain? The very point there omitted; namely, the time: *Seventy weeks* are determined upon thy people, etc. These facts are sufficient to show the connection of Daniel 9 with the vision of chapter 8. But how do the words of Gabriel, Seventy weeks are determined upon thy people etc., explain the period of the 2300 days? The answer is, The word rendered determined, signifies literally, *cut off*. Gesenius, in his Hebrew Lexicon, thus defines it: Properly, to *cut off*; tropically, to divide, [53] and so to determine, to decree. The Englishman's Hebrew Concordance says, Determined, literally divided. From what period are the seventy weeks divided, or cut off? From the 2300 days; for there is no other period given from which they can be taken; and this is placed beyond a doubt by the connection of the two chapters, which has already been proved.

Having now ascertained that the 70 weeks of Daniel 9 are the first 490 years of the 2300 days, and that consequently the two periods commence together, we further learn that this period of weeks dates from the going forth of a commandment to restore and build Jerusalem. Daniel 9:25. If then we can definitely locate this commandment, we have the starting point for the great period of the 2300 years. The Bible furnishes us with four tests by which to determine when the true date is found:

1. From the time of the commandment, 49 years were to witness the completion of the street and wall of Jerusalem. Daniel 9:25

2. Threescore and two weeks from this time, or, in all, 69 weeks, 483 years, were to extend to Messiah the Prince.

3. Sixty-nine and a half weeks were to extend to the crucifixion — the cessation of sacrifice and oblation in the midst of the week. Verse 27.

4. The full period of 70 weeks was to witness the complete confirmation of the covenant with Daniel's people.

In the seventh of Ezra, we find the decree for which we seek. It went forth in B.C. 457. Much concerning this decree, and the date of its promulgation, might here be said. But a more full explanation of it may more properly be given in another place. I will [54] say, however, that, admitting that B.C. 457, is the correct date for the commencement of the 2300 years, which is susceptible of the clearest proof, none will fail to see how William Miller came to the conclusion that this prophetic period would close in the year 1843.

From	2300
Take	457
And there remains	1843

"With the solemn conviction," writes Mr. Miller, "that such momentous events were predicted in the Scriptures, to be fulfilled in so short a space of time, the question came home to me with mighty power regarding my duty to the world, in view of the evidence that had affected my own mind. If the end was so near, it was important that the world should know it. I supposed that it would call forth the opposition of the ungodly; but it never came into my mind that any Christian would oppose it. I supposed that all such would be so rejoiced, in view of the glorious prospect, that it would only be necessary to present it, for them to receive it. My great fear was, that, in their joy at the hope of a glorious inheritance so soon to be revealed, they would receive the doctrine without sufficiently examining the Scriptures in demonstration of its truth. I therefore feared to present it, lest, by some possibility, I should be in error, and be the means of misleading any.

"Various difficulties and objections would arise in my mind, from time to time. Certain texts would occur to me, which seemed to weigh against my conclusions; and I would not present a view to others, while any difficulty appeared to militate against it. I therefore continued the study of the Bible, to see if I could sustain any of these objections. My object was not merely to [55] remove them, but I wished to see if they were valid.

"Sometimes, when at work, a text would arise like this: Of that day and hour knoweth no man, etc., and how then, could the Bible reveal the time of the advent? I would then immediately examine the context in which it was found, and I saw at once that, in the same connection, we are informed how we may know when it is nigh, even at the doors; consequently, that text could not teach that we could know nothing of the time of that event. Other texts, which are advanced in support of the doctrine of a temporal millennium, would arise; but, on examining their context, I invariably found that they were applicable only to the eternal state, or were so illustrative of the spread of the gospel here, as to be entirely irrelevant to the position they were adduced to support.

"Thus, all those passages that speak of the will of God being done on earth as in Heaven, of the earth being full of the knowledge of the glory of God, etc., could not be applicable to a time when the Man of Sin was prevailing against the saints, or when the righteous and wicked were dwelling together, which is to be the case until the end of the world. Those which speak of the gospel being preached in all the world, teach that, as soon as it should be thus preached, the end was to come; so that it could not be delayed a thousand years from that time, nor long enough for the world's conversion after the preaching of the gospel as a witness.

"The question of the resurrection and Judgment was for a time an obstacle in the way. Being instructed that all the dead would be raised at the same time, I supposed it must be so taught in the Bible; but I soon saw it was one of the traditions of the elders.

"So also with the return of the Jews. That question [56] I saw could only be sustained by denying the positive declarations of the New Testament, which assert, There is no difference between the Jew nor Greek, bond nor free, male or female; but that if ye are Christ's then are ye Abraham's seed, and heirs according to the promise. I was, therefore, obliged to discard an objection which asserts there *is* a difference between the Jew and Greek; that the children of the flesh *are* accounted for the seed, etc.

"In this way I was occupied from 1818 to 1823, in weighing the various objections which were being presented to my mind. During that time, more objections arose in my mind, than have been advanced by my opponents since; and I know of no objection that has been since advanced, which did not there occur to me. But, however strong they at first appeared, after examining them in the light of the divine word, I could only compare them to straws, laid down singly as obstacles, on a well-beaten road. The car of truth rolled over them, unimpeded in its progress."

He continued to make the Bible his daily study, and became more and more convinced that he had a personal duty to perform respecting what he conceived the Bible to teach of the nearness of the advent. These impressions he thus describes:

"'When I was about my business it was continually ringing in my ears, Go and tell the world of their danger. This text was constantly occurring to me: "When I say unto the wicked, O wicked man, thou shalt surely die; if thou dost not speak to warn the wicked from his way, that wicked man shall die in his iniquity; but his [57] blood will I require at thy hand. Nevertheless, if thou warn the wicked of his way to turn from it, if he do not turn from his way, he shall die in his iniquity; but thou hast delivered thy soul." Ezekiel 33:8, 9. I felt that if the wicked could be effectually warned, multitudes of them would repent; and that, if they were not warned, their blood might be required at my hand. I did all I could to avoid the conviction that anything was required of me; and I thought that, by freely speaking of it to all, I should perform my duty, and that God would raise up the necessary instrumentality for the accomplishment of the work. I prayed that some minister might see the truth, and devote himself to its promulgation; but still it was impressed upon me, Go and tell it to the world; their blood will I require at thy hand. The more I presented it in conversation, the more dissatisfied I felt with myself for withholding it from the public. I tried to excuse myself to the Lord for not going out and proclaiming it to the world. I told the Lord that I was not used to public speaking; that I had not the necessary qualifications to gain the attention of an audience; that I was very diffident, and feared to go before the world; that they would not believe me, nor hearken to my voice; that I was slow of speech, and of a slow tongue. But I could get no relief.'

"As Mr. Miller's opinions respecting the nearness and nature of the millennium became known, they naturally elicited a good deal of comment among his friends and neighbors, and also among those at a distance. Some of their remarks, not the most complimentary to his sanity, would occasionally be repeated to him.

"Having heard that a physician in his neighborhood had said that Esquire Miller, as he was familiarly called, [58] was a fine man and a good neighbor, but was a monomaniac on the subject of the advent, Mr. Miller was humorously inclined to let him prescribe for his case.

"One of his children being sick one day, he sent for the doctor, who, after prescribing for the child, noticed that Mr. Miller was very mute in one corner, and asked what ailed him.

"'Well, I hardly know, doctor. I want you to see what does, and prescribe for me.'

"The doctor felt of his pulse, etc., and could not decide respecting his malady; and inquired what he supposed was his complaint.

"'Well,' says Mr. Miller, 'I don't know but I am a monomaniac; and I want you to examine me, and see if I am, and, if so, cure me. Can you tell me when a man is a monomaniac?'

"The doctor blushed, and said he thought he could.

"Mr. Miller wished to know how.

"'Why,' said the doctor, 'a monomaniac is rational on all subjects but one; and when you touch that particular subject he will become raving.

"'Well,' says Mr. Miller, 'I insist upon it that you see whether I am in reality a monomaniac; and if I am, you shall prescribe for and cure me. You shall, therefore, sit down with me two hours, while I present the subject of the advent to you, and, if I am a monomaniac, by that time you will discover it.'

"The doctor was somewhat disconcerted; but Mr. Miller insisted, and told him, as it was to present the state of his mind, he might charge for his time as in regular practice.

"The doctor finally consented; and, at Mr. Miller's request, opened the Bible and read from the 8th of Daniel. As he read along, Mr. Miller inquired what the [59] ram denoted, with the other symbols presented. The doctor had read Newton, and applied them to Persia, Greece, and Rome, as Mr. Miller did.

"Mr. Miller then inquired how long the vision of those empires was to be.

"'2300 days.'

"'What!' said Mr. Miller, 'could those great empires cover only 2300 literal days?'

"'Why,' said the doctor, 'those days are years, according to all commentators; and those kingdoms are to continue 2300 years.'

"Mr. Miller then asked him to turn to the second chapter of Daniel, and to the seventh, all of which he explained the same as Mr. Miller. He was then asked if he knew when the 2300 days would end. He did not know, as he could not tell when they commenced.

"Mr. Miller told him to read the ninth of Daniel. He read down till he came to the 21st verse, when Daniel saw the man Gabriel, whom he had seen in the vision.

"'In what vision?' Mr. Miller inquired.

"'Why,' said the doctor, 'in the vision of the eighth of Daniel.'

"'Wherefore, understand the matter, and consider the vision. He had now come, then, to make him understand that vision, had he?'

"'Yes,' said the doctor.

"'Well, seventy weeks are determined; what are these seventy weeks a part of?'

"'Of the 2300 days.'

"'Then do they begin with the 2300 days?'

"'Yes,' said the doctor.

"'When did they end?'

"'In A.D. 33.'

"'Then how far would the 2300 extend after 33?' [60]

"The doctor subtracted 490 from 2300, and replied, '1810. Why,' said he, 'that is past.

"'But,' said Mr. Miller, 'there were 1810 from 33; in what year would that come?'

"The doctor saw at once that the 33 should be added, and set down 33 and 1810, and, adding them, replied, '1843.'

"At this unexpected result, the doctor settled back in his chair and colored; but immediately took his hat and left the house in a rage.

"The next day he again called on Mr. Miller, and looked as though he had been in the greatest mental agony.

"'Why, Mr. Miller,' said he, I am going to hell. I have not slept a wink since I was here yesterday. I have looked at the question in every light, and the vision must terminate about A.D. 1843; and I am unprepared, and must go to hell.'

"Mr. Miller calmed him, and pointed him to the ark of safety; and in about a week, calling each day on Mr. Miller, he found peace to his soul, and went on his way rejoicing, as *great a monomaniac* as Mr. Miller. He afterward acknowledged that, till he made the figures 1843, he had no idea of the result to which he was coming.

His Public Labors

The public labors of Mr. Miller, according to the best evidence to be obtained, date from the autumn of 1831. He had continued to be much distressed respecting his duty to go and tell it to the world, which was constantly impressed on his mind. One Saturday, after breakfast, he sat down at his desk to examine some point, and, as he arose to go out to work, it came home to him with [61] more force than ever, Go and tell it to the world. He thus writes:

"The impression was so sudden, and came with such force, that I settled down into my chair, saying, I can't go, Lord. Why not? seemed to be the response; and then all my excuses came up — my want of ability, etc.; but my distress became so great, I entered into a solemn covenant with God that if he would open the way, I would go and perform my duty to the world. What do you mean by opening the way? seemed to come to me. Why, said I, if I should have an invitation to speak publicly in any place, I will go and tell them what I find in the Bible about the Lord's coming. Instantly all my burden was gone, and I rejoiced that I should not probably be thus called upon; for I had never had such an invitation. My trials were not known, and I had but little expectation of being invited to any field of labor.

"In about half an hour from this time, before I had left the room, a son of Mr. Guilford, of Dresden, about sixteen miles from my residence, came in, and said that his father had sent for me, and wished me to go home with him. Supposing that he wished to see me on some business, I asked him what he wanted. He replied that there was to be no preaching in their church the next day, and his father wished to have me come and talk to the people on the subject of the Lord's coming. I was immediately angry with myself for having made the covenant I had; I rebelled at once against the Lord, and determined not to go. I left the boy without giving him any answer, and retired in great distress to a grove nearby. There I struggled with the Lord for about an hour, endeavoring to release myself from the covenant I had made with him; but I could get no [62] relief. It was impressed upon my conscience, Will you make a covenant with God, and break it so soon? The exceeding sinfulness of thus doing overwhelmed me. I finally submitted, and promised the Lord that, if he would sustain me, I would go, trusting in him to give me grace and ability to perform all he should require of me. I returned to the house, and found the boy still waiting. He remained till after dinner, and I returned with him to Dresden.

"The next day, which, as nearly as I can remember, was about the first Sabbath in August, 1831, I delivered my first public lecture on the second advent. The house was well filled with an attentive audience. As soon as I commenced speaking, all my diffidence and embarrassment were gone, and I felt impressed only with the greatness of the subject, which, by the providence of God, I was enabled to present. At the close of the services on the Sabbath, I was requested to remain and lecture during the week, with which I complied. They flocked in from the neighboring towns; a revival commenced, and it was said that in thirteen families all but two persons were hopefully converted.

"On the Monday following I returned home, and found a letter from Elder Fuller, of Poultney, Vt., requesting me to go and lecture there on the same subject. They had not heard of my going to Dresden. I went to Poultney, and lectured there with similar effect.

"From thence I went by invitation to Pawlet, and other towns in that vicinity. The churches of Congregationalists, Baptists, and Methodists, were thrown open. In almost every place I visited, my labors resulted in the reclaiming of backsliders, and the conversion of sinners. I was usually invited to fields of labor by the ministers of the several congregations who I visited, who gave [63] me their countenance; and I have never labored in any place in which I was not previously invited. The most pressing invitations from the ministry, and the leading members of the churches, poured in continually from that time, during the whole period of my public labors, and with more than one-half of which I was unable to comply. Churches were thrown open everywhere, and I lectured to crowded houses, through the western part of Vermont, the northern part of New York, and in Canada East; and powerful reformations were the results of my labors."

Conversion of One Hundred Infidels

"With the 1st of January, 1838, he commenced a second course of lectures at Lansingburgh, N.Y., in compliance with the urgent request of the Baptist church in that place, and of E.B. Crandall, their pastor. The lectures continued nine days, and were listened to by crowded and attentive audiences. The result also was most heart-cheering. Infidelity had several strongholds in that neighborhood, and many of that class attended his lectures, and were greatly affected by them. In a letter dated on the 25th of that month, two weeks after the close of the lectures, a gentleman of that place writes to Mr. Miller:

"'I have never witnessed so powerful an effect in any place as in this, on all who heard. I am of the opinion that not less than one hundred persons who held infidel sentiments are brought to believe the Bible. Infidelity is dumb in this place, as if frightened, and converts are many.'

"The following testimony of one who was converted from infidelity during these lectures, is copied from the [64] Boston Investigator (an infidel paper) of January, 1845:

"'Mr. Editor: I was a warm supporter of the views of Abner Kneeland, attended his lectures and *protracted dances*, disbelieved in Divine revelation and a future existence, and fully accorded with Mr. Kneeland's views of religion. Having read every work of note that I could obtain, and having heard many lectures opposed to God and the Bible, I considered myself prepared to overthrow the Christian faith, and feared no argument that could be brought form the Bible. With these feelings, I attended a full course of Mr. Miller's lectures. He gave his rules of interpretations, and pledged himself to prove his position. I approved of his rules, — to which I refer you, — and the result was, he established the fact that the Bible is what it purports to be — the word of God — to my mind, beyond a doubt;

and I have taken it as the man of my counsel. I notice your doubts of the truth of the statement in relation to hundreds of infidels being converted under the preaching of Mr. Miller. This may possibly be owing to your never having given Mr. Miller a candid and thorough hearing. He is a man mighty in the Scriptures, and has done terrible execution in the ranks of the "King's enemies," with the sword of the Spirit, which is the word of God. I am personally acquainted with nearly one hundred who held to similar views with Abner Kneeland, who were converted under the preaching of Mr. Miller; and we did not yield the point without a struggle, nor without due consideration. Each and every prop and refuge of infidelity and unbelief was taken away from us, and our sandy foundation was swept by the truth of the Almighty as chaff is driven by the wind. Yet we parted with them much as a man parts with a *diseased tooth*. We tried to cure and keep it there, and when made to [65] know that the *root* and foundation was rotten, it was painful to part with; but we rejoiced and felt better after the separation; for there is balm in Gilead — there is a Physician there.'

"From the 24th to the 28th of May, Mr. Miller lectured in Groton, Mass., and from the 3rd to the 9th of June, in Lynn, Mass. In connection with his visit to this place, he made the following entry in his memorandum book: 'Thus ends my tour into Massachusetts, making eight hundred lectures from October 1, 1834, to June 9, 1839 — four years, six months, nine days.' The editor of the Lynn Record gave the following notice of Mr. Miller, and his visit to that place:

Miller and the Prophecies

"'We took a prejudice against this good man when he first came among us, on account of what we supposed a glaring error in interpreting the Scripture prophecies so that the world would come to an end in 1843. We are still inclined to believe this an error or miscalculation. At the same time we have overcome our prejudices against him by attending his lectures, and learning more of the excellent character of the man, and of the great good he has done and is doing. Mr. Miller is a plain farmer, and pretends to nothing except that he has made the Scripture prophecies an intense study for many years, understands some of them differently from most other people, and wishes, for the good of others, to spread his views before the public. No one can hear him five minutes without being convinced of his sincerity, and instructed by his reasoning and information. All acknowledge his lectures to be replete with useful and interesting matter. His knowledge of Scripture is [66] very extensive and minute; that of the prophecies, especially, surprisingly familiar. His application of the prophecies to the great events which have taken place in the natural and moral world is such, generally, as to produce conviction of their truth, and gain the ready assent of his hearers. We have reason to believe that the preaching or lecturing of Mr. Miller has been productive of great and extensive good. Revivals have followed in his train. He has been heard with attention wherever he has been.

"'There is nothing very peculiar in the manner or appearance of Mr. Miller. Both are at least equal to the style and appearance of ministers in general. His gestures are easy and expressive, and his personal appearance every way decorous. His Scripture explanations and illustrations are strikingly simple, natural, and forcible; and the great eagerness of the people to hear him has been manifested wherever he has preached.'

"On his way home he lectured at the following places: Commencing on the 16th of June at Westford, Vt.; the 23rd, at Cambridge, Vt.;

and on the 30th, at Colchester, Vt. As a result of his labors in Colchester, twenty-three were added to the Baptist church between that time and the 2nd of December following.

"The letters addressed to him and his son at this period show that a report was in circulation that he was dead; and as soon as that was successfully contradicted, another was current, that, on re-examining his calculations, he had discovered a mistake of one hundred years. Both of these rumors were several times subsequently revived, and had to be as often contradicted.

"On the 15th of September, in compliance with the wish of many in Rutland, Vt., who were very anxious to hear his course of lectures, he visited that place, and [67] lectured each day, to the 22nd, when he returned to his family, and made arrangements for a second visit to Massachusetts.

"He commenced his labors at Groton, Mass., on the 13th of October, and lectured ten days. In reference to these lectures and others in neighboring towns, Silas Hawley, Congregational minister, wrote from Groton, on the 10th of April, 1840, as follows:

"'Mr. Miller has lectured in this and adjoining towns with marked success. His lectures have been succeeded by precious revivals of religion in all those places. A class of minds are reached by him not within the influence of other men. His lectures are well adapted, so far as I have learned, for shaking the supremacy of the various forms of error that are rife in the community.'

"Closing his lectures in Groton, Mr. Miller gave a third course of lectures in Lowell, continuing from the 23rd of October to the 1st of November. These, like the previous lectures in that place, were attended with precious fruits.

"From the 2nd to the 10th of November, he lectured in Haverhill, Mass., where he made the acquaintance of Elder Henry Plummer, pastor of the Christian church, who embraced his views, and was a steadfast friend till Mr. Miller's decease.

"On the 11th of November, Mr. Miller commenced a course of lectures in Exeter, N. H., which continued till the 19th. On the 12th, a Conference of the Christian connection was in session there, and they called on Mr. Miller in a body. He was a stranger to nearly all of them; and few of them regarded his views with anything more than mere curiosity. Several of them questioned him respecting his faith; but they were speedily [68] silenced by the quotation of appropriate texts of Scripture.

"He arrived in Boston on the 7th of December, and from the 8th to the 16th lectured in Chardon-street chapel, — his first course of lectures in that city.

"On the 12th of December, Mr. Miller writes from Boston to his son: 'I am now in this place lecturing twice a day, to large audiences. Many, very many, go away unable to gain admittance. Many, I am informed, are under serious convictions. I hope God will work in this city.'

"On the 19th of November, he commenced a course of lectures in New Haven, Ct., in the M.E. Church, Rev. Mr. Law, pastor. On Sunday, the 20th, although the house was large, it was crowded; and in the evening many were unable to gain admittance. He continued there till the 26th, the interest continuing during the entire course. *The Fountain*, a temperance paper published in that city, gave the following account of the meeting:

"'Mr. William Miller, the celebrated writer and lecturer on the second advent of our Saviour, and the speedy destruction of the world, has recently visited our city, and delivered a course of lectures to an immense concourse of eager listeners in the First Methodist Church. It is estimated that not less than three thousand persons were in attendance at the church, on each evening, for a week; and if the almost breathless silence which reigned throughout the immense throng for two or three hours at a time is any evidence of interest in the subject of the lectures, it cannot be said that our community are devoid of feeling on this momentous question.

"'Mr. Miller was accompanied and assisted by Elder [69] J.V. Himes, who is by no means an inefficient coadjutor in this great and important work. We did not attend the whole course, the last three lectures being all we had an opportunity of hearing. We are utterly disappointed. So many extravagant things had been said of the "fanatics" in the public prints, and such distorted statements published in reference to their articles of faith, that we were prepared to witness disgusting and perhaps blasphemous exhibitions of Millerism, as the doctrine of the second advent is called.

"'In justice to Mr. Miller we are constrained to say, that he is one of the most interesting lecturers we have any recollection of ever having heard. We have not the least doubt that he is fully convinced of the truth of the doctrine he labors so diligently to inculcate, and he certainly evinces great candor and fairness in his manner of proving his points. And he proves them, too, to the satisfaction of every hearer; — that is, allowing his premises to be correct, there is no getting away from his conclusions.

"'There was quite a number of believers in attendance from other places, and a happier company we have never seen. We have no means of ascertaining the precise effect of these meetings on this community, but we know that many minds have been induced to contemplate the Scripture prophecies in a new light, and not a few are studying the Bible with unwonted interest. For our own part, this new view of the world's destiny is so completely at variance with previous habits of thought and anticipation, that we are not prepared to give it entire credence, though we should not dare hazard an attempt to disprove it.

"'The best part of the story is, that a powerful revival has followed the labors of Messrs. Miller and company. [70] We learn that over fifty persons presented themselves for prayers at the altar of the Methodist church on Sunday evening. On Monday evening the number was about eighty.'"

"From the 6th to the 9th of March [1842], Mr. Miller lectured in Medford, Mass. While here, a friend took him to the phrenologist in Boston, with whom he was himself acquainted, but who had no suspicion whose head he was about to examine. The phrenologist commenced by saying that the person under examination had a large, well-developed, and well-balanced head. While examining the moral and intellectual organs, he said to Mr. Miller's friend:

"'I tell you what it is, Mr. Miller could not easily make a convert of *this man* to his hair-brained theory. He has too much good sense.'

"Thus he proceeded, making comparisons between the head he was examining and the head of Mr. Miller, as he fancied it would be.

"'Oh, how I should like to examine Mr. Miller's head!' said he; 'I would give it one squeezing.'

"The phrenologist, knowing that the gentleman was a particular friend of Mr. Miller, spared no pains in going out of the way to make remarks upon him. Putting his hand on the organ of marvelousness, he said: 'There! I'll bet you anything that old Miller has got a bump on his head there as big as my fist;' at the same time doubling up his fist as an illustration.

"The others present laughed at the perfection of the joke, and he heartily joined them, supposing they were laughing at his witticisms on Mr. Miller.

"He pronounced the head of the gentleman under examination the reverse, in every particular, of what he declared Mr. Miller's must be. When through, he [71] made out his chart, and politely asked Mr. Miller his name.

"Mr. Miller said it was of no consequence about putting his name upon the chart; but the phrenologist insisted.

"'Very well,' said Mr. M.; 'you may call it Miller, if you choose.'

"'*Miller, Miller*,' said he; 'what is your first name?'

"'They call me William Miller.'

"'What! the gentleman who is lecturing on the prophecies?'

"'Yes, sir, the same.'

"At this the phrenologist settled back in his chair, the personation of astonishment and dismay, and spoke not a word while the company remained. His feelings may be more easily imagined than described."

Concerning his personal appearance and private character, we must do the reader the service of giving him the following portrait, drawn by a delicate pencil:

"I have just had the privilege of meeting with this humble servant of God, at the fireside of a friend, and I can truly say that my earnest expectations were more than realized in the interview. There is a kindness of soul, simplicity, and power, peculiarly original, combined in his manner, and he is affable and attentive to all, without any affectation of superiority. He is of about medium stature, a little corpulant, and in temperament a mixture of sanguine and nervous. His intellectual developments are unusually full, and we see in his head, great benevolence and firmness, united with a lack of self-esteem. He is also wanting in marvelousness, and is NATURALLY skeptical. His countenance is full and round, and much like the engraving we have seen, while there is a peculiar depth of expression in his blue [72] eye, of shrewdness and love. Although about sixty-two years of age, his hair is not grey, but of a light glossy auburn, his voice is full and distinct, and his pronunciation somewhat northern-antique. In his social relations, he is gentle and affectionate, and insures the esteem of all with whom he mingles. In giving this charcoal sketch to the public, I have merely sought to correct numerous misstatements, and gratify the honest desire of many distant believers, with a faint outline of the character and appearance of the man whom God has chosen to give the 'Midnight Cry' to a sleeping world." — *Midnight Cry.*

Here we must leave William Miller for the present, to be introduced again in a brief sketch of the rise and progress of Adventism.

My Public Labors

On returning from the great camp-meeting in Eastern Maine, where I heard with deepest interest such men as Miller, Himes, and Preble, I found myself happy in the faith that Christ would come about the year 1843. I had given up all to teach the doctrine to others, and to prepare myself to do this was the great object before me. I had purchased the chart illustrating the prophecies of Daniel and John, used by lecturers at that time, and had a good assortment of publications upon the manner, object, and time of the second advent. And with this chart hung before me, and these books and the Bible in my hands, I spent several weeks in close study, which gave me a clearer view of the subject.

In October, 1842, an Advent camp-meeting was held in Exeter, Me., which I attended. The meeting was large, tents numerous, preaching clear and powerful, [73] and the singing of Second-Advent melodies possessed a power such as I never before witnessed in sacred songs. My Second-Advent experience was greatly deepened at this meeting, and at its close I felt that I must immediately go out into the great harvest-field, and do what I could in sounding the warning. I therefore prepared three lectures, one to remove such objections as the time of the advent not to be known, and the temporal millennium, one of the signs of the times, and one of the prophecy of Daniel.

I had neither horse, saddle, bridle, nor money, yet felt that I must go. I had used my past winter's earnings in necessary clothing, in attending Second-Advent meetings, and in the purchase of books and the chart. But my father offered me the use of a horse for the winter, and Elder Polley gave me a saddle with both pads torn off, and several pieces of an old bridle. I gladly accepted these, and cheerfully placed the saddle on a beech log and nailed on the pads, fastened the pieces of the bridle together with malleable nails, folded my chart, with a few pamphlets on the subject of the advent, over my breast, snugly buttoned up in my coat, and left my father's house on horseback.

I gave from three to six lectures in four different towns around Palmyra. Speaking, with the blessing of God, gave me freedom and confidence, and as the subject opened to me by study, reflection, and in speaking, I found it necessary to divide subjects, so that I added one discourse, at least, to the little series, at each place. I had a good hearing at all these places, but saw no special results.

A school-mate of mine had engaged to teach school in the town of Burnham; but by accident had lost an eye, [74] and was told by his physician that he should rest at least one week before teaching. He urged me to teach for him one week. I consented, and on the first day of school gave an appointment for evening lectures. The school-house was crowded. I gave seven lectures, which were listened to with interest and deep feeling.

At this place I began to feel the burden of the work, the condition of the people, and love for precious souls, as I had not before. Previous to this time I had taken great delight in dwelling upon the evidences of the Advent hope and faith. But now I realized that there was a solemn power in these evidences, to convict the people, such as I did not expect to realize. At the close of my last lecture, sixty arose for prayers. I felt deeply the condition of the people. But what could I do for them? I had not anticipated that I should ever have upon my hands sixty repenting sinners, and was wholly unprepared to lead them any farther. My little pond of thought, in the course of seven lectures, had run out, and I dared not undertake to preach a practical discourse for fear it would prove a failure, and injure the well-begun work. In this state of things it occurred to me to send for my brother, who had been in the ministry five years before me, and was favorable to the Advent doctrine. He came and labored six weeks, baptized, and organized a large church, for which they paid him sixty dollars. I paid, at the close of my week's teaching and lecturing, one dollar for horse-keeping, and left for the Kennebeck. My brother afterward told me that everyone he baptized dated their experience from my lectures.

At one of the places near my native town, where I had given lectures, I met a gentleman who seemed very much interested in the soon-coming of the Lord, who [75] gave me an urgent invitation to visit Brunswick, Me. He stated that there had been no preaching on the subject in that part of the State, and that the Freewill Baptists, who were very numerous on the west side of the Kennebeck river, from Augusta to Brunswick, would willingly give me a hearing. From that moment I felt inclined to make my course toward Brunswick. So, in January, 1843, I left on horseback, thinly clad, and without money, to go more than a hundred miles among strangers.

Night came on as I drew near Augusta, the capital of the State, and I inquired at a humble cottage for entertainment, stating that I was a penniless preacher, and wished to find rest with some Christian, who would willingly care for me and my tired horse without charge. "I am a member of the Christian church of this place," said he, "please stop with me." I gladly accepted the cordial invitation.

During the evening my friend stated that Elder Pearl, a Christian minister, was to preach on the next Sunday, and invited me to stop and give evening lectures in the school-house, and spend the Sunday with my old friend and acquaintance, Elder Pearl. I did so, and had a good hearing, and was kindly received by Elder Pearl, who loved the doctrine of Christ's soon coming. I was also invited to speak in the school district east of that, near the Kennebeck river. The house was filled, and many stood outside at the open windows. A Universalist opposed the doctrine I was presenting to the people, and finding he could prevail nothing, brought a Mr. W., the editor of the Augusta *Age*, a noted Universalist, to oppose me, and, at the close of my lecture, introduced him to the people, and invited them to stop and hear what he had to say. I was too hoarse to reply, [76] and stated that I had no further claims on the congregation. A dozen voices cried, "Clear the way, and let us pass out." Only about twenty-five, and those of the baser sort, remained to hear Mr. W. They were, of course, ready to receive what the speaker chose to say, who, being grieved and angry with the youthful lecturer for leaving, and with the people for following me, was in a state of mind to excite in them a mob spirit.

The reader may think me rash in depriving the editor of the *Age* of a hearing. But I was an inexperienced youth, and feared a battle, and took this course to avoid it. But a battle came the next evening of a different kind. Mr. W.'s hearers decided before leaving the school-house to get all to join them who would, and on the next evening break up the meeting.

As I was about to go to the house the next evening, several of my friends came to me and stated that a mob of at least three hundred was around the school-house. They warned me, as I regarded my life, to remain away from the meeting. I went before the Lord with the matter, then told my friends that I should go to the school-house, trusting in God to defend me. And as I drew near the house I heard the shouting of the mob, and was again warned by the friends who accompanied me to take their advice, and go no further lest I lose my life. I then stated to them that I believed the Lord would in some way defend me, and pressed forward. My friends had resolved that if I went to the place of meeting they would go with me, and stand by me to the last. We found the school-house filled with women, all the windows taken out, and the house surrounded by men enough to fill three such houses. I pressed through the crowd and made my way to the desk. The greatest fear [77] prevailed within the house, while unearthly yells seemed to be the delight of the mob without. The Universalist, who had taken the trouble to get Mr. W. to the place to oppose me, stood close to the desk, and, as I entered it, said to me:

"This, sir, is the result of your conduct last evening, in refusing to hear the gentleman I brought here to reply to you. Your meetings will be broken up."

I replied, "Very well, sir, if it is the will of God, let it be so." I then called the meeting to order, and prayed, standing upon my feet. This I did for two reasons. First, want of room to kneel, and, second, it was safer for me to stand with my eyes open and watch this infuriated Universalist, who seemed to have all he could do to keep from striking me.

While praying, a snow-ball whistled by my head and struck on the ceiling behind me. I read my text from Peter, relative to the burning day of God, and commenced commenting upon it, but could be heard by only a few near me, in consequence of the shouting of the mob. Many snow-balls were thrown at me through the open windows, but none hit me. I raised my voice above the noise of the mob, but while turning for my proof-texts they seemed to gain advantage over me. And there was too much excitement and fear for my proofs to tell on any mind.

My clothing and also my Bible were wet from the melted fragments of a hundred snow-balls which had broken upon the ceiling behind me, and had spattered over me and it. That was no time for logic, so I closed my Bible and entered into a description of the terrors of the day of God, and the awful end of the ungodly. These opened before me wonderfully. Language and power of voice seemed to be given me for the occasion. [78]

I was nearly lost to all around me, while the naked glare of the fires of the day of God seemed to light up the field of slaughter of the ungodly men before me. I cried, "Repent and be converted, that your sins may be blotted out, or you will drink of the wrath of God. Repent, and call on God for mercy and pardon. Turn to Christ and get ready for his coming, or in a little from this, on rocks and mountains you will call in vain. You scoff now, but you will pray then."

The mob seemed more quiet. The night before, a spike was thrown at me and hit me on the forehead, and fell into my Bible, and I put it into my pocket. Inexpressible pity and love for the crowd came over me, and as I was pointing sinners to the Lamb of God, with tears, I held up the spike, saying, "Some poor sinner cast this spike at me last evening. God pity him. The worst wish I have for him is, that he was this moment as happy as I am. Why should I resent his insult when my Master had them driven through his hands," and at the moment raising my arms and placing my hands upon the ceiling behind me, in the position of Christ on the cross.

The Spirit of God accompanied the words and the gesture to the hearts of the crowd. Some shrieked, and a general groan was heard. "Hark! hark!" cried a score of voices. In a moment all was silent. In tears I was calling on sinners to turn and live. I spoke of the love of God, the sacrifice of Christ; his undying pity for vile sinners. I then spoke of his coming in glory to save all who would seek him now. More than a hundred were in tears. "Do you want to see a happy man," said I; "please look at me." Many were weeping aloud, and I was getting so hoarse that I could hardly be heard for the penitent cries and sobs of those [79] around me. "Who are willing to seek Christ," said I, "and with me suffer persecution, and be ready for his coming? Who in this crowd wish me to pray for them, that this may be their happy portion? As many as do, please rise up." Nearly one hundred arose. It was nine in the evening, and I was hoarse and weary. I closed with benediction, took my chart and Bible, and made my way out through the subdued crowd. Someone locked arms with me to assist and guard me. His countenance seemed impressively familiar, yet I did not know him. When I had passed the crowd, I missed him, and, from that evening, who he was, or how he left me, and where he went, have been mysterious. Was it an angel of God, sent to stand by me in the perils of that evening? Who can say it was not?

My lectures continued in this place three or four evenings without the least opposition, and a general reformation followed. In about eight weeks I returned to the place again, and as I entered the door of an especial friend, near the old scene of battle, I recognized my Universalist friend. He had been driving some exciting conversation with the lady of the house about me. Both appeared greatly agitated as I entered. The lady greeted me cordially, but with expressions of astonishment that I was in her house again. The Universalist made for the door, and left in a most abrupt manner. The lady then stated that this man had been talking of me to her in a most abusive manner, and that the last statement he made as I came to her door was as follows: "White is a rascal. He has been overtaken in crime, and is safe in jail. One of my neighbors told me that he saw him yesterday in Augusta jail."

This man was overtaken in his guilty folly in a manner [80] he little expected. He had certainly succeeded poorly in his war against me. I did not see this Universalist, neither did I hear of him after his hasty retreat homeward, showing as much shame as the face of a guilty man is capable of silently expressing. But let the reader go back with me over these eight weeks to the time I closed my labors in this place.

An invitation came for me to visit Sidney, and lecture in the Methodist meeting-house. Cheerfully I accepted, and found a large house filled with attentive hearers. The first evening I spoke on the millennium with freedom. And as I entered the house the second evening, I was told that Elder Nickerson, the presiding elder, would be present that evening. I felt my youth, my lack of general knowledge of the Scriptures, and my brief experience in the things of God. I trembled for the result of that meeting, as I learned that this presiding elder was opposed to the doctrine I was teaching. I was on Methodist ground. This led me to pray most earnestly to God for help. My confidence that the Lord would be with me grew firm as I entered the pulpit.

"I learn," said I, "that Elder Nickerson is in the congregation. Will he please take a seat with me, and join in the services of the evening?" He cheerfully came forward, and I gave him an Advent hymn from the Methodist book to read, and found him willing to pray. I then sung an Advent melody, and took this text: "But of that day and hour knoweth no man, no, not the angels of Heaven, but my Father only." Matthew 24:36. I stated,

1. That the subject was the second advent.

2. That God had not revealed the day nor the hour of that event.

3. That Christ did say, in this connection, that when [81] his people should see the signs in the sun, moon, and stars, that they should know that His coming was near, even at the doors, as truly as men know that summer is near when they see the trees of the field send forth their buds and unfold their leaves.

4. That, as it was in the days of Noah, so should it be at the coming of the Son of man.

The work of warning the people of the coming flood was given to righteous Noah. And in order for him to know when to build the ark, and when to raise his warning voice, the year of the flood was given to him. So shall it be at the coming of the Son of man. The world is to be warned of its approaching doom. And to this end the prophecies of Daniel and John especially point to this time. The signs in the heavens, on earth, in the church, and a wicked world, all show that Christ and the day of vengeance are at hand.

The people of that place were divided between Methodism and Universalism, and it seemed a favorable time to show up from Matthew 24 the view held by Universalists that Christ came at the destruction of Jerusalem. In this I had had some experience, and succeeded in pleasing Elder

Nickerson, who made a few general remarks, not directly opposing me, for fear, as I supposed, of pleasing the Universalists, who evidently felt stirred at my discourse. The meeting closed with good feelings between us. But as I left the house, I received an urgent request by several gentlemen to call at the hotel the next morning, at nine, to answer some questions relative to what I had said of Universalism.

At the hour appointed, I found myself surrounded by several Universalists, who were evidently in an unfriendly mood, and as many Methodists, who had come to see that the young stripling should be well treated. [82] This was kind in my Methodist friends. The interview lasted till the clock struck twelve. My Methodist friends expressed themselves satisfied with my answers. The landlord, who was the leading spirit among those professing Universalism, then arose and said to me:

"Mr. White, please walk out to dinner. This afternoon I wish to show you that there is no connection between the Old and New Testaments."

I was surprised to find that this professed champion of Universalism was really an infidel, and declined dining with him, stating that my mission was to those who received the sacred Scriptures of both Testaments as a harmonious revelation from God. This closed our interview.

My Methodist friends charged me to be on my guard lest the Universalists take advantage of some unguarded expression, and hurt my influence. This was indeed kind in them, and for which I have ever felt to respect them. I gave a few more lectures, and parted with the Christian people of that place, with their thanks for my labors among them, and their expressions of joy that Universalism had been fearlessly exposed without giving its adherents chance to hurt me.

My mind was still on the field of labor farther down the river toward Brunswick. My labors thus far in Augusta and Sidney seemed more accidental, or providential, than in accordance with my design when I left home. And now, with the peace of God ruling in my heart, I journeyed on. As I passed a neat cottage in the town of Richmond, the impression came upon me powerfully, as distinctly as if a voice said to me, "Call into this house." I obeyed, and asked for a drink of water. A middle-aged lady laid down the paper she was reading, and upon it placed her glasses, and gravely [83] said to me, "Please be seated." As she stepped to another room to wait upon me, I took up her paper, and to my joyful surprise, saw that it was the *Signs of the Times*, published by J.V. Himes, No.14 Devonshire street, Boston. And as I took the water, the following conversation, in substance, commenced:

"I see you have the *Signs of the Times*, which teaches the peculiar sentiments of one William Miller. Are you a subscriber for it?"

"I am, and I think it an excellent periodical. Would you like to read it?"

I took the paper from her hand, and enjoyed reading several stirring articles from able pens, then passed it to her, and, with an air of indifference, asked, "What do you do with the long-cherished opinion of nearly all great and good men, of all denominations, that the temporal millennium, in which the conversion of the whole world and the complete triumph of the church is to take place prior to the second advent?"

"I reject the doctrine. And you are mistaken, sir, as to the millennium being a long-cherished sentiment. It is an unscriptural fable of recent date. It has not been the faith of the church until the last century. The parable of the wheat and tares, as explained by our Lord, and his declaration that as it was in the days of Noah so should it be at the coming of the Son of man, forbids the idea. In fact, the prophets of the Old Testament, and the apostles of the New, describe the last days as dark, gloomy and perilous, with the church fallen, and far from God, and the world filled with crime and violence."

"Admitting that you are right on this point, is it not very wrong to set the time, as Mr. Miller has done?"

"Bro. Miller, in searching the Scriptures, has found [84] by the prophetic periods, as he thinks, the time of the end, and, as an honest man, has taken the cross to teach it to the world. He also sees by the signs of the times that Christ's coming is near, even at the doors, and takes the safe side of the question to be ready, and to warn others to get ready. And all those texts usually quoted to show that men are to know nothing of the period of the second advent, do not prove what they are said to prove."

It was evident that this woman was mistress of the subject, and as she proceeded to give the proofs in support of definite time, I interrupted her, stating that I would no longer conceal from her my faith and mission. "I am," said I, "a full believer in the second advent of Christ as taught by Wm. Miller, and have left all to proclaim it."

"Thank the Lord!" she exclaimed, "my prayer is answered in sending you here. My husband is a Freewill Baptist minister, and will be glad to have you speak to the people of his charge here upon the coming of Christ. Let me have your coat and hat. I will send for someone to care for your horse, and will send an appointment to the school for you to lecture this evening."

"What is your husband's name?" I inquired.

"Andrew Rollins," was the reply.

"Is he a believer in the advent doctrine?"

"He does not oppose, and is favorable."

Soon Elder Rollins came in, and his wife introduced me to him as a Second-Advent lecturer. He asked me a few questions in a grave manner, and looked me over closely, as much as to say, "You are a young stripling to go abroad to lecture upon the prophecies." I saw that he was a strong man, watching all my words; therefore thought it best for me to be guarded. [85]

The appointment flew through that portion of the town, and, at the time appointed, what has ever been known as the Reed meeting-house, was filled with both the pious and the curious. And as I sung an Advent melody, all listened with solemn silence, and some wept. Elder Rollins then prayed in a most solemn and fervent manner for the blessing of God to rest upon the youthful stranger who was about to speak to the people. This prayer drew me nearer to him, and I began to feel that in this minister I had found a true friend. And so it proved.

At the close of my lectures, there was a general interest and deep conviction upon all minds. The school children committed to memory all my texts, and almost everywhere you might hear them repeating this one from Daniel 8: "Then I heard one saint speaking, and another saint said unto that certain saint which spake, How long shall be the vision concerning the daily sacrifice, and the transgression of desolation, to give both the sanctuary and the host to be trodden under foot? And he said unto me, Unto two thousand and three hundred days, then shall the sanctuary be cleansed."

As I was about to leave, Elder Rollins said to me, "In two weeks our quarterly meeting, embracing about thirty churches in this locality, will hold its session at Richmond village. I would like to have you give some lectures before the preachers, delegates, and brethren who will be present. I will call the matter up in a business session, and they will probably vote you room, if you will decide to be present and speak to us." "Certainly, I shall be glad of the opportunity to speak what I regard important truth to the heads of your denomination in this part of the State, and will, Providence permitting, be at the meeting in season." This said, I [86] rode off on horseback to fill appointments in Gardiner and Bowdoinham.

After filling these appointments, I returned to the quarterly meeting in Richmond. And as I entered the place of worship, Elder Rollins, who was seated beside the pulpit at the further end of the house, arose and said: "Bro. White, you will find a seat here by me." After the sermon, liberty was given for remarks, and I spoke with freedom upon the Christian life, and the triumphs of the just at the second advent of Christ. Many voices cried, "Amen! amen!" and most in that large congregation were in tears.

The Freewill Baptists in those days were indeed a free people, and many in that congregation were exceedingly anxious to hear upon the subject of the advent. And as I spoke, they seemed to be finding relief from their pent-up feelings in hearty responses and tears. A portion, however, seemed unmoved, unless it was to show in their countenances that they were displeased. Elder Rollins then informed me that his brethren had voted in favor of a lecture at that meeting, and the next day rescinded the vote. This displeased him much, and his statement to me relative to the action of his people as to my speaking to them explained to me the existing state of things. Near the close of that meeting, after getting my consent, Elder Rollins arose and said:

"Bro. White, who sits at my right side, will speak at the Reed meeting-house this evening, upon the second coming of our Lord Jesus Christ. Come up, brethren, and hear for yourselves. We have sufficient room to entertain you all. Come up, brethren — it will not harm any of you to hear upon this subject."

He had as much influence as any minister in that quarterly meeting, and, being disappointed and hurt that [87] his brethren should vote against my lectures, and shut the Advent doctrine out of their meeting, was willing they should feel it. He very well knew that most of his brethren would leave their meeting in the village, and go three miles to hear me, and that their appointed business session would be broken up. And so it was. Three-fourths of the ministers, and nearly every delegate, left, and the Reed meeting-house at an early hour was crowded. My subject was Matthew 24. The interest was wonderful.

As I closed with an exhortation to Christians to fully consecrate themselves, and be ready, and to sinners to seek Christ, and get ready for the coming of the Son of man, the power of God came upon me to that degree that I had to support myself with both hands hold of the pulpit. It was a solemn hour. As I viewed the condition of sinners, lost without Christ, I called on them with weeping, repeating several times, "Come to Christ, sinner, and be saved when he shall appear in his glory. Come, poor sinner, before it shall be too late. Come, sinner, poor sinner, come."

The place was awfully solemn. Ministers and people wept — some aloud. At the close of every call to the sinner, a general groan was heard throughout the entire assembly. I had stood upon my feet explaining the chapter and exhorting for more than two hours, and was getting hoarse. I ceased speaking, and wept aloud over that dear people with depth of feeling such as he only knows whom God has called to preach his truth to sinners. It was nine o'clock, and to give liberty to others to speak, would be to continue the meeting till midnight. It was best to close with the deep feeling of the present, but not till all had a chance to vote on the [88] Lord's side. I then called on all in the congregation who would join me in prayer, and those that wished to be presented to the throne of mercy, that they might be ready to meet the Saviour with joy at his second coming, to rise up. Every soul in that large house, as I was afterward informed by persons in different parts of it, stood up. After a brief season of prayer, the meeting closed.

The next morning I returned to the village, accompanied by at least seven-eighths of that Freewill Baptist quarterly meeting. Everyone was telling what a glorious meeting they attended the evening before. This did not help the feelings of the few who remained away, who had been instrumental in closing the pulpit at the village against the doctrine of the soon coming of Christ. Their course only increased the interest to hear me. The independent stand taken by Elder Rollins resulted in their having a taste of that spiritual food for which they hungered.

At intermission, delegates and ministers invited me to join them in making arrangements as to time when I could lecture to the several congregations in that quarterly meeting who had commodious houses of worship. It was then in the middle of February, and it was decided that there remained not more than six weeks of firm sleighing, giving the people a good chance to attend meetings. Twelve of the most important places were selected for my labors in six weeks. I was to give ten lecturers, which would require of me to speak twenty times a week. This gave me only half a day each week, which I generally found very necessary to travel fifteen or twenty miles to the next place of meeting.

At Gardiner, near the river, Elders Purington and Bush were holding a protracted meeting with poor success, and were ready to hear me. So were most of the [89] church. Some opposed, stating their fears that the Advent doctrine would destroy their reformation. They had, after tugging at the wheel several days, on the third or fourth evening of their meeting, after inviting and coaxing for half an hour, prevailed on two persons to take what was called the anxious seat. In this, however, I saw no reformation to spoil. I told these ministers I was ready to commence my work. They hesitated. I proposed to go where the people were all anxious to hear me. They would not consent to have me leave. I waited one day longer, and spoke several times in social meeting. Many urged me to lecture. I sent them to the ministers. They labored with the opposition privately. Their meeting was becoming divided. I decided to bring the matter to the point of decision, so that I might at once enter upon my work, or leave the place. The ministers held on to me, and also labored with the opposition.

I finally stated before the entire congregation that I had been invited to the place, and had been held there one day by their ministers and most of the congregation, waiting for a few individuals to consent to have me lecture; that I should wait no longer; that if I could not commence lectures that evening, I should go where they wanted to hear. I called for a vote of the congregation. Nearly all voted for me to remain and commence that evening. The ministers said, "Go on with your lectures, and we will stand by you."

As I took the stand that evening, I requested all who loved Christ, and the doctrine of his soon coming, to pray for me, and stated that I would excuse those who did not love him enough to see him come in glory from praying for me, as I thought they could to better advantage [90] and profit pray for themselves. Every ear was open, and every heart felt. The Lord gave perfect freedom in presenting proofs of the advent near, and in exhorting the people to prepare for that day. Many were in tears. I left the pulpit, exhorting the people, and calling on them to come forward to the front slips. About thirty came forward. Many of them wept aloud. I then turned to the ministers in the stand saying:

"These fears, expressed by some unconsecrated ones, that the glorious doctrine of the second coming of Jesus would kill a reformation, are without foundation. Do you think the work of reform has been injured here this evening?"

"No! no! Go on, Bro. White; go on. The Lord is here."

This meeting, apparently, swept away all opposition, and the way was prepared for a good work. But other appointments would not allow me to remain longer than to give three or four lectures more. The protracted meeting then progressed with success.

At Richmond Corners I gave seven lectures in their new meeting-house, just dedicated, and at the close, two hundred arose for prayers. During the progress of the meetings, a Baptist deacon opposed. When I was commenting upon Daniel 7, I stated that it was a historical fact that on February 10, 1798, at the close of the 1260 days, Berthier, a French general, entered the city of Rome and took it, and that on the 15th of the same month the Pope was taken prisoner and shut up in the Vatican; and gave Dr. Adam Clarke as one of my authorities. An educated Catholic broke in upon me, charging me with falsehood, and offered me five dollars if I would read such a statement from Clarke's comments on Daniel. With the promise that I would read Clarke [91] the next evening, and by the entreaties and threats of his neighbors, this enraged Irishman was kept quiet.

The next evening I entered the pulpit with Clarke's Commentary under my arm, and, after calling the people to order by singing an Advent melody, read what Clarke had said upon taking away the dominion of the little horn, which fully sustained what I had stated the previous evening. I then offered the volume to anyone who would see if I had read correctly, stating that I had not been to the trouble of going five miles for the Commentary in order to claim the five dollars. That I chose to let the gentleman keep his money, and have the truth on the subject besides. There was no reply. A gentleman of fine feelings and good influence in the community, who made no pretensions to piety, arose and said:

"I wish to call the attention of this congregation to this one fact, that no persons in this community have manifested opposition to the lectures of Mr. White but a Baptist deacon and a Roman Catholic."

Many were converted in the vicinity, a strong company of believers was raised up, and a Second-Advent camp-meeting was held there in the autumn of 1844.

At Bowdoinham Ridge my labors were well received. A protracted meeting was being held with that church by Elders Quinnum and Hathern. They and the church fully co-operated with me, and a good work followed. On the last day I spent in this place I spoke forenoon and afternoon, then invited sinners to come forward for prayers, and joined in prayer for them. When we arose from our knees the sun was just setting, and I had sixteen miles to go to my next appointment, which was that evening. A friend held my horse at the door. I had labored excessively, and was so hoarse that I could [92] hardly speak above a whisper, and my clothes were wet with sweat. I needed rest. But there was my next appointment. The people would be together in about an hour, and I had sixteen miles to go. So I hastily said farewell to the friends with whom and for whom I had labored, mounted my horse and galloped away toward Lisbon Plains, in a stinging cold February evening. I was chilled, but there was no time to call and warm. My damp clothing nearly froze to me, but I galloped on.

As I rode up to the door of the house of worship, an aged Freewill Baptist minister was saying to the crowd:

"I am sorry to say to the congregation that we are disappointed. The speaker we expected to hear this evening has not come."

As this minister raised his hands to dismiss the people with the benediction, I cried: "Hold! I am here!"

"Good!" cried the minister; and the people sat down. They had been waiting for me more than an hour. With a few words of explanation of my late arrival, I commenced a speak; but I was so thoroughly chilled that my chattering teeth would cut off some of my words. However, I soon warmed up, and felt freedom in speaking.

But there was my poor horse. His turn had come to be wet with sweat, and to shake with cold. A friend stood at the door watching for my arrival, who took the poor creature, and, as I supposed, took care of it. But he simply ties it to the fence with a rope. Heated, wet, and without blanket, it had to stand in the keen wind one hour and a half, trembling with cold until it was ruined. The next morning there was seen in the poor creature a clear case of chest-founder. It is a shame to treat God's poor creatures thus. I learned from this sad [93] circumstances never to leave my horse without full directions as to its wants.

The large house of worship was crowded with attentive hearers three times each day, till my time came to hasten to the next place. On Sunday, the Presbyterian minister had thirteen hearers. On Monday he came to hear me, and as I passed down the symbols of Daniel 8, and began to apply the specifications of the little horn of that chapter to the historical facts of Rome, he broke in upon me, saying:

"You mislead your hearers. Antiochus, and not Rome, is the subject of this prophecy."

"Please wait, sir," was my reply, "till I have finished speaking, then you can talk as long as the people wish to hear you. Be patient, and hear me while I show that Rome, and not Antiochus Epiphanes, is the subject of the prophecy."

The matter was made quite plain, and the minister was told that he could speak. He rose, but his subject was the temporal millennium. All his propositions and proof-texts, which he tediously brought forward, had been examined in my first lecture. But it seemed necessary to briefly reply, notwithstanding it was little more than to repeat the same in the ears of nearly the same congregation. As I closed, a tall, rough-looking, red-shirted lumberman rose up in the house and said:

"The difficulty with Elder Merrill is that he is not ready, and is afraid the Lord will come."

The benediction repeated, the meeting closed. Good fruits followed in this place.

At Brunswick, I had a candid hearing in what was called Elder Lamb's meeting-house, a very large house of worship. My stay was brief, and most of the members of that numerous church were rich and worldly. [94]

They had not sufficient interest to even oppose me. So they heard me with a degree of apparent interest, amounting to little more than curiosity, and let me go.

At Bowdoin, Elder Purington received me as a brother, and stood by me till my work was done in that place. The large house of worship was crowded. The people listened with deep interest and feeling. The Universalists sent a few questions to the desk in writing, which I enjoyed answering. Sinners manifested their desire for salvation, and those who loved Christ and his appearing rejoiced in the Advent hope and faith.

Litchfield Plains was my next place of labor. The house was crowded the first evening. In fact, it was with difficulty that I found my way to the pulpit. To call the people to order, the first words they heard from me were in singing,

"You will see your Lord a coming,
You will see your Lord a coming,
You will see your Lord a coming,
In a few more days,
While a band of music,
While a band of music,
While a band of music,
Shall be chanting through the air."

The reader certainly cannot see poetic merit in the repetition of these simple lines. And if he has never heard the sweet melody to which they were attached, he will be at a loss to see how one voice could employ them so as to hold nearly a thousand persons in almost breathless silence. But it is a fact that there was in those days a power in what was called Advent singing, such as was felt in no other. It seemed to me that not a hand or foot moved in all the crowd before me till I had finished all the words of this lengthy melody. Many [95] wept, and the state of feeling was most favorable for the introduction of the grave subject for the evening. The house was crowded three times each day, and a deep impression was made upon the entire community.

West Gardiner was my next point. Elder Getchel received me like a brother, and seemed to have a good interest in the subject. The people in this part of the town were nearly all Freewill Baptists. There had been one large church in the place, composed mostly of farmers possessing more wealth than piety. A part of the church had wanted a popular minister, and because they were opposed in this by a more humble portion, drew off in a church by themselves, built a fine house, and employed a preacher that pleased them. Here stood in full view two Freewill Baptist meeting-houses, each occupied every Sunday by two ministers of the same denomination, not always on friendly terms. It was a hard place to labor.

While the members of these churches had been occupied with the division in their midst, they had been destitute of the spirit of reformation, and their children had grown nearly to manhood without conversion. These were much affected by my lectures, and sought the Lord, while their parents seemed unmoved. I will leave this place in my narrative, for the present, to return again, as I have something more to relate of the good work here in its proper place.

According to arrangements at the quarterly meeting at Richmond village, I filled all my appointments, and saw in every place more or less of the work of God before I left. But the lectures were usually followed by protracted meetings, and large accessions were made to these churches. At the next quarterly meeting it was publicly stated that within the limits of that quarterly [96] meeting, one thousand souls dated their experience from my lectures during that six weeks.

The second day of April, 1843, I mounted my poor chest-foundered horse, and started for my native town, much worn by the labors of the winter. The snow was very deep. My horse's feet were much of the time, while passing over the drifts, higher than the tops of the fence-posts. My only suit of clothes was much worn, and I had no money. I had not received the value of five dollars for my labors. Yet I was happy in hope. As I journeyed homeward, my horse became very much irritated with frequent turning out into the deep snow and sharp crust in passing teams. Several times while passing women and children he crowded nearly into the sleighs where they were. And fearing that he might seriously injure someone, I decided that it was safest, as teams approached, to dismount, crowd the horse out of the road, and hold him with a firm hand until they passed.

As I was entering the city of Augusta, a farmer was returning home with an empty hay-sled, drawn by six oxen. I chose to ride past this team. The driver sat on the fore part of the sled, and the oxen kept the middle of the road. On being crowded out of the road, my horse became very angry, and as the sled was passing, threw himself over the first set of stakes on to the sled. Seeing strong probabilities that I should be thrown on some one of the second set of sharp stakes, into the snow on the other side. The team continued to move along with my horse fairly loaded upon the sled; and, by the time I had rescued myself from the snow, was several rods from me. [97]

"Halloo!" cried I. "Please stop your team and let me have my horse."

The good farmer stopped his oxen, and assisted me in unloading my horse, which, when I had mounted, galloped off as well as before.

Rain came on, and the firmly-trodden drifts became soft, so that my horse with my weight upon him would frequently sink to his body in the snow. I rode all day with my feet out of the stirrups, and as he would plunge into the snow, I would instantly slide off and relieve him of my weight, that he might better struggle out, or if he could not do this alone, assist him by lifting where most needed.

April 5, I reached my father's house, and, after resting a few weeks till the ground settled, returned to my field of labor, and was rejoiced to learn that the spirit of reformation had swept over the entire field. But the time had fully come for the people in farming districts to hasten out upon their lands, and I found but little chance to get a general hearing excepting on Sunday. However, I soon had a call to labor in East Augusta.

But before going to this place I dreamed that an ox, with very high horns, was pursuing me with very great fury, and that I was fleeing before him for my life. He followed me so closely that I sprang into a house nearby and bolted the door. The ox broke down the door and entered. I left the house through an open window, and escaped to the barn. The ox broke down the barn door and entered. I escaped by another door, and as my last resort for safety, crept under the barn floor. The ox tore up the planks with his horns, and drove me from under the barn. And as he was pursuing me in the open field, I felt his horns goading my back. At that moment wings were given me, and I arose and flew with [98] ease to the roof of the house. The disappointed ox stood looking at me, frequently shaking his horns, and appeared wild with rage. My deliverance was complete, and exultingly I flew from the house near the head of the ox, then quickly arose to the roof of the barn. This repeated several times, I awoke. This dream made quite an impression upon my mind, but soon passed from me, and I thought no more of it until brought to my mind by what occurred in connection with my labors at East Augusta.

As I entered the school-house to meet my first appointment, the only person present was a tall, athletic man, in the middle age of life. As it was a cool evening, he was kindling a fire. He spoke to me in a tone of kindness, but eyed me closely. I was afterward told that Walter Bolton, for this was his name, was an infidel. He was regarded as a good citizen, but had never before been known to take any interest in religious meetings. He attended all my lectures, and seemed deeply interested, and I often heard remarks from his neighbors like this: "What has got hold of Walter Bolton to call him out to these meetings? I never saw him in a religious meeting before, unless it were a funeral." We will leave Mr. Bolton for the present, and pass to other features of this series of meetings.

During the week I gave lectures each evening to small congregations. But Sunday morning, at an early hour, the house was crowded. My subject was the millennium. I labored to show,

1. That those texts usually quoted to prove the conversion of the entire world, did not prove what they are said to prove.

2. What those texts do teach. In speaking upon Isaiah 65, I showed that it was not in this mortal state, [99] upon this old sin-cursed earth, that the leopard would lie down with the kid, and the lion eat straw like the ox, but in the new earth, as plainly declared by the prophet. That beasts, restored from the effects of the curse, would be no more out of their proper places in the earth restored, than when created upon it before the fall.

3. That certain texts in the Old and New Testaments, in most distinct and emphatic language, teach that at no period of man's fallen condition will all men be holy.

At the close of this discourse, a Universalist preacher present arose and said:

"I want five minutes to show that this doctrine has no foundation in the Bible, or in common sense."

He had been a regular Baptist minister, had engaged in trade, and in the sale of liquor, had backslidden, and was preaching the unconditional salvation of all men.

"You will want more than five minutes, sir, to do that," I replied. "It is already half past twelve, and the people need rest and refreshment. When I have closed this afternoon, you can speak as long as they wish to hear you."

"No; this is just the place and time for me to speak, and the people want to hear me."

"We will submit the matter to the congregation, and let them decide it for us," was my reply. I then asked those who agreed with me that the gentleman had better wait till afternoon, to rise up. Nearly the entire congregation were at once on their feet. I then asked those who chose to have him speak immediately to arise. Ten or twelve young men, who looked like finished ruffians, arose. The congregation was immediately dismissed for one hour.

In the afternoon I spoke upon Matthew 24, and, expecting [100] a battle with the Universalist preacher, gave some time to the examination of the view that Christ came the second time at the destruction of Jerusalem. My arguments told on the congregation, and the minister felt it. When I had closed my discourse, I said "There is now room for that gentleman to speak as long as the people wish to hear him." He arose embarrassed, and said in substance:

"I do not want to act the part of the scoffer, or fall under the denunciation of him who says 'My Lord delayeth his coming, and smites his fellow servant;' but I wish to make a few remarks relative to a portion of scripture commented upon by the speaker this forenoon., which you will find in the sixty-fifth chapter of Daniel."

He immediately commenced to ridicule the idea of beasts in Heaven. I saw at once that it was Isaiah 65, and not Daniel, that he referred to. And after he had gotten fairly under way, I called his attention to the fact that he had made a mistake in giving the prophet Daniel credit for speaking of the lion and the ox both feeding on straw, and the leopard and the kid lodging together. It was not Daniel, but another prophet who had thus spoken. He rebuked me for interrupting him. I stated that as he should proceed to show in five minutes that the doctrine I preached had no foundation in scripture, or in common sense, I should see that his reference was all correct. But he affirmed that he was right in quoting Daniel, and went on with his remarks in a style well calculated to disgust the people, and turn them in strong sympathy with me. And when his unsanctified tongue was moving off at full speed, I called to him again, saying, "I am not willing the gentleman shall proceed any further till he reads from Dan. 65, the scripture from which he is speaking. Please turn [101] and read, sir, and satisfy us all that you are correct, and I will consent for you to go on."

He took up his Bible and turned from one side of it to the other, colored up, appeared greatly agitated, and said, "The book of Daniel is torn out of my Bible."

"Here, sir, is mine, said I, and reaching it toward him, said to those seated near me, "Please pass it to him. Mine has the book of Daniel in it." As my Bible was being passed from seat to seat toward this man, he looked distressed. He could not readily find the book of Daniel, not being familiar with his Bible, and evidently made the false statement for the occasion, that this book was torn from his Bible.

He took my Bible and searched from one lid to the other several times for the book of Daniel, but was so agitated that he could not find it. The people fixed their eyes upon him, some with pity, others with apparent anger, while still another class laughed at him. My pity was moved toward him, and I stated that I could help the gentleman. That it was Isaiah, and not Daniel, that he wished to quote. That there were but twelve chapters in all the book of Daniel, and that he wished to speak upon Isaiah 65:17-25. I then quoted these nine verses from memory, and said, "This is what you want, is it not?" "Yes," was the reply, and after a few broken remarks which showed his complete confusion, he sat down and covered his face with his hands. The people were ashamed of him, and seemed astonished that I should know from his remarks what chapter and verses he wanted, and that, without my Bible, I could repeat nearly half a chapter.

If the dream of the ox applied to the effort on the part of this Universalist minister to crush me, then by this time I had all that victory over him represented by [102] my soaring above him on wings. I then exhorted this poor apostate to turn from his sins, and seek a preparation for the coming of Christ. And as I felt the condition of the people, as there was scarcely a praying man or woman present, I exhorted them for half an hour. Nearly all wept. The minister did not raise his head.

I gave an appointment for another evening meeting. Seventy men and women were present. At the close of the lecture I asked those who felt the need of Christ and desired my prayers, that they might become Christians, to rise up. Every one arose, the Universalist minister and all. He then stated as follows:

"I was once a Christian, and was called of God to preach, and if at last I wail in hell, I shall have this to comfort me, that I have been a means in the hands of God of the salvation of sinners."

The reader may judge that by this time this man's faith in universal salvation had become very much shaken. I then asked all among those who had risen, who would esteem it a privilege to come forward and bow with me, to come to the front seats. All seventy started, and soon the floor in front of the seats was crowded so as to give no one a chance to kneel down. I then told them to go back to their seats and kneel down there as best they could, and give their hearts to the Lord. As I knelt every soul present bowed with me. There was no one in all that congregation to join me in vocal prayer, for not one of them enjoyed communion with God.

The next day I called at the house of Walter Bolton. He and his family received me kindly, and conversed with me freely relative to the meetings, and upon the [103] subject of religion in general. Before I left, Mr. Bolton said:

"Mr. White, when you rode into this place I knew you by sight as if I had been acquainted with you for years. Your countenance, hat, coat, horse, saddle and bridle, looked familiar to me. Just before you came here to lecture, I dreamed that a young man rode into this place on horseback, to speak upon the second coming of Christ. I noticed particularly his appearance and dress. The people asked him many questions, which he readily answered in a manner that carried strong conviction to their minds that the doctrine was true. Among these questions were those upon the millennium, suggesting the view that there was to be a thousand years of peace and prosperity to the church, during which time all men were to be holy. They were the very points you examined in your discourse last Sunday forenoon, which called out that Universalist minister. When I saw you, as you rode to this place, my dream came to my mind with such force that I felt that I must hear you speak. This is the reason why I have attended all your meetings, and have watched their progress with interest. Especially when you quoted the very texts which I heard you quote in my dream, and when you made the very remarks upon those texts which I distinctly remember of hearing you make, my feelings were beyond description."

From anything Mr. Bolton said during this interview with him and family, no one would receive the idea that he had been troubled with infidelity. He was under deep conviction, and seemed to choose the religion of the Bible as the theme of conversation. I bowed with this dear family in prayer, and parted with them in tears. The case of Walter Bolton furnishes an illustration [104] of the simple means by which the

Lord sometimes softens the hearts and enlightens the minds of those shut up in the hardness and blindness of infidelity, and prepares them for the reception of light and truth.

In a few days I returned to Palmyra, where I received ordination to the work of the ministry from the hands of ministers of the Christian denomination, of which I was a member. But I soon returned back to East Augusta and baptized three persons. A fourth candidate stood ready to go into the water, but not being satisfied that she was sincere, I refused to baptize her in the presence of a large congregation at the water. This young woman was disappointed, and joined her parents in expressions and manifestations of anger. They sent for Elder Hermon Stinson, an educated Freewill Baptist mister of note, who came to the place, baptized the young woman, and organized a small church. And in just four weeks from that time, Elder Stinson was again called to the place to sit in counsel in the case of this woman, when she was dismissed from the church for bad conduct. Fearing that the bitter feelings of this family toward me might involve me in difficulty, I did not visit the place again.

During the summer of 1843, I was not able to awaken especial interest at any new place upon the subject of the second advent. I visited the congregation of believers in Portland and Boston, labored in the hay-field to earn clothing for the winter, and preached in different places where I had the previous winter given lectures.

In the autumn of that year, in company with my father and two sisters, I attended the Maine Eastern Christian Conference, of which I was a member, held in the town of Knox. Before we reached the place, as [105] night drew on, a heavy shower of rain compelled us to call at a hotel. In those days singing was our delight. My father had been a teacher of vocal music, and my sisters were first-class singers. And as time began to hang heavily upon our hands, we found relief in singing some of the most stirring revival melodies of those times.

The landlord, his family, and many who had been driven in by the rain as we had been, seemed to enjoy our singing, and when we had finished one piece, they would call for another. In this way the evening passed off pleasantly. And when my father called for our bill the next morning, the landlord told him there was none for him to settle, as we had paid him the evening before in singing. He also stated that at any time we would put up with him he would entertain us, and take his pay in singing.

The Christian denomination in Maine, as well as in other States, had been deeply imbued with the spirit of the Advent hope and faith. But it was evident before that conference closed, that many, especially among the ministers, were drawing back, and were partaking of the spirit of opposition. The religious meetings and business sessions, however, passed off with a good degree of apparent harmony. No one preached or spoke in favor of the soon advent of Christ in a manner to offend anyone, and no one directly opposed. But a lack of freedom of spirit was felt by that portion of the conference who were decided believers. This class constituted a majority, and on Sunday, the last day of the meeting, I was urged to preach. But I was young, and well knew that according to custom the ablest men present were already selected to preach to the crowd on that day, yet I felt assured by the Spirit of God, that I had the word [106] of the Lord to speak to the people on that occasion.

Just as the afternoon service was to commence, I felt so deeply impressed with duty to preach, that several ministers noticed it in my appearance, and came to me, saying: "It is your duty to speak, and we will try to secure the time to you this afternoon." I then retired from the crowd in and around the house, to pray over the matter, and while bowed before the Lord, decided that I would press my way directly toward the pulpit, and if the ministers gave me room, and the time, I would speak. As I came toward the pulpit, I saw that the sofa was filled with ministers, and that one of experience in the ministry sat in the center, directly behind the large Bible. This man had been selected to give the last discourse. He had opposed me when lecturing in the west part of the State, and I concluded that he would not consent to give me the time.

But as I drew near the pulpit, my brother Samuel, who was then a member of the conference, and a Bro. Chalmers, stepped down from the pulpit, took hold of my arms, and urged me to take a seat upon the sofa, stating to me that if I wished to preach I should have a chance. I replied that if one of them would read Advent hymns, the other pray, and I could get hold of the large Bible, I would speak. My brother read a hymn, and while Bro. Chalmers was praying, I took the Bible from the stand and turned leaves to certain proof texts. When the prayer was finished, some uneasiness was manifested by several ministers as they saw me in possession of the Bible. The second hymn was read and sung, while I held fast the Bible. My intentions to preach were by this time well known to all the ministers, yet no one offered to take the Bible, or speak to me in reference to occupying the time. The way seemed [107] fully open, and I moved forward with freedom, while responses of "Amen," were heard in different parts of the house from those who cherished the blessed hope of the soon-coming of Jesus.

At the close of this service, the Lord's supper was to be celebrated, and while the friends of Jesus were gathering around his table, I joined with my sisters in singing,

"You will see your Lord a coming," etc.

Our voices were in those days clear and powerful, and our spirits triumphant in the Lord. And as we would strike the chorus of each verse — "With a band of music," — a good Bro. Clark, who ever seemed to have resting upon him a solemn sense of the great day of God near at hand, would rise, strike his hands together over his head, shout "Glory!" and immediately sit down. A more solemn appearing man I never saw. Each repetition of this chorus would bring Bro. Clark to his feet, and call from him the same shout of glory. The Spirit of God came upon the brethren, who by this time were seated ready to receive the emblems of our dying Lord. The influence of the melody, accompanied by Bro. Clark's solemn appearance and sweet shouts, seemed electrifying. Many were in tears, while responses of "Amen," and "Praise the Lord," were heard from almost everyone who loved the Advent hope. The emblems were passed, and that yearly meeting closed.

In a few weeks I returned to my old field of labor, and gave lectures at Brunswick and Harpswell, where a good degree of interest was manifested. The field of labor seemed to open before me as winter drew near. I had become acquainted with Bro. John Pearson, Jr., of Portland, who had been laboring a portion of his time [108] giving lectures upon the advent near, and I invited him to join me. We labored together in different parts of Maine much of the time for nearly one year. At the Reed neighborhood, in Richmond, we saw a good work. Elder E. Cromwell, the pastor of the church, embraced the faith in full. I there baptized several.

We labored at Litchfield and saw a good work. Many professed Christians embraced the faith, and sinners were converted. The Congregationalist minister felt that the work was against his interests, and in private circles opposed. On returning to the place, after an absence of some weeks, I met this minister in the road, and as we passed he seemed to be surprised to meet me again, and said,

"Why, Mr. White, are you yet in the land of the living?"

"No, sir," was the reply, "I am in the land of the dying, but at the soon coming of the Lord I expect to go to the land of the living." We each went our way.

The year 1843, Jewish time, which was supposed to reach, as stated by Mr. Miller, from March 21, 1843, to March 21, 1844, passed, and many were sadly disappointed in not witnessing the coming of the Lord in that year. But these soon found relief in the clear and forcible application to the existing disappointment of those scriptures which set forth the tarrying time.

It was as early as 1842 that the prophecy of Habakkuk suggested the idea of the prophetic chart to the mind of that holy man of God, Charles Fitch. No one, however, then saw in this prophecy the tarrying time. Afterward they could see both the chart and the tarry. Here is the prophecy:

"Write the vision, and make it plain upon tables, that he may run that readeth it. For the vision is yet [109] for an appointed time, but at the end it shall speak and not lie. Though it tarry, wait for it; because it will surely come, it will not tarry." Chap. 2:2, 3.

True believers were also much comforted and strengthened by that portion of the prophecy of Ezekiel which seemed exactly to the point, as follows:

"And the word of the Lord came unto me, saying, Son of man, what is that proverb that ye have in the land of Israel, saying, The days are prolonged and every vision faileth? Tell them, therefore, Thus saith the Lord

God, I will make this proverb to cease; and they shall no more use it as a proverb in Israel. For I am the Lord, I will speak, and the word that I shall speak shall come to pass. It shall be no more prolonged, for in your days, O rebellious house, will I say the word, and will perform it, saith the Lord God. Again the word of the Lord came to me saying, Son of man, behold, they of the house of Israel say, The vision that he seeth is for many days to come, and he prophesieth of the times that are far off. Therefore, say unto them, Thus saith the Lord God, There shall none of my words be prolonged any more, but the word which I have spoken shall be done, saith the Lord God." Chap. 12:21-28.

There was a general agreement with those who taught the immediate coming of Christ, in applying the parable of the ten virgins of Matthew 25 to the events connected with the second advent. And the passing of the time of expectation, the disappointment and the delay, seemed to be forcibly illustrated by the tarrying of the bridegroom in the parable. The definite time had passed, [110] yet believers were united in the faith that the event was near. It soon became evident that they were losing a degree of their zeal and devotion to the cause, and were falling into that state illustrated by the slumbering of the ten virgins of the parable, following the tarrying of the bridegroom.

The first of May I received an urgent call to visit West Gardiner, and baptize. A messenger was sent twenty miles for me. He stated that there were ten or twelve children there, who were convicted by my lectures, who had held their little meetings by themselves, and sought and found the Lord, and who had decided to have me baptize them. Their parents opposed the idea, and told them that Elder Getchel, the pastor of the church, would baptize them. They held a little counsel and decided that they would not go into the water unless they could have me to immerse them. Their parents yielded and sent for me. But before I reached the place, an effort was made to intimidate these dear children, and, if possible, to frighten them, and thus keep them from doing their duty. "What kind of an experience does Mr. White suppose those babies can tell?" said a Baptist minister of the most rigid stamp of past times.

The large school-house was crowded at the time appointed, and there were three unfriendly ministers present to watch the proceedings. "Please vacate these front seats," said I, "and give those who are to be baptized a chance to come forward." Twelve boys and girls, from seven to fifteen years of age, came forward. It was a beautiful sight, which stirred the very depths of my soul, and I felt like taking charge of them as I would of a class in school. I was determined to help [111] the feelings of those dear children as much as possible, and rebuke their persecutors.

After taking my text, "Fear not little flock, it is your Father's good pleasure to give you the Kingdom," Luke 12:32, a text quite applicable to the occasion, I stated that I should not require the children before me to relate their experiences before the congregation. That it would be cruel to decide their fitness to follow the Lord in the ordinance of baptism by the confidence and freedom they might have in speaking before those professed Christians present who felt unfriendly toward them, and that I should, at the close of my discourse, ask them a few questions. The children were much comforted and cheered by the discourse. In fact I was enjoying decidedly a good time with those lambs of the flock. They then arose in their turn and answered some questions, and related particulars as to their conviction of sin, the change they had experienced, and the love of Jesus they felt, until the congregation heard twelve intelligent and sweet experiences. It may be proper for me here to state that questions asked these children at the very point in the relation of their experiences when they were becoming confused, and were about to cut their story short, gave them confidence, and helped them to enter into all parts of their experiences.

I then called upon all present who felt opposed to the baptism of the little flock before me, to rise up. Not one arose. I stated to them that the present was the time to object if they had objections. But if they did not then and there object, to forever be silent. I then said to the children that no one objected, and that the way was fully open before them, and no person from that day had any right to object to their baptism. We [112] went to a beautiful body of water, where I led those dear children down into the liquid grave, and buried them with their divine Lord. Not one of them strangled or seemed the least agitated. And as I led them out of the water and presented them to their parents, the children met them with a heavenly smile of joy, and I praised the Lord with the voice of triumph. This meeting, and that sweet baptism, has lived among the most pleasing memories of the past, and when laboring for the youth in different States, I have probably rehearsed more or less of the particulars of that sweet meeting, and that happy baptism, a hundred times.

In the month of June, 1844, a Second-Advent Conference was held at Poland, Me., which I attended in company with Elder Pearson. I had traveled extensively in the heat and dust of summer, until my plain clothing was much soiled and worn. And not enjoying my usual freedom of spirits, I chose to remain silent and give others the time. I enjoyed the preaching, however, and the social seasons of this excellent conference, and at its close felt my usual spiritual strength and freedom.

There was present at this conference an Elder H., from Eastern Maine, who had much to say in his peculiar, noisy style. He professed to be a man of great faith, and wonderfully filled with the Holy Spirit. If noise, harsh expressions, rough language generally, and frequent empty shouts of "Glory, hallelujah," constituted the sum total of the fruits of the Spirit, then this Elder H. was an exceedingly good man. But if love, peace, long-suffering, gentleness, goodness, meekness, and temperance, are among the fruits of the Spirit, this poor man was sadly deficient. In fact, these precious fruits were not exhibited in him. He enjoyed a shout with those [113] who would join with him, and ever appeared to feel strong and sure of Heaven. Self appeared in this man, and not Christ. He had much to say of humility; but his was evidently on the outside. His style of worship, and pretended humility, are well-described by the apostle as "Voluntary humility and will-worship." At times he was so very humble (?) that he chose not to seat himself at the table with others to take food; but, forgetting the words of the apostle, "Let all things be done decently and in order," he would take food from the table, and go behind the door and eat it, attracting attention to his wonderful humility by shouts. But if corrected for his faults, however carefully, the demon in him was aroused at once. This man had no words of tenderness and comfort for the weak and fainting. So far from this, he even boasted of running over, as he expressed it, this one and the other. He spoke and acted as if he regarded himself as being on exhibition at that meeting as a wonderful specimen of faith and goodness. His career since that time, in following the spirit that seemed to possess him at that conference, has proved that the man was laboring under the sad mistake of supposing himself led by the Spirit of God, while being controlled by Satan.

The reader may be disappointed at the introduction of this unpleasant matter, choosing to read only of those incidents with which are connected the victories of the work and power of God. But it may be for the safety and sure advancement of young disciples, and those of little experience in the conflicts of the Christian life, to learn of the trials of the way, and of the wiles of the Devil, as to know only of the power and love of God, and the triumphant victories of his truth and people. The various attacks of Satan, in order to mislead and finally [114] destroy even honest men and women, may with propriety, in consequence of their numbers, bear the name of legion. And the duty of all is, as stated by our Lord, "Watch and pray, lest ye enter into temptation."

But he who is filled with pride in spiritual things, and is unteachable — thinks himself especially led by the Spirit, and understands all about the work of the Lord, who regards himself as an eminent Christian, yet is easily tempted, and becomes jealous of being slighted and even ugly if he does not receive a large share of attention — is a tool for the Devil, and an exceedingly dangerous man. He is a medium in the hands of Satan through which to affect and mislead the precious flock of Christ. Let all beware lest they, in some way, be brought more or less under the influence of such, and, in consequence, weave into their experience uncomely stripes of vain religion.

Such things ever have existed, and ever will exist during the entire period of Satan's efforts to wrest precious souls from the hands of Jesus Christ. "For there must be also heresies among you," says Paul, "that they which are approved may be made manifest among you." These, in the Lord's providence, constitute a portion of the fuel to heat the furnace of affliction in which the true Christian loses his dross and is refined, so as to reflect in his life the meekness and purity of the loving Lamb of God.

Therefore let not the beloved of the Lord think it strange concerning the fiery trial which is to try them, as though some strange thing had happened unto them. But rejoice, inasmuch as they are partakers of Christ's sufferings, that when his glory shall be revealed, they may be glad with exceeding joy. 1 Peter 4:12, 13.

The reader will please return to Poland conference. [115] One morning about forty brethren and sisters bowed at the family altar, at the house of Bro. Jordan, while Elder H. led in prayer. A portion of that strange prayer was in substance as follows:

"O Lord, have mercy on Bro. White. He is proud, and will be damned unless he gets rid of his pride. Have mercy upon him, O Lord, and save him from pride. O Lord have mercy, and wean him from the pride of life. Break him down, Lord, and make him humble. Have mercy upon him. Have mercy."

He went on telling a long story about me, informing the Lord of my pride, and how sure I was of destruction unless I should speedily repent, and closed up with vehement cries of "Have mercy! Have mercy! Mercy! Mercy!" This was his way of treating those who did not seem to receive him with feelings of great reverence for his special humility and extra holiness. His object in this was to cast fear upon those around him, and thus bring them directly under his influence, that they might show him all that respect which his especial endowments demanded.

But he did not succeed in my case. After the company had arisen to their seats, and had for a while painfully pondered in silence what these things could mean, I drew my chair near Elder H., and in a kind manner said to him:

"Bro. H., I fear you have told the Lord a wrong story. You say I am proud. This I think is not true. But why tell this to the Lord? He knows more about me than you do. He does not need to be instructed in my case. But this was not your object. You wished to represent me before these brethren and sisters as proud, and have chosen to do so through the medium of prayer to God. Now, sir, if I am proud, so much so [116] that you are able to give the Lord information on the subject, you can tell me before these present in what I am proud. Is it in my general appearance, or my manner of speaking, praying, or singing?"

"No, Bro. White, it is not in those things."

"Well, is it manifested by these worn and soiled clothes? Please look me over. Is it in my patched boots? my rusty coat? this nearly worn-out vest? these soiled pants? or that old hat I wear?"

"No; I do not see pride in any of these things you mention. But, Bro. White, when I saw that starched collar on you, God only knows how I felt."

And here the man wept as though his heart would break. This was for effect. It was his usual resort when he had points to carry in a difficult case. In an extremity, tears are not unfrequently woman's closing and most powerful argument. In her, if her cause be just, they are excusable, and even appropriate and beautiful. But to see a coarse, hard-hearted man, possessing in his very nature but little more tenderness than a crocodile, and nearly as destitute of moral and religious training as a hyena, shedding hypocritical tears for effect, is enough to stir the mirthfulness of the gravest saint.

"But let me explain to you, Bro. H., about this starched collar. I may be able to help you. When I came to this conference, sister Rounds offered to do my washing, and as I had no clean change, she kindly lent me her husband's shirt, which unfortunately has a starched collar. Mine have only a narrow binding round the neck. I wear no collars only in cases of necessity like the present. It is this, sir, that has given rise to all your ado this morning. I usually wear a black alpaca bosom, but am not the owner of a single collar. You have certainly told the Lord a wrong story about [117] me, under circumstances the most inexcusable. And I think your first and most important work is to settle this matter with him."

Elder H. dropped upon his knees, and said, in substance:

"O Lord, I have prayed for Bro. White, and he is displeased with me for it. Have mercy upon him! Have mercy! Mercy! Mercy!"

And seeing that none joined with him, not even so much as to kneel, he felt that his effort was proving a failure, and in a subdued tone came to me and said:

"Why did you not kneel with me? O Bro. White, I have felt for you, prayed for you, and have wept over you, and I hope you will not be offended."

"Certainly, I am not offended. There is nothing in all this to offend anyone. I pity you. You are suffering from unsanctified feelings arising from an unfortunate application of false ideas. Your prayers are no more to me than the howling of the winds. And when you, under such circumstances, plead your tears, feelings of shame and inexpressible disgust and pity for you come over me. I advise you to carry this matter no further; and I hope you will learn a good lesson from the folly you have manifested this morning.

By this time I seemed to lose sight of that gloom and despondency under which I had been suffering for several days, and I enjoyed the closing portion of the conference exceedingly well, and from that time felt my usual freedom of spirits. This was my first experience in meeting and rebuking fanaticism, which served to prepare me to deal with it in its ever-varying forms in after time.

That fanaticism did arise about this time, and labor to attach itself to the Advent cause, I would not deny. [118] I, however, by no means admit the truthfulness of the highly-colored reports of the bitter enemies of the cause. Not more than one in ten of the slanderous reports had the least semblance of truth in them. Men filled with prejudice and with bitterness against the proclamation of the immediate second advent of Christ, mingled with fear that it might be true, were totally unfitted to fairly represent the faith, motives and actions of believers. And there are no good reasons why he who gives a faithful sketch of Advent history, should hesitate to admit all the facts relative to fanaticism which have arisen from the bigotry and blind zeal of such men as Elder H., and those more designing and shrewd, who have borne the Advent name, and have professed the Advent faith.

Is it not one of the plainest facts in sacred history, that when God has especially wrought for his people, Satan has ever improved the opportunity to make especial efforts? And, during the entire period of the controversy between Christ and his angels, and Satan and his angels, when the sons of God come to present themselves before the Lord, may they not expect that Satan will come also? Has not this ever been true in the history of the people of God? And does not the sad experience of the church of Jesus Christ, since the time where sacred history leaves it, agree with that of the patriarchs and prophets?

We read of Luther's perplexities, and of his anguish, in consequence of the conduct of fanatics, and the terrible influence the course of these men had on the great reformation, and count these things among the evidences that God was especially with Martin Luther. And there were the Wesleys, and a host of other good men, who have lifted at the great wheel of reform, and have [119] blessed the world with the inspiring influence of their living faith. These men who kept pace with the spirit of reform, have, in their turn, been annoyed at every step by Satan close at their heels, pushing unguarded souls, over-zealous and illy-balanced ones, into fanaticism. The experiences of these men are in harmony with that of the holy men of old, and attest the fact that when and where God works for his people, just there is the time and place for Satan to practice his impositions upon those he can get under his foul influence.

Did Satan stir up fanaticism in connection with the Advent movement? This is one of the proofs of the genuineness of the work. What! He suffer the world to be warned of their and his approaching doom, and he not be stirred in consequence of it? The church be aroused to action, and to readiness for the day of God, and sinners by thousands leaving his ranks and seeking a preparation to meet the King of kings, and he remain quiet? No. He knows his time is short, hence not only his wrath, but his wiles in all their forms. This is well illustrated by what is said to be a dream. A traveler saw Satan seated upon a post, in front of a house of worship, asleep. He aroused him from his slumbers and addressed him as follows:

"How is it that you are so quietly sleeping? This I conclude is unusual for you, considering your reputation for activity in your kind of work. Is it not?"

"Yes," was the reply, "but the people in this house of worship are asleep, and the minister is asleep, and I thought this a good time for me to take a nap."

Let the people be aroused to the living truths of the word of God, and to a life of faith and holiness; let them with gladness receive the news of the return and peaceful reign of the Just One; let them consecrate [120] themselves and all they have to the Lord, and with one united voice swell the note, "Behold he cometh," and you will have good evidence that the powers of darkness are all astir. Satan will not sleep then. With vigilance will he manifest his wrath, and, calling to his aid all the fallen angels of his realm, his wiles will be imposed upon all connected with the people of God who are not properly instructed and guarded.

But it should be distinctly understood that the proclamation of time in the message symbolized by the first angel of Revelation 14:6, 7, and in the cry "Behold the Bridegroom cometh," given in great power in the autumn of 1844, did not produce fanaticism. In those solemn movements, believers were sweetly united in the one blessed hope, and the one living faith. It was when they were left without definite time, during the summer of 1844, that extravagant views of being led by the Spirit prevailed, and to some extent brought in fanaticism, division and wild-fire, with their blighting results, among the happy expectants of the King of glory. But when the proclamation of definite time came in the autumn of 1844, fanaticism, ultra holiness, unhappy divisions, and their results, melted away before it like an early autumn frost before the rising sun.

Rise and Progress of Adventism

A wide field is before me, and I must study brevity upon this subject, or it will crowd more important matter out of this volume. I can therefore give but a brief sketch of the most prominent features of this great movement. I shall be principally indebted to an article published in the *Advent Shield* for May, 1844, written by J. Litch, for what is said upon this subject. The [121] first period of expectation had just passed, when Mr. Litch reviewed the entire ground, and presented facts in the case for the edification and encouragement of believers. These facts can never lose their interest to all true believers, till the Advent hope shall be consummated.

"The rise of the Advent cause, as it has been developed by Mr. Miller, may be dated A.D. 1831. For although he discovered his principles as early as 1818, it was not until 1831 that he first began to publish them abroad.

"His first step in this work was the publication of a series of articles on the subject of Christ's second coming, which appeared in the *Vermont Telegraph*, a Baptist paper, published in Brandon, Vt. Those articles were written to rid himself of the strong impression which followed him, that he must go and publish this thing to the world.

"But after writing and publishing the above, instead, as he expected, of finding relief from his responsibilities, he only found the inward monitor the more earnestly pressing him, saying, 'Go and tell it to the world, or their blood will I require at thy hand.' To rid himself of this strong impression, he wrote a synopsis of his views, and in the spring of 1832 he published it in pamphlet form, and spread it over the country, and sent it to different parts of the world among the missionary stations."

Invitations for Mr. Miller to lecture came in from all directions, which he accepted, and he continued to travel and labor with great success among the people, but with little encouragement from the ministry.

"In 1836 Mr. Miller found a friend who undertook [122] the publication of a volume of lectures, the series which he usually gave as a course. The publication of those lectures constituted a new era in the history of the Advent cause; for, from that time, wherever he went and lectured, the written lectures which were left behind continued to preach and establish those who were partially convinced of the truth. His labor, by this means, ceased to be like writing upon the sand, as formerly. It is one of those strongly-marked demonstrations which history presents of the power and influences of the press for good or evil.

"Those books gradually spread abroad, where he had never been in person, and created an interest in the public mind to investigate the subject for themselves. It was not, however, until the winter of 1837-8, that the work attracted much attention in Massachusetts. About the month of February, in 1838, several copies of the lectures found their way into Massachusetts, and awakened quite a sensation. One copy fell into the hands of the editor of the *Boston Daily Times*, and most of the lectures were re-published in that paper, and obtained quite an extensive reading. The effect was so great that it was found necessary to provide an antidote, in the shape of two letters from the pen of Rev. Ethan Smith."

Mr. Litch introduces his own interesting experience in the Advent cause in the following language:

"About the time of the appearance of those lectures in the *Boston Times*, a copy of the work was put into the hands of the present writer, with a request that he should read it and give his opinion of its merits. The idea of an attempt to discover the time of Christ's second advent was to him so strange, that he could scarcely make up his mind to give the book a perusal. No doubt [123] came into his mind but what he could entirely overthrow the whole system in five minutes. For, thought he, according to Paul, [2 Thessalonians 2,] the falling away must first come, and the Man of Sin be revealed; which the great body of commentators understood to be the Papal system. But, according to Daniel and John, that power is to continue for 1260 days, or years; and the date assumed by the most learned writers of the age, for the commencement of the period, was 606, and consequently it would not end until 1866. This was a decisive argument.

However, to gratify a friend, and from a curiosity to know what arguments could be adduced in support of so novel a doctrine, the book was read. There was no difficulty in adopting most of the sentiments advanced in the first lecture. Prejudice began to give way, and the idea of the glorious reign of Christ on the earth renewed, was most delightful. From that, the 1260 days came up, and the evidence presented, by which it was clearly shown that those days terminated in 1798, having begun in 538. The great argument against the coming of the Lord, which had appeared so strong and invulnerable, soon vanished; and a new face shone forth from Paul's argument. The substance of it was, the predicted period having gone by, and the Papacy having been consumed away by the spirit of the Lord's mouth, he is next to be destroyed by the brightness of Christ's coming. Then there can be no millennium until Christ comes — for the reign of the Man of Sin and a glorious millennium cannot coexist. Thus the old fabled millennium was lost.

"Before concluding the book, I became fully satisfied that the arguments were so clear, so simple, and withal so scriptural, that it was impossible to disprove [124] the position which Mr. Miller had endeavored to establish.

"The question of duty then presented itself thus: 'If this doctrine is true, ought you not, as a minister of the gospel, to understand and proclaim it?' Yes, certainly I had. 'Then why not do so?' Why, if it should after all, prove false, where will my reputation be? And besides, if it is not true, it will bring the Bible into disrepute, after the time has gone by. But there is another view to be taken of this subject. How shall we know whether it is true or false? Can it be known except by the testimony of the Scriptures? What do they teach? This is the true question. If it is true that the Lord is coming so soon, the world should know it: if it is not true it should be discussed, and the error exposed. I believe the Bible teaches the doctrine; and while I believe thus, it is my duty to make it known to the extent of my power. It is a scriptural subject, and one full of interest; and the discussion of it cannot do harm. These prophecies and periods are in the Bible, and mean something — if they do not mean this, what do they mean? Thus I reasoned, until the Lord, in a night-dream, showed me my own vileness, and made me willing to bear reproach for Christ, when I resolved, at any cost, to present the truth on this subject."

As soon as Mr. Litch came to this decision, he published a synopsis of Mr. Miller's views in a pamphlet, entitled the *Midnight Cry*. He continued to lecture, and also published a second work of 204 pages, entitled "The Probability of the Second Coming of Christ about A.D. 1843."

"It was in this work that the calculation on the fall of Ottoman supremacy on the 11th of August, 1840, was first given to the world. So also the argument on the [125] 1260 days, showing how all the events which were to precede the time, times and a half, centered in 538, while the decree of Justinian was given in 533.

"This work circulated through New England, and excited something of an interest. The subject rested here, with the exception of a few newspaper articles published in *Zion's Herald*, of Boston, and *Zion's Watchman*, of New York, until the spring of 1839.

"In that year (1839) Mr. Miller was invited into Massachusetts to lecture. In that tour he visited and lectured in Randolph, Lowell, Groton, and Lynn. His introduction was principally through the influence of Elder T. Cole, of Lowell, a minister of the Christian connection. Again, in the autumn and winter of the same year, he returned and lectured in Exeter, New Hampshire, and Haverhill, Massachusetts, where a good effect was produced.

"It was at this Exeter meeting that he first became acquainted with Elder J.V. Himes, and received his first invitation to visit Boston and give a course of lectures in the Chardon-Street Chapel. His first course of lectures in that place constituted altogether a new era in the history of Adventism. An excitement was produced in Boston which demanded light, and prepared the public mind to sustain the enterprise of hiring the Marlboro' Chapel for a course of lectures. From that point an influence was extended through all the adjacent country; and such was the demand for light that it was determined to issue a new and revised edition of the lectures. This work was undertaken, without fee or reward, by that devoted friend of the cause. He cheerfully undertook the revision of the work and the superintendence of publication, which a Boston publisher agreed to do if he could have the profits arising [126] from an edition of five thousand copies. This he had. Mr. Miller has often been blamed for securing the copyright, and hence it is but just to him and the cause to say, that it was the only condition on which the publisher would undertake to issue the work. After selling the five thousand copies, Mr. Mussey, the publisher, concluded that the demand was over. For the purpose of supplying the public, Mr. Himes then undertook, at the earnest solicitation and advice of friends, the publication of the work himself. At the same time he abandoned the copyright, and thus, to save reproach on the cause, exposed himself to the competition of any and all who chose to compete with him. The same course has been pursued in reference to all his other publications. Notwithstanding all this, all that the tongue of slander could invent has been heaped upon him for the stand he took and the self-denying course he pursued on this subject.

"During Mr. Miller's lectures in Boston, a work entitled 'Illustrations of Prophecy, by David Campbell,' appeared. Some other works of an ephemeral character, from Orthodox, Infidel, Universalist, and other *ists*, appeared about the same time, and accomplished each their work, by overthrowing — not Mr. Miller — but one another.

"Under these repeated attacks from the pulpit and press, it was felt that some organ of communication should be opened, by which the public mind could be disabused in reference to the varied reports which were circulated in reference to Mr. Miller and his views. He had long sought for someone to take the supervision of a paper through which he could speak to the public; but such a man could not be found, who for love or [127] money would undertake the task, and bear the scorn of an unbelieving world.

The Signs of the Times

"At this juncture, when the storm of opposition grew heavy, the providence of God raised up a man for this work also. The unwearied friend of this cause, J.V. Himes, who has so nobly stood in the front of the hosts and the hottest of the fire, came forward and threw himself into the enterprise, to make up the breach. On the 20th of March, 1840, without money, patrons, or scarcely friends, he issued the first number of the *Signs of the Times*. The appearance of that sheet was hailed with joy by many a longing heart, waiting for the consolation of Israel. The paper was sustained for the first year at a considerable expense to the editor, besides his own unrequited toil. As might be expected, the enemies of the cause were greatly discommoded by the appearance of such a weapon, both offensive and defensive. Nothing which a heart surcharged with gall could invent, or the tongue of envy utter, was left unsaid or unwritten against the editor. But his language was, None of these things move me. He was sufficiently convinced of the truth of the doctrine to know that it was worthy, at least, of a full and candid investigation, and this he determined it should have, so far as he was able to gain thus much for it.

"The paper thus started was published for two years as a semi-monthly, and, since then, as a weekly periodical. It has been read by multitudes throughout the United States, and in the British provinces, with the deepest interest, and has been to thousands an angel of [128] mercy and love; the good it has accomplished will only be known in the great day of the Lord.

"During the same winter (1839-40) Mr. Miller was invited to lecture in Portsmouth, N.H., and Portland, Me. In both these places, as well as in Boston and vicinity, his labors were attended with refreshing showers of divine grace. Numbers embraced the doctrine of the Lord's speedy coming, who are yet strong in the faith, giving glory to God. This winter's campaign produced an excitement throughout New England, and raised up friends in almost every town.

"As the spring opened and the summer came, the entire community were excited, and expectation on tiptoe, in reference to the 11th of August and its anticipated events, the fall of the Ottoman empire, etc., etc. Many were the predictions that when that day should have passed by, as it certainly would do, without the event being realized, then the spell would be broken, and Adventism would die. But the time came; and it must be confessed it was for a few weeks a time of trial to many. Yet 'He who tempers the wind to the shorn lamb,' had compassion on his little ones, and did not suffer them to be tempted above what they were able to bear. And few, very few, even under that trial, shrunk from their faith. The time came and passed by; and, as a matter of course, the distance from Constantinople could not be passed without consuming some considerable period of time. But when the fact did reach us, it was found that on the very day anticipated, the 11th of August, a transfer was made of the supremacy of that empire from Mahometan hands. This fact entirely discomfited the hosts of the enemy. The cause again revived, and careered on its way with still greater power than ever before." [129]

UNITED EFFORT

"Up to this period all that had been done was accomplished by individual effort. In this depression of affairs, it was determined to hold a 'Second-Advent Conference' in Boston, where the friends of the cause could congregate and give expression to their feelings, and put forth an effort to arouse the country and the world to a sense of its coming doom. This meeting was assembled in the Chardon Street Chapel, on the 15th of October, 1840, and continued two days. This was styled 'The First General Conference of Second-Advent Believers.' It was a season of comfort and refreshing to the lovers of the glorious appearing of our blessed Lord.

"In the spring of 1840, the writer of this article wrote and published a third work, entitled 'An Address to the Clergy.' It embraced in a short compass an exposition of the nature of the kingdom of God; also an article on the return of the Jews, and their title to the land promised to Abraham for an everlasting possession. It presented the subject in a light somewhat different from what it had ever been presented before in this country. The effect of it on the clergy was considerable; some were moved by it to give the subject an examination, and became satisfied that it was the true position. It also contained the argument on the fall of the Ottoman empire. The second edition, published in 1841, was revised by giving the historical facts, showing the fulfillment of the calculation."

June 15-17, 1841, the second General Conference of Advent believers was held in Lowell, Mass. It was a time of deep interest, and gave a new impulse to the cause. [130]

During the ensuing summer Mr. Litch visited the seats of the four New England Methodist Episcopal Annual Conferences, and gave lectures which called out more or less of the ministry to hear him. His efforts in this direction removed prejudice, and made a good impression.

"The course of Adventism was steadily onward, both among clergy and laity, throughout New England.

"It was in the autumn of this year that that devoted and beloved brother, C. Fitch, returned again to the examination of the question of the Lord's coming, and came out a decided advocate of the doctrine. He at once entered the field, and has proved an efficient auxiliary to the cause.

"Bro. William Miller continued his labors in various parts of the country with great success. Bro. Himes also devoted as much time as his pastoral and other duties would allow, to lecturing on the subject.

"In October another conference was held in Portland Me., which gave a new impulse to the work in that section of the country. Another conference was appointed and held in the Broadway Tabernacle, New York city, which was the first successful effort ever made in that city.

"From New York city we proceeded to Low Hampton, the residence of Bro. Miller, and commenced another conference. It was a season of refreshing to all, and more especially to Bro. Miller himself. It was the first conference he had ever attended; and to find around him such a host as were congregated there, from east, west, north, and south, from Canada as well as the States, raised up to proclaim this truth, by the blessing of God on his labors, was to him most refreshing and encouraging. [131]

"During the winter of 1841-2, conferences were held in various places, which were all attended with good: Boston, Mass.; Dover, N.H.; Sandy Hill, N.Y.; Pomfret, Ct.; Colchester, Vt.; Ashburnham and Lunenburg, Mass., etc. The result of them, eternity will unfold; but much fruit was immediately apparent. A large number of ministers of the gospel were awakened, during the winter, to a sense of their duty to investigate the subject, and were induced to preach it more or less in their pulpit ministrations; and some of them devoted themselves entirely to the Advent cause, and became efficient lecturers.

"As the spring opened, Bro. Himes determined on sounding the cry abroad more fully in the city of New York; and accordingly, in the month of May, himself with Bro. Miller went to that city to commence their operations. The Apollo Hall, on Broadway, was rented at a heavy expense, and they commenced their work.

The labors of the preceding visit were so far obliterated that none could be found to invite them to their house and give them a night's lodging. They accordingly took an ante-room adjoining the hall as a sitting and lodging room for a part of the time, until friends were awakened and brought in, who furnished a cot-bed, and thus relieved them from the hard floor. Two weeks, under these circumstances, laboring night and day, paying most of their own expenses (for the public collections were very small), were necessary before an impression could be made. One fact should be here recorded: An impression had gone abroad respecting the Adventists, that they were monsters, or almost anything but civilized beings. So strong was his impression, and so general, that a number of days had passed and scarcely a lady dared to make her appearance in the [132] meetings. The religious press had sounded the alarm, and spread a panic through the community which it was difficult to remove. But as one after another ventured to look in, and then to listen, the prejudice began to give way, and the congregation to enlarge, and before the meetings closed on anniversary week, the house was well filled with attentive hearers, and a permanent interest secured. It was a great undertaking, but the victory was at length achieved, and a great and glorious harvest has been gathered in. This meeting closed under encouraging circumstances, and filled all who were present with hope as to the future."

Camp-Meeting Era

"While the meetings were progressing in New York, the friends in Boston determined on a general rally in that city during anniversary week. Accordingly, the Melodeon was secured for the occasion, and our meetings began under the most auspicious circumstances. Adventism had never seen a brighter day. The attendance was large throughout the entire meeting. Although the interests of the week were great, yet none had a larger share of attention than the Advent Anniversary Conference. During that week, among the various other interests which came up for discussion, was the question of holding a camp-meeting, or camp-meetings, during the ensuing summer. This was thought, by many, a great undertaking. What, a little handful of Adventists hold a camp-meeting! Why, they are hardly able to hold a house-meeting, much less a camp-meeting! However, there was sufficient faith and zeal in the meeting to say TRY. Arrangements were accordingly made by the appointment of a camp-meeting committee, [133] to carry the plan into effect. It was determined to make a most vigorous effort during the summer, for the spread of this great light. For we then thought it doubtful whether we ever should reach another anniversary week, in time.

"Immediately after the anniversary meetings were over, the writer started for Canada East, to fulfill an engagement in Stanstead. He left Boston on Monday morning, and arrived at Stanstead, and began his meeting on Wednesday. The interest steadily increased from the beginning, and before two weeks were passed, the country, for thirty or forty miles around, was awake to the subject of the Lord's coming. Immense concourses assembled both in Canada and in Derby, Vermont, where a course of lectures was given. Such was the interest to hear, and the awakening among the people, that it was determined at once to hold a camp-meeting in Canada. In accordance with this determination, a place was selected, the ground prepared, and the meeting held in the township of

Hadley, Canada East. Such was the good effect of this first meeting, that the people of Bolton wished one to be held in their town. This was begun the next week after the Hadley meeting closed, and ended on the third of July. During that month's labor, as near as could be estimated, five or six hundred souls were converted to God.

"The last week in June, the first Advent camp-meeting held in the States commenced in East Kingston, New Hampshire, where an immense multitude assembled to hear the word of the kingdom, and worship the God of Abraham. Thus, instead of one Advent camp-meeting during the season, which the unbelief of some thought could hardly be carried through, within one month of the determination to *try*, three such meetings [134] had actually been successful. Besides these camp-meetings, there were immense gatherings of the people all through the northern part of Vermont and New Hampshire, and onward through the State of Maine."

The Great Tent

"While these operations were going forward, the plan was started for constructing a large tent sufficient to accommodate four thousand persons, with which to go onto the cities where no house was open for lectures. This proposition was at once received by the people, and Bro. Himes, with the help of other friends, undertook the work. Such a tent was completed and pitched in Concord, New Hampshire, in the latter part of July. The excitement produced by such a movement was still greater that that occasioned by the Advent camp-meetings.

"The tent was next pitched in Albany, New York; then in Springfield, and Salem, Massachusetts, and Benson, Vermont. And finally, for the last time in the season, in Newark, New Jersey. In all these places the word took effect, and produced the greatest and most beneficial results. Besides the great tent-meetings and numerous courses of lectures, there were held some six or eight camp-meetings, in New England, during the summer and fall. The work spread with a power unparalleled in the history of religious excitements.

"During the season, Bro. C. Fitch made a visit to Oberlin Institute, where he proclaimed the doctrine of the Lord's coming to the students, as well as faculty of the institution, and in various other places in Ohio. While on this tour, the Lord wonderfully blessed his labors, and gave him favor in the sight of the people. [135] It was arranged for him to remove his family into that region of country to spend the winter, and lecture in Cleveland and vicinity. This movement awakened an interest in that part of the country, which has been increasing to the present time.

"After the close of the Newark camp or tent-meeting, the cold weather set in, and rendered it impracticable longer to continue these public, out-door meetings, and the laborers began to arrange for a winter's campaign. Bro. Himes, together with Bro. Miller and others, returned to New York, and commenced a course of lectures in the church, corner of Catherine and Madison streets, where Bro. Storrs had been laboring with great success for a number of weeks. The interest still continued to increase beyond all expectation. An invitation was also given for a course of lectures in the Methodist Protestant church, in Anthony street, under the pastoral care of Bro. E. Jacobs. This invitation was accepted by Bro. A. Hale, and attended with a great blessing. Bro. Jacobs, and many of his church, embraced the doctrine, and began immediately to proclaim it with power.

The Midnight Cry

"Such was the interest in New York City, that it was determined by Bro. J.V. Himes, to commence a daily Advent paper, and publish it at least for four weeks, in which the principal arguments sustaining our views were to be embodied and given to the public in a cheap and popular form. The paper was commenced in the latter part of November, 1842, entitled *The Midnight Cry*. It was principally under the editorial supervision of our beloved and faithful brother, N. Southard. The [136] twenty-four-four numbers were published, and ten thousand copies of each number circulated. Most of these were gratuitously distributed through the post-offices at the expense of the publisher. Of course, such a distribution could not fail to awaken an interest throughout the country, of the most salutary character. Thousands were enlightened and instructed, and embraced the doctrine, who never heard a lecture on the subject. The '*Cry*' has been continued as a weekly paper up to the present time, and has each successive week been extending its sphere of usefulness, and cheering the hearts of thousands of lonely pilgrims in every part of the land.

"In February, 1843, Bro. Miller and Bro. Himes visited Philadelphia, and gave a course of lectures, with very great effect. The city was convulsed throughout with the influence of the lectures. Saints rejoiced, the wicked trembled, backsliders quaked, and the word of the Lord ran and was glorified. It is doubtful whether Mr. Miller ever gave a course of lectures with greater effect than at that time. It placed the cause on a permanent foundation in the city, and prepared the way for extending it into the South and West. A bookroom was opened in the city early in January, and a small penny paper, the *Philadelphia Alarm*, was issued. Thirteen numbers of it were published, about four thousand copies per number.

Efforts were now made in Washington, D.C, and Pittsburgh, Va. "Indeed, the whole West seemed ripe and ready for harvest. Letters written from Pittsburgh, and published in the *Midnight Cry*, soon aroused the friends at the East, and a number of lecturers immediately started for that field of labor. The Advent banner was unfurled in Cincinnati, and from thence the [137] light has been spreading all over the western and southern country.

"Returning from Pittsburgh, about the middle of March, the *Philadelphia Alarm* was merged in the *Trumpet of Alarm*, a paper containing the diagrams of the visions of Daniel and John, and a connected view of the Advent doctrine, gotten up for the express purpose of circulating in the West and South. From twenty-five to thirty thousand copies of it have been circulated.

"While these things were going on at the West, the Lord was still at work in the East. By his gracious Providence, those beloved brethren, N.N. Whiting, J.B. Cook, and F.G. Brown, were brought into the faith and began to proclaim it aloud. The effect of it was electrical. Very many, who had previously looked upon the subject as beneath their notice, began to feel that it was possible, after all, that there might be something in it. This induced examination of the evidence, and that again produced conviction of the truth of the doctrine.

"In a manner too rapid to record, the Advent cause went forward during that winter. I am aware that history loses more than half its interest from the absence of its detail; but such are the limits to which this sketch must be confined, it is impossible to enter into the minutiae of the thing. All that can be done will be to record the outlines of the story.

"Then, again, Bro. Fitch's mission in Ohio resulted in the establishment of a Second-Advent paper in Cleveland, which has proved an instrument of great good to the cause in that section of the country. Brn. H.B. Skinner and L. Caldwell, who spent the winter [138] in Canada East, also commenced a paper there devoted to the cause.

"As the summer opened, preparations were made for tabernacle and camp-meetings. East, West, and North, they were appointed and held; most of which were attended with the special blessing of God on the people, and greatly extended the knowledge of the Advent views. The same anxiety to hear on the subject, which has characterized the doctrine from its beginning, marked it still. Not only in places where it had gained a foothold, but in new places where it had never been proclaimed, the greatest anxiety to hear was manifested.

"Bro. Himes undertook the task of again sustaining *the great tent*, and going with it into western New York. This he, in connection with other brethren, carried through. Up to that time, no permanent interest had been created in that part of the country. But from the holding of the tent-meetings in Rochester and Buffalo, the subject took a strong hold on the community through that region of country, and has been steadily going forward ever since.

"From Buffalo, the tent was taken to Cincinnati, Ohio, and a full exposition of the Advent doctrines given to the people. Several courses of lectures, however, had been previously delivered in that city, and the people were thus prepared to improve the privilege of the tent-lectures. There had also been several camp-meetings in the vicinity of the city; so that a great interest prevailed in the country to obtain light on the subject.

"In connection with each of the tent meetings, an Advent paper was published, in which the main points of the Advent doctrine were given to the people, with great effect. [139]

"We have not space for a full account of the numerous incidents which marked the labors of the summer and autumn of 1843. But it must be recorded, to the praise of the God's glorious grace, that the work of the Lord went steadily forward, bearing down all opposition, from whatever source.

"We were deprived, during the entire spring and summer, of the labors of our beloved Bro. Miller, who was confined to his house by a painful sickness for a number of months. In the fall of the year, as his health improved, he again commenced his arduous work: first making a tour through New England, and then into western New York. During the eight weeks which he spent in the latter tour, he preached eighty-five times, besides all the other duties which devolved upon him, incidental to such a journey. Never were his labors attended with better results, or received with greater pleasure, than during that journey. 'The good seed,' 'the word of the kingdom,' still found good ground, into which it fell, took root, and brought forth fruit.

"During this visit to the west, among other places, he visited Lockport, New York, the residence of Elder E. Galusha, so well-known in the Baptist church in the United States. He had been for several months more or less exercised on the subject of the coming of the Lord, and had given it a very candid examination, but had never fully committed himself to it until Bro. Miller's lectures in the church of which he had the pastoral charge. He, from that time, became a decided advocate of the doctrine, and has since devoted himself to its advocacy." [140]

Mr. Miller's Visit to Washington

"It had long been in contemplation, by Bro. Himes, in company with Bro. Miller, to visit Washington city, District of Columbia, and sound the alarm in the capital of the nation; but no opportunity presented itself for so doing until the past winter. Commencing in Boston, they lectured in that city, and from thence came to New York, delivering a course of lectures to a numerous audience; from thence visited Philadelphia, spent a week, and gave a course of lectures to an immense concourse of people, with very great effect. From Philadelphia, he, in company with the writer, went to Washington and commenced a course of lectures, February 20, 1844. Two weeks were spent in different sections of the city, in presenting the doctrines of Adventism, and the evidences of the speedy coming of the Lord. The attendance was good, and the interest to hear, deep. A greater revolution in public sentiment has rarely been witnessed in so short a time, than was brought about in Washington, in reference to the Advent doctrine.

"During our stay in Washington, besides the papers and books which were carried on from the North, a paper was commenced there, called the *Southern Midnight Cry*. Two numbers were published and circulated in Washington and vicinity, and another in Baltimore, while Bro. Miller was giving his course of lectures in that city. Thus ended the winter of 1843-4, and brought us to the point which had so long been before us — the end of the Jewish year 1843." [141]

The Termination of the Prophetic Times

"As might be expected, as the crisis, the 21st of March, approached, there was a very general expectation of an entire overthrow of the whole system of Adventism. It was supposed that those who had embraced it, if the appointed time should pass, would yield the whole question. But they had not so learned the Bible. The doctrine does not consist in merely tracing prophetic periods, although that is an important part of the work. But the whole prophetic history of the world is given in the pages of inspiration, is recorded in history, and affords indubitable evidence of the fact, that we have approached a crisis. And no disappointment respecting a definite point of time can move them, or drive them from their position relative to the speedy coming of the Lord. And it yet remains to be shown that our calculations of time are not correct, and are only in error relative to the event which marked its close. This is the most likely. There are, at present, some who falter, but comparatively few, however, who have given up the cause. Most stand unmoved amidst all the scoffs and jeers of a reviling world."

Modes of Opposition

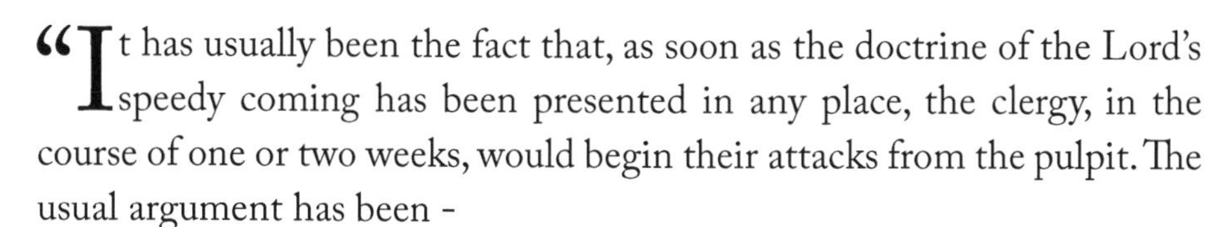

"It has usually been the fact that, as soon as the doctrine of the Lord's speedy coming has been presented in any place, the clergy, in the course of one or two weeks, would begin their attacks from the pulpit. The usual argument has been -

"1. 'Of that day and hour knoweth no man;' yet these men profess to know the very time when the Lord [142] is to come. Yes, they profess to know more than the angels, or even the Son of God himself.

"2. The Lord cannot come until after the millennium, during which the whole world is to be righteous, and the lion eat straw like the ox, etc.

"3. The Jews must be brought in, and restored to Palestine, before that day comes.

"4. It is to come as a thief, as a snare, etc., on all them that dwell on the earth. But now there are so many who are looking for it, that it cannot come as a snare.

"5. It cannot come now, because there are so many learned and holy ministers and Christians, that if it should come now, it would take them by surprise. The Lord will not come without their knowing it.

"6. The world is yet in its infancy; the arts and sciences are just beginning to come to maturity, and fit the world to live, and it cannot be that the Lord will come now and destroy it all.

"7. Then again there is so much waste land to be occupied in the western country, land which has never yet been cultivated at all, that it is not at all reasonable that the Lord should destroy it all before it has been improved.

"8. But the great argument, the one which has proved the most effectual, has been, that this vision of Daniel 8 has nothing to do with the coming of Christ, or setting up of God's everlasting kingdom. It simply refers to Antiochus Epiphanes, and his persecution of the Jews, and desecration of the temple, some 160 odd years B.C. Thus we have the abomination of desolation spoken of by Daniel the prophet, for which the Saviour taught his people to look, about two hundred years before the instruction was given. [143]

"To the foregoing might be added a number more of the same class, *professedly* drawn from reason and Scripture, but none of them more formidable than those already recorded. Do you smile, gentle reader, at the idea of calling these arguments? Yet, you may be assured that each of them in turn has been urged by grave men, calling themselves doctors of divinity.

"But the most wonderful and overwhelming of all arguments which have ever been presented against the doctrine, is, 'Mr. Miller has built some stone wall on his farm!!' But, I forgot myself; I said the most wonderful; there is another quite its equal: 'Mr. Miller refuses to sell his farm!!' How, oh! how can Christ come, when Mr. Miller will not sell his farm?

"But this is not all; for the truth is, 'Mr. Himes has published and scattered (a large part of them gratuitously) more than five millions of books and papers. He must be engaged in a speculation; and how can the Lord come? Oh! how can he come?'

"But to be serious; a word on this subject is due these men, and the cause whose advocates they have been. For those who have known William Miller, and have known his personal history, it is not needful we should write. But there are those who know him not; on their account it is, that this memento is here inserted.

"When Mr. Miller first commenced the advocacy of the Advent doctrine, he was engaged in agricultural pursuits. He had a farm of his own, was surrounded by an interesting family, and possessed all that could make life easy and agreeable. When the Lord called and thrust him out into this work, he was in the decline of life, without the advantages of an academical education, without experience as a public speaker, without ecclesiastical [144] preferments, except as a valued and worthy lay member of the Baptist church; the prejudices of both the church and world were decidedly against all attempts to understand the prophetic scriptures, with many other discouraging circumstances. Yet, in the face of all discouragements, he went forth taking nothing; but as freely did he bestow on others the light which God had given, as he had received it.

"For a number of years after he began this work, he traveled extensively, lectured frequently, endured privation and scoffing, and paid all the expenses of his journeys from his own funds. At the same time he had a large family dependent on him for their subsistence, besides keeping open doors for all the Lord's servants who should choose to come under his roof; where they were always sure to find a hearty welcome.

"After pursuing this course for some years, he arranged his domestic affairs, by giving up his farm into the hands of his sons, so as to sustain his family, and have an annuity of one hundred dollars, to clothe himself and meet his other incidental expenses. In this way he continued to travel far and near, wherever Providence opened the way, and for the most part bearing his own expenses. This he did until his journeys became so numerous, long and expensive, as to exceed his income. Then he permitted the people among whom he labored to pay his traveling expenses. But he has not received enough, since he began his work, to sustain him in it. From the sale of his books he has received no profit. It has been no part of his business to lay up treasures on earth, or accumulate wealth by the gospel of God's grace.

"Amidst all the vile and reproachful epithets which have been heaped upon him, all the false and scurrilous [145] reports which have gone the rounds of both pulpit and press, as well as private circles, he has gone on, still pursuing the even tenor of his way, accomplishing the mission on which he set forth. If his remarks concerning the attacks which have been made upon him, have sometimes seemed severe, it will not be wondered at, when it is recollected that it is nothing else but the severity of truth. We will not pretend to say that he has never erred; but this we do say, while we confess, that 'to err is human,' few men have gone through an enterprise like this, with fewer errors or blemishes than William Miller.

"So, likewise, in exposing and reproving the growing corruptions of the church and ministry, he has been thought by many too severe. But this, too, has consisted in the severity of truths which few, in an age of degeneracy like this, had either the independence or courage to speak out. He has spoken aloud what others have thought and repeated only in private. Yet, after all, who that knows the man, but loves him? Take him all in all, where could an instrument be found better qualified for the station he has filled?

"A few words respecting that faithful and devoted friend of the cause of Adventism, J.V. Himes, must close this part of the present work. From the position he has occupied in the front of the battle, the most deadly shafts of the enemy have been aimed at him. The generous spirit of self-sacrifice with which he came forward and exerted every nerve for the advancement of this great work, excited at once the envy, the wrath, the anger and calumny of the whole host of foes to the doctrine. And no means which could be devised to blast his influence has been wanting from that to the present time. But through grace he has thus far triumphed. [146] I believe the providence of God raised up J.V. Himes as an associate and fellow helper of Mr. Miller, in the great work of arousing the church and the world to prepare for the coming of the Lord; and that he has performed the work with fidelity to God and man, and honor to himself."

Extent of the Work

"We look upon the proclamation which has been made, as being the cry of the angel who proclaimed 'the hour of His judgement is come.' Revelation 14:6, 7. It is a sound which is to reach all nations; it is the proclamation of 'the everlasting gospel,' or 'this gospel of the kingdom.' In one shape or other, this cry has gone abroad through the earth wherever human beings are found, and we have had opportunity to hear of the fact. Within the last six years, publications, treating on the subject, have been sent to nearly every English and American missionary station on the globe; to all, at least, to which we have had access.

"Then again, the great religious papers of the country have all aided in this work; for some of them have published our views, as written by friends, and others have published reviews and overthrows, in which our arguments must be presented, in order to refute them.

"By these the truth has been spread into many places where it could not have reached by the ordinary means. Then again, the caricatures which have been scattered among the rabble, have carried the great point with them, the coming of the Lord to judgment, and the time of his coming.

"The secular press has contributed, in no small degree, to increase and spread an interest on the question. [147] Even the foolish and false statements which have been put forth, have, in some instances, only turned out for the advancement of the work of God. The story, for instance, which was started by the New York *Sun*, that Mr. Miller had fixed on the 23rd of April, 1843, as the time for Christ to come, although entirely false and baseless in itself, yet was so widely circulated, that there was scarcely a place known where the report was not heard and an interest awakened."

Advent Books

"These have been greatly multiplied within the last four years. As already remarked, the first and most important work published, was Mr. Miller's lectures. That volume may be regarded as the seed from which all the rest have germinated. The works of Miller, Ward, Hale, Bliss, Fitch, Storrs, Brown, Hervey, Cook, Whiting, Starkweather, Hawley, Litch, Fleming, Cox, Sabine, etc., constitute the Second Advent Library, and exhibit the views which have been presented to the public by the lectures. Other sheets and pamphlets have been published.

"Some of the sheets which have been published and circulated have accomplished a vast amount of good. The 'Clue to the Time,' written by Bro. L. Hersey, a shoemaker in Boston, and a city watchman, with a diagram, has been the means of great good. Eternity alone will reveal the many precious souls who have been led to look for the Lord's coming from the reading of one of those sheets." [148]

Lecturers and Writers

"The mass of lecturers who have been raised up and thrust forth into this work, have been men of sound minds, warm hearts, full of zeal for God and the salvation of men. They have made no great pretentions to learning, in its common acceptation; but yet, as a general thing, they have been close students of the Bible making it a self-interpreting book. Nor have they been altogether inattentive to history as their time and means have allowed. It is true that, so far as they have been successful in their work, the excellency of the power has been of God.

"But there have been some raised up among us of commanding talents and acquirements; men, who need not blush to stand by the side of the wise and learned of the earth. These were raised up at a time when such assistance was needed, and God has accomplished his work by them. The Advent writings exhibit minds accustomed to think and reason, as well as read. Although the mass of the books lay no claim to literary merit, yet they have done more to promote a sound, healthy, moral literature, than any other books of the age. They have so selected and arranged historical incidents, in connection with the prophetic scriptures, which embrace the history of the world, as to invest that history with an interest which the mass of readers never before saw or felt. If they have promoted the study of history, much more have they induced a careful study of the Scriptures.

"It is a lamentable fact, that although this is an age of Bibles, yet the great body of professing Christians know but little what that Bible contains. And wherever [149] Advent books have been circulated, instead of superseding the use of the Bible, as most books do, they almost invariably send the reader to the sacred storehouse. Nothing ever given to the public has excited so much interest in the study of the Bible as the proclamation of 'the hour of His judgement.' A course of lectures in a village, would open a door for the sale of more Bibles in a week than would have been sold before for years. Whatever may be the final issue of this question, so far its fruits have been of the best character.

What Adventism Has Accomplished

"1. When the cry first commenced, the prophecies were generally looked upon as a book of mysteries, which it was presumption, if not sacrilege, to attempt to understand or explain. That spell has been broken, and the Christian public understand that those deeply interesting portions of the word of God are also a part of his revelation to man. And even the clergy, of all orders, have been constrained to speak out and give some explanation of the prophecies, however crude it might be.

"2. The fable of the world's conversion, and the universal triumph of Christianity, which almost universally prevailed ten years ago, has been exploded, and the church now understands that the Man of Sin is to remain in the world until the Lord comes and destroys him by the brightness of his coming. That there is to be no millennium until 'the first resurrection,' at the coming of the Lord. That idea cannot be made to grow again as it has done.

"3. That kindred doctrine, the return of the Jews to Palestine, where they are again to be exalted to peculiar [150] privileges, is exposed, and the old apostolic doctrine, that there is no respect of persons with God, is made to stand out in bold relief, so that the church must see and acknowledge it to be the truth of God.

"4. It has produced a very general conviction on the public mind, that we are near the end of time, and just ready to appear before the bar of God. The general outlines of prophecy, as exhibited in the four great kingdoms, is seen and acknowledged by very many to be nearly accomplished. And hence the conviction fastens on the mind, that the end of all things is at hand.

"5. It has developed a vast amount of German rationalism, neology and infidelity in the church, and has demonstrated the fact, that nearly or quite all the theological schools are under its influence. And it has proved, that if the Lord does not come speedily and end the strife, that the country must soon be flooded with this system of neology.

"6. Wherever it has gone, the Advent doctrine has awakened sinners, reclaimed backsliders, quickened believers, and promoted the cause of God generally. Thousands on thousands can witness the truth of this remark in their own experience; and will have cause to bless God eternally for the Advent doctrine and Advent preaching.

"7. It has shown professedly orthodox ministers to be so degenerate in their sentiments as to make common cause with infidels and Universalists against the coming of the Lord. And has also shown the church to be so degenerate as to cast out her children for looking for and speaking of the return of her Lord.

"8. It has given to the church and world a simple, plain, common-sense system of interpretation of the sacred [151] canon, so that every man, who will take the trouble of reading the Bible and collating the different portions of it, may understand the word of God without the aid of learned commentaries."

Permanency of the Work

"No provision has been made for the establishment of permanent institutions among Adventists. Indeed, we have no means of ascertaining the number of ministers, and others, who have embraced the Advent faith. We only know that there are several hundred congregations, and a still larger number of ministers, who have publicly professed the faith, besides many who still remain in the churches of the land. Those who have espoused this cause have honestly believed in the coming of the Lord 'about A.D. 1843;' and as honest men they have kept to their work of sounding the alarm. All peculiarities of creed or policy have been lost sight of, in the absorbing inquiry concerning the coming of the heavenly Bridegroom. Those who have engaged in this enterprise are from all the various sects in the land — Protestant Episcopal, Methodist Episcopal, Methodist Protestant, Primitive Methodist, Wesleyan Methodist, Close Communion Baptist, Calvinistic and Armenian Baptists, Presbyterians, Old and New School Congretionalists, Old and New School Lutheran, Dutch Reformed, etc., etc. All these have agreed to work together for the accomplishment of a certain object; and the organization to which this has given rise, so far as there is anything which may be called an organization, is of the most simple, voluntary and primitive form. While the engrossing and scriptural character of the grand object has kept those who have been brought under [152] its influence above the considerations which so generally divide the household of faith, it has also made them frank and kind in expressing their minor differences, and forbearing toward each other on subordinate questions upon which they may not see alike. And in this is their strength.

"In 1842, Robert Winter, an Englishman by birth, and a Primitive Methodist by profession, fell in with the Adventists in this country and embraced the doctrine. In the fall of the year he resolved to return to England, and proclaim the coming of the Lord. He did return, and commenced the work. God owned his truth, and it took effect, and many have been raised up to join with him in spreading the light through these islands of the sea. Last summer camp or field meetings were held in different parts of England with great success.

"Books and papers to a large amount have been sent to England, and scattered abroad through the country; and several books and papers have been republished in that country with great effect.

"The British provinces adjoining the United States, have been visited and furnished with the light. Our beloved brother Hutchinson, in Montreal, has published a large amount of matter in his paper, *The Voice of Elijah*, and sent it over the United Kingdoms.

"But I must close this brief sketch of the rise and progress of Adventism, or my space will be more than full. But a few only out of the multitude of incidents which should enter into a work of this kind have been noticed. But this is all we have room to give in the present sketch. The Judge is at the door, and will make a more full and accurate development of this great work than human heart can indite or hand record. Concerning [153] Adventism, it may be truly said, 'What hath God wrought?'

"No cause of a moral or religious character, probably, ever made so rapid advances as the cause of Adventism. Its votaries have usually been the most humble, pious, devoted members of the different churches; men and women who love their Lord, and to whom the thought of his glorious advent has been a source of sweetest pleasure. The hand of Providence has everywhere opened the way, and provided the means for doing all that human means could do. None of the lecturers have made themselves rich, or even held what little they had when they embarked in the enterprise. Everything has been freely sacrificed when the cause demanded it. Never have a set of men labored more faithfully and zealously in the cause of God, or with purer motives. But their work is with the Lord, and their record on high.

"It is asked what we intend to do, now the time is expired? Our answer is, we intend, by the Lord's help, to spread the glad tidings of the kingdom of God until it appears. The arguments which have been presented on the prophetic history and periods, together with the signs of the times, have lost none of their strength; and we purpose to continue presenting them until the Master comes, that we may be found giving his 'household meat in due season.'"

The Exeter, N.H., Camp Meeting

It was in the month of August, 1844, that the memorable Second-Advent camp-meeting was held at Exeter, N.H. This meeting was large. It was the occasion [154] of a general rally from all parts of New England, and many were present from other States and from the Canadas. There were many tents upon the ground, some of them resembling houses of worship, in size and shape, more than the small tents usually seen upon Methodist camp grounds. These furnished ample accommodations for the thousands of believers present.

There was a general agreement with all Adventists at that time, that the special providence of God had directed the Advent movement. But the farthest point to which the Jewish year could be extended, reaching from March, 1843, to March, 1844, had passed, and believers were left in a state of suspense and uncertainty, evidently not enjoying all the inspiring influence of the Advent hope and faith they felt under the proclamation of definite time. And there were other things besides the passing of the time, that cast a degree of general gloom over the Second-Advent cause at that time.

Storrs' Six Sermons on the immortality question were being widely circulated among Adventists, and the doctrine of man's unconsciousness in death and the destruction of the wicked, was being adopted by some and regarded with favor by many. The time had come, in the providence of God, for this question to be agitated. But its importance could not then be seen by any as it is now regarded since the rise and wide-spreading, desolating influence of Spiritualism. Those Second-Advent editors and lecturers, such as Litch, Hale, Bliss, Himes, and Miller, who did not agree with Mr. Storrs, not only failed to see that good could result from the agitation of the subject, but were grieved that the once united and happy flock, who were looking for the immediate return of the great Shepherd, should have their minds divided by this question. And these men, who felt the responsibilities [155] of the great Advent cause, are not to be censured too much for their fears, nor blamed too severely for their efforts to avoid the discussion of so sensitive a question.

And while it was being feared that a portion of the Advent body were having their minds diverted from the all-important work of warning the world of the soon-coming of the Son of man, by an unnecessary discussion of the immortality question, others were causing divisions, and were bringing much labor and perplexity upon the leading men in the cause, by urging upon the flock extreme views of entire consecration, of Christian perfection, then taught by the Methodists, the men of the Oberlin school, and others. And not a few men and women appeared in the Advent ranks who professed to be wonderfully led by the Holy Spirit. These took their position in advance of their brethren. Many of them soon became self-righteous, and, notwithstanding their apparent humility, were proud of their spiritual attainments. So wonderfully impressed to do this or that, and so directly taught by the Holy Spirit in relation to their entire duty, how could they err? The idea of mistakes on their part, in doctrine or in duty, was banished from them.

Viewing themselves far in advance of their brethren, they were ready to teach even their teachers. And supposing themselves directly taught by the Holy Spirit, they were ready to reject the instructions and corrections of those who labored to help them. Such persons usually advance rapidly in their wild career. They soon fall under the direct power of Satan, to be impressed and tempted by him to do this or that thing which may be sinful. They labor under the terrible deception that all their impressions are from the Holy Spirit, and must at [156] all hazards be promptly obeyed. God pity the poor fanatic, who is thus goaded on by the Devil to disgrace himself and wound the cause of Christ. In no case could Satan strike the Advent cause so stunning a blow, and so completely cover it with reproach, as to lead on certain ones who bore the Advent name in the wild career of fanaticism.

And he knows when to strike. The world had just trembled before the solemn message of the Judgment hour, proclaimed with great boldness and power. And believers had lifted up one united voice in confident testimony relative to the period of their joyful expectations. But the time had passed, the world breathed easier, the scoffer triumphed, and believers felt that they had all they could do to hold fast, and not draw back to perdition. This was just the time for Satan to strike.

More or less had embraced the Advent faith from all those religious bodies where the idea was prevailing that Scriptural sanctification, purity and holiness, consisted chiefly in happy flights of feeling, and being led in the minutiae of the Christian life by impressions. These had been stirred to the very depths of the soul by the proclamation of the second coming of Christ, and felt that if they ever needed holiness it was then necessary, to enable them to stand when he should appear, and that if they should ever follow the leadings of the Holy Spirit, it was then, as they were engaged in the preparatory work for the Judgment. And with their false notions of entire consecration, they were in readiness for the torch of fanaticism. If Satan could control these, and bring reproach upon the Advent cause, and sadden the hearts of those he could not destroy, he would gain a victory that would cause wicked men and demons to triumph. [157]

There was upon the Exeter camp-ground a tent from Watertown, Massachusetts, filled with fanatical persons, as briefly described above. At an early period in this meeting, they attracted much attention by the peculiar style in which they conducted their seasons of social worship in their tent. These were irregular, very lengthy, frequently extending into hours of intermission and rest, continuing nearly all night, and attended with great excitement, and noise of shouting and clapping of hands, and singular gestures and exercises. Some shouted so loud and incessantly as to become hoarse, and silent, simply because they could no longer shout, while others literally blistered their hands striking them together.

The tent's company from Portland, Me., of which I was one of the number, had pitched close by this tent from Watertown, before the condition of those who occupied it was generally known, little thinking of the annoyances they were to suffer from these fanatical persons. But these they endured for a while in the hope that they would be corrected and reproved. Seeing, however, that they were not the persons to be reformed, and that they grew no better, but, rather worse, the Portland brethren moved their tent to a distant part of the ground. But this act, showing the assembled thousands that we had no union with those we left, created sympathy for these fanatics, in not a few who viewed all the dangers of the way on the side of those who were disposed to formality. These joined with the Watertown people in the cry of persecution, and shouted glory to God over it, as if a new and brilliant victory had been gained.

By this time a general gloom was coming over the meeting, and ministers who had the burden of the work [158] upon them, felt deeply. The wildfire was spreading, and how to stop it was the question. The people were told of the dangers of spiritual magnetism, and were warned to keep away from that tent. But this only caused a crowd of the curious, incautious, and those who claimed a right to investigate, and felt that they were responsible to no one, to gather round this tent. And it was evident that every hour some were being brought under this influence, several of whom were suffering impulse to ride over reason.

A minister, possessing more natural eloquence than piety and real moral worth, while attempting to preach from the stand, was rebuked by a clear voice from this tent, and thrown into confusion. "Don't let me fall, brethren," said he to the large congregation who were turning their attention to the tent from which came the voice. "Pray, and keep your minds upon the subject." He did fall in spirit and freedom, and his effort was a decided failure.

Elder Plummer, of Haverhill, Mass., who had the especial charge of the meeting, made appropriate remarks upon the condition of things, with great solemnity and deep feeling. He then prayed, calling on God for guidance and help in that critical hour. He prayed like a strong man in agony, whose only hope of deliverance was in God. He then stated something of his opinion of the spirit of fanaticism on the ground, and exhorted the people to look to God for help, and not suffer their minds to be diverted by the interruptions and general noise of the faction on the ground, who were not in harmony with the great objects of the meeting.

He stated, in the most solemn manner, that he had no objections to shouts of praise to God, over victories won in his name. But when persons had shouted [159] "Glory to God" nine hundred and ninety-nine times, with no evidence of one victory gained, and had blistered their hands in striking them together with violence, he thought it was time for them to stop. But if they would not change their course, it was time for all who wished to be consistent Christians to withdraw their sympathy from them, and show their disapproval of their course by keeping entirely away from them.

These remarks helped the people generally, but not those who were wild with fanaticism. But none among the preachers and speakers generally had shown up to this time that they had the burden of the meeting upon them, excepting what was seen in Elder Plummer, in reproving existing wrongs. Several spoke from the stand, but they failed to move the people. God evidently had a special message for that people, to be attended with his signal blessing. Men of ability spoke of the great lines of prophecy, which proved that the advent of Christ was the next great event, and of the signs that the event was at the door; but this was as familiar to that crowd of intelligent believers as the alphabet. Just then, as one was speaking with but little force and interest, and the people were becoming weary of being told, in a dull, prosy style, what they already knew, a middle-aged, modest-appearing lady arose in the centre of the audience, and in a calm manner, and with a clear, strong, yet pleasant voice, addressed the speaker as follows:

"It is too late Bro. -------. It is too late to spend our time upon these truths, with which we are familiar, and which have been blessed to us in the past, and have served their purpose and their time."

The brother sat down, and the lady continued, while all eyes were fastened upon her. [160]

"It is too late, brethren, to spend precious time as we have since this camp-meeting commenced. Time is short. The Lord has servants here who have meat in due season for his household. Let them speak, and let the people hear them. 'Behold the Bridegroom cometh, go ye out to meet him.'"

This testimony seemed electrifying, and was responded to by choked utterances of "Amen," from every part of the vast encampment. Many were in tears. What former speakers had said was forgotten, and the spirit of fanaticism, which an hour before lay upon the burdened feelings of the brethren and sisters like a ponderous leaden weight, was also forgotten. The attention paid to those in fanaticism, and the opposition they were able to call out, were just the coveted fuel to feed the unhallowed flame. And they were destined to triumph, unless the attention of the people could be fastened in another direction. This done, and their power was broken.

By the request of many brethren, the next morning, the arguments were given from the stand, which formed the basis of the tenth day of the seventh-month movement. The speaker was solemn and dignified, and showed to the entire satisfaction of that vast body of intelligent believers -

1. That all the evidences which had been relied upon as proof that the 2300 prophetic days of Daniel 8, would end in the year 1843, proved that they would terminate in 1844. The entire body of believers had been united, agreeing with William Miller that the 2300 days dated from the going forth of the commandment to restore and to build Jerusalem, B.C. 457. This point settled, the figures 1843 were readily found: [161]

From	2300
Take	457
And there remains	1843

But the speaker showed an error in this calculation. He stated that it would require 457 *full* years *before* Christ, and 1843 *full* years *after* Christ, to make 2300 full years, so that if the 2300 years commenced with the first day of B.C. 457, they would reach to the first day of A.D. 1844.

2. That this prophetic period did not commence with the year 457, in the spring, but in the autumn of that year. His reasons were —

a. That as the seventy prophetic weeks are the first 490 years of the 2300, and as the first seven weeks of the seventy, mark the time of the work restoring and building Jerusalem in troublous times, the great period must commence with the commencement of the work of restoring and building, which did not commence in the spring, on the first month, when Ezra started from Babylon, but after he had reached Jerusalem, in the autumn, probably on the seventh month. "For upon the first day of the first month began he to go up from Babylon, and on the first day of the fifth month came he to Jerusalem." Ezra 7:9. This would give more than two months for necessary preparations for the work of restoring and building to commence on the seventh month, immediately after the great day of atonement.

b. That as the words of the angel to the prophet Daniel — "in the midst of the week he shall cause the sacrifice and the oblation to cease," — mean that in the middle of the last week of the seventy, Christ should be crucified; and as he was crucified in the spring, that prophetic week of seven years must commence and [162] close in the fall. Consequently the seventy weeks commenced and closed in the fall, and, therefore, the 2300 days terminate in the fall.

3. The speaker then introduced the arguments drawn from those types of the law of Moses which point to Christ, to prove that the second advent of Him who was then our High Priest would take place in the autumn, even on the tenth day of the seventh Jewish month. He reasoned that as the spring types, pointing to the great events connected with the first advent of Christ, were fulfilled, not only as to their nature and order, but as to time, so would the autumnal types, pointing to the second advent, be fulfilled as to time. See Leviticus 23. The slaying of the passover lamb was a type of the crucifixion of Christ. Paul says, Christ our passover is sacrificed for us. 1 Corinthians 5:7.

The sheaf of the first fruits of the harvest, which was waved before the Lord, was typical of the resurrection of Christ. Paul again says, in speaking of the resurrection of the Lord and all his people, Christ, the first fruits, afterward they that are Christ's at his coming. 1 Corinthians 15:23. As this sheaf was like the grain in all the wide harvest-field, only that it was the first ripe grain, so Christ arose from the dead a sample of all the just to be raised at his second coming. Then all the saints will have glorious bodies, like that of their divine Lord. Philippians 3:21

The new meat offering was a type of the descent of the Holy Spirit on the day of Pentecost.

The speaker stated that Christ was offered a sacrifice for sinners on the fourteenth day of the first Jewish month, the very day and month on which the passover lamb had been slain for sixteen long centuries. That he was raised from the dead a sample of all the resurrected just on [163] the very day of the month upon which the earliest ripe grain was waved before the Lord. And that the descent of the Holy Spirit on the day of Pentecost, — Pentecost meaning fifty, — was on the day of the month in which the new meat-offering was presented unto the Lord. That new meat-offering was fifty days from the presentation of the wave sheaf. The descent of the Holy Spirit upon the waiting disciples was on the day of Pentecost, or fiftieth day from the resurrection of their divine Lord. And, therefore, as the high priest, on the tenth day of the seventh month, on the great day of atonement, came out of the sanctuary and blessed the people, so Christ, our great High Priest, would upon the same day of the same month, come from Heaven to bless his waiting people with immortality. The conclusion seemed irresistible. And what gave it still greater force was the harmony of this position with the proofs presented, that the prophetic period of 2300 days would terminate in the fall.

The deepest solemnity pervaded the entire encampment. But one view was taken of the subject presented, by nearly all present, namely, that in all probability the speaker was correct, and that in a few short weeks human probation would close forever.

But what of the Watertown fanatics? In the intense interest upon the subject of time, taken by the entire crowd, these were forgotten. No one seemed to be affected by them, or troubled about them. In fact, they were quiet till they left the ground, and as dumb as if the special rebuke of the Lord was upon them. This fact, that fanaticism dried up before the solemn and searching time-message of 1844, like the morning dew before the midsummer's sun, is of importance to those [164] who suppose that that stirring proclamation caused fanaticism.

The next day, by unanimous request of the people, the same speaker repeated, with still greater clearness and force, the same proofs in support of the position that the fast-approaching autumn was the time for the great prophetic periods to terminate, and that the types pointed to the tenth day of the seventh month as the time for our great High Priest to come out of Heaven and bless his waiting people.

This was followed with solemn and stirring discourses in harmony with the time, from Elders Heath, Couch, and Eastman. The specifications of the parable of the ten virgins, down as far as the cry at midnight, seemed to have a natural and forcible application to the great Advent movement up to the time, and the words, "Behold the bridegroom cometh, go ye out to meet him," already being heard from the lips of those who were looking to the seventh Jewish month for the coming of the Lord, had a solemn, subduing power in them, such as no others had. The first portion of the parable, and the application of it then made, I will here give:

"Then shall the kingdom of Heaven be likened unto ten virgins, which took their lamps and went forth to meet the bridegroom. And five of them were wise, and five were foolish. They that were foolish took lamps, and took no oil with them; but the wise took oil in their vessels with their lamps. While the bridegroom tarried, they all slumbered and slept. And at midnight there was a cry made, Behold the bridegroom cometh; go ye out to meet him. Then all those virgins arose and trimmed their lamps." Matthew 25:1-7.

1. The ten virgins represent those then interested in the subject of the immediate second coming of Christ. [165]

2. The lamps which the virgins took to light their way at the hour of midnight, represent the prophetic word of the Lord. "Thy word is a lamp unto my feet, and a light unto my path." Psalm 119:105. "We have also a more sure word of prophecy, whereunto ye do well that ye take heed as unto a light that shineth in a dark place." 2 Peter 1:19

3. The five wise virgins, who took oil in their vessels with their lamps, represent those who had faith, and the work of the grace of God wrought in them.

4. The five foolish virgins represent those professed believers who lacked true faith, and who had not the work of the grace and Spirit of God in them.

5. The tarry of the bridegroom, the delay in the parable, and the slumbering and sleeping of the virgins, represent the passing of the Jewish year, 1843, the disappointment, the suspense and uncertainty which resulted in loss of faith and zeal, manifested by believers before the time passed. It appeared evident that the period of hope deferred and general gloom since the close of the Jewish year, 1843, was the night of sleeping and slumbering.

6. The cry at midnight in the parable, "Behold the bridegroom cometh; go ye out to meet him," represented the solemn message of the tenth day of the seventh month time, 1844, already being heard. It was suggested that the night of tarry in the parable represented half of the prophetic day, or six months, extending from the passing of the time in the spring, to the seventh month in the fall, and that the then present work of waking up under the cry, "Behold the bridegroom cometh, go ye out to meet him," commenced in July, in the middle of the tarrying time, or at midnight.

And now the work of waking up the slumbering believers, [166] and giving the last warning to the world, seemed to be crowded into a few weeks. Those who received the message felt the burden of the work. Language cannot describe the solemnity of that hour. And no one can have any just idea of it, only eye-witnesses upon the grounds, who saw, heard, and felt for themselves. The time for shouting, and display of talent in speaking, singing, and praying, seemed to be past. The brethren and sisters calmly consecrated themselves and their all to the Lord and his cause, and with humble prayers and tears sought his pardon and his favor. All those unhappy divisions and extravagances, which had threatened the prosperity of the Advent cause, were lost sight of, and the watchmen, and the people also, were beginning to lift up one united voice, with strength and heartfelt solemnity, "Behold the Bridegroom cometh; go ye out to meet him."

On returning from the Exeter camp-meeting, I visited the Advent congregation at Poland, Me., and attended camp-meetings at Litchfield and Orington. At these two camp-meetings ministers and people became imbued with the spirit of the seventh-month message. The evidences upon which it was based seemed conclusive, and a power almost irresistible attended it; and the fruits of this message everywhere were alike excellent. Whatever of differences of opinion, division in feelings and plans of action, or schisms of any kind that had sprung up during the time of suspense represented by the tarrying of the bridegroom, and the slumbering of the virgins, were now being swept away and lost sight of in the onward course of this mighty movement. The hearts of the believers were being united as never before.

The first evening of the Orington meeting I spoke to the people, and stated my convictions that Christ would [167] come on the tenth day of the seventh Jewish month of that year. There was a tent's company on the ground affected more or less with the spirit of fanaticism, and there was a great want of that solemnity in most all present, which characterized the recent camp-meeting at Exeter, N.H., where the evidences in favor of the tenth day of the seventh month had been presented.

As I spoke of the disappointment, the tarry, the slumbering and sleeping, and the cry, "Behold the bridegroom cometh, go ye out to meet him," a death-like stillness reigned throughout the entire encampment. The application of Advent history thus far to these specifications of the parable seemed so natural and forcible as to convict all.

And there was no more heard the irreverent shout of the fanatic, nor the heartless prayer of the formalist, after that evening meeting. As in the days of Christ's first apostles, all were pricked in the heart, and the inquiry of all seemed to be what they should do to be saved. The labor of that meeting, from that time onward to its close, was the presentation of the evidences that the 2300 prophetic days of Daniel would end that autumn, that the types pointed to the tenth day of the seventh Jewish month as the time for the second advent, and that we had reached the point in Second-Advent history where the slumbering ones were to be aroused by the midnight cry. To this were added practical sermons and solemn exhortations, setting forth the necessity of giving up the world, and consecrating all to the Lord. Social meetings were marked with great solemnity. Sins were confessed with tears, and there was a general breaking down before God, and strong pleadings for pardon, and a fitness to meet the Lord at his coming. And the humble disciples of the Lord did not seek his [168] face in vain. before that meeting closed, hundreds testified with tears of joy that they had sought the Lord and found him, and had tasted the sweets of sins forgiven.

The parting was most solemn. That was the last camp-meeting the brethren expected to attend on these mortal shores. And as brother shook the hand of brother, each pointed the other to the final gathering on the immortal shores at the grand encampment of the saints in the New Jerusalem. Tears flowed profusely, and strong men wept aloud. God grant that those who read these lines may see as good a day. And even now, although more than twenty years have passed since that meeting, and that parting scene, as I write, my being seems to be inspired with its solemn, humble spirit, and my tears will flow.

The ministers all fully believed that time was short, and now the work before us was to fly to every part of that wide field, sound the alarm, and wake the slumbering and sleeping ones. In company with one who professed the truth, I visited two towns each day, and sometimes spoke the same day in three different towns. Congregations were crowded, and every meeting was wonderfully marked with the presence of the Holy Spirit.

Character of the Work

As to the character of the work which resulted from giving what was called the midnight cry, it evidently was the special work of God. It was not, as many supposed, the result of fanaticism.

1. Because it bore the marks of the especial providence of God. It was not characterized by those [169] extremes ever manifested where human excitement, and not the word and Spirit of God, has the controlling influence. It was in harmony with those seasons of humiliation, rending of heart, confession and complete consecration of all, which are matters of history in the Old Testament, and are made matters of duty in the New.

2. Because it was subversive of all those forms of fanaticism which had made their appearance somewhat in connection with the Second-Advent cause. And it is a fact, that Satan had crowned upon some who bore the Advent name, almost every stripe of fanaticism he had ever invented. But these were at once swallowed up by the solemn power of the midnight cry, as the rods of the magicians were by the rod of Aaron.

3. Because the work was marked with sobriety, humility, solemnity, reverence, self-examination, repentance, confessions and tears, instead of lightness, exaltation, trifling, irreverent expressions, self-justification, pride in spiritual things, voluntary humility and will worship, which generally characterize the conduct of fanatics.

4. Because the work bore the fruit of the Spirit of God, as set forth in the New Testament. It was evidently guided by wisdom from above. The apostle James declares this wisdom from above. The apostle James declares this wisdom to be "first pure, then peaceable, gentle, and easy to be entreated, full of mercy and good fruits, without partiality, and without hypocrisy." Chap. 3:17. Paul says that the fruit of the Spirit is love, joy, peace, long-suffering, gentleness, goodness, faith, meekness, temperance. Galatians 5:22, 23. These are the good fruits of the work and Spirit of God, and these did all appear in an eminent sense as the results of the midnight cry. [170]

But fanaticisms are the works of the flesh, the power of Satan being brought to bear upon the carnal mind.

It is true that Satan seeks to clothe his work, as far as possible, with that which may resemble garments of truth and righteousness. But the experienced observer will not fail to see that he, and those who are brought under his influence, come infinitely short of counterfeiting the work of God. He may succeed in blinding the eyes of men, so that they may not be able to discern the difference between the work of God and his imperfect mimicry. But the work of high Heaven he cannot imitate. And when the work of Satan in fanaticism is carried out, and its terrible fruit is ripened into bitterness, its contrast with the fruit of the work and Spirit of God will be seen as wide as Beelzebub with Christ, perdition with all its terror and blackness of despair with the matchless glories of the kingdom of God.

Reader, there is a difference between the road to life, and that leading to death. And these do not lie side by side. They are in opposite directions. Do not be deceived by those who mix fanaticism with the work of God, and affirm that the compound all came from Heaven. Neither be deceived by those who, seeing evidence of fanaticism in some who have been connected with the Advent cause, denounce the entire movement as being the work of men, or of Satan. I here enter my solemn protest against making one grand Second-Advent chowder of all that in any way has been connected with the great Advent movement, of truth and error, of wisdom from Heaven, and the spirit and work of fanaticism, and then presenting it to the people as being all the work of Satan, or all the work of God. Such insult God by making him the author of fanaticism and confusion. They also please the Devil, by attributing the [171] work of God which he has tried to mar, to his satanic power. That they might do this, and make no difference between the pure work of God and the results of his miserable efforts at counterfeiting, is the spur of his ambition.

But of all the great religious movements since the days of the first apostles of our Lord, none stand out more pure and free from the imperfections of human nature, and the wiles of Satan, than that of the autumn of 1844. In fact, after looking back upon it for more than twenty years as the greenest spot on all the way in which God has led his people, I do not see how it could have been better, at least so far as the direct providence and work of God is concerned. It was beyond the control of human hands, or human minds. Men and demons sought to hinder and to mar this work, but the power that attended it brushed away their influence, as you would remove a spider's web, and there stood the work of God free from the print of a man's hand.

But as the reader will be better edified by reading the statements and experience of those ministers who had the burden of the work upon them, and were imbued with the spirit of that solemn message, I will here let them speak in confirmation of the foregoing statements.

Elder George Storrs, New York, September 24, 1844, says:

"I take up my pen with feelings such as I never before experienced. *Beyond a doubt*, in my mind, the *tenth day* of the *seventh month* will witness the revelation of our Lord Jesus Christ in the clouds of heaven. We are then within a *few days* of the event. Awful moment to those who are unprepared, but glorious to those who are ready. I feel that I am making the *last* [172] *appeal* that I shall ever make through the press. My heart is full. I see the ungodly and sinner disappearing from my view, and there now stands before my mind the *professed believers* in the Lord's near approach. But what shall I say to them? Alas! we have been *slumbering* and *sleeping*, both the *wise* and the *foolish*; but so our Saviour told us it would be; and 'thus the Scriptures are fulfilled,' and it is the last prophecy relating to the events to precede the personal advent of our Lord; now comes the true midnight cry; the previous was but the alarm. Now the real one is sounding; and oh, how solemn the hour! The 'virgins' have been asleep or slumbering; yes, all of us. Asleep on the time; that is the point. Some have indeed preached the seventh month, but it was with doubt whether it is this year or some other; and that doubt is now removed from my mind. 'Behold the bridegroom cometh,' this year, 'go ye out to meet him.' We have done with the nominal churches and all the wicked, except so far as this cry may affect them; our work is now to wake up the 'virgins' who 'took their lamps and went forth to meet the bridegroom.' Where are we now? 'If the vision tarry, wait for it.' Is not that our answer since March and April? Yes. What happened while the bridegroom tarried? The virgins all slumbered and slept, did they not? Christ's words have not failed, and 'the Scriptures cannot be broken,' and it is of no use for us to pretend that we have been awake. We have been slumbering; not on the fact of Christ's coming, but on the time. We came into the tarrying time; we did not know 'how long' it would tarry, and on that point we have slumbered. Some of us have said in our sleep, 'Don't fix another time;' so we slept. Now the trouble is to wake us up. Lord, help, for vain is the [173] help of man. Speak thyself, Lord. Oh! that the 'Father' may now 'make known' the time.

"To illustrate the position we have occupied. Time — the preaching of definite time for the coming of our Lord, was what led us to take our lamps, and go forth to meet the Bridegroom. The great truth, our Lord Jesus Christ is coming again, personally, to this earth, was, so to speak, the rope let down from Heaven, made fast to the throne of God, equally immovable as that throne; by faith, as with both hands, we took hold of that rope; under our feet we had solid platform, time, where we stood, and all opponents could not remove it, nor make us let go of the rope. There we stood, and rejoiced in the 'blessed hope.' What our opponents never could and never did do, the end of the supposed Jewish year 1843 effected, viz: swept away our platform from under us, and left us with nothing but the rope to hold on by. Did we let go? Some have, and drawn back to perdition. But many have continued to hold by the rope. The scoffing winds have beat against us severely, and we have swung in the air, the sport of our opponents. They told us we were now with them, looking for the Lord's coming, but without any definite time; and we have been compelled to admit it, but have refused to let go the rope, saying, 'If the vision tarry, wait for it.' But we have not known how long we were thus to swing upon the rope, without a foundation for our feet; and we have not felt the same joy and glory that we did when we stood on definite time. God has been trying our faith, to see if we would hold on. Now, once more, he offers us a platform on which to stand. It is in the twenty-fifth chapter of Matthew. Here we have the chronology of the tarrying time, and its duration. 'If ye shall receive it,' you will find once more [174] your feet upon a rock, and the glory that the first belief in time produced in our breast, returns with a large addition to it, even a 'joy unspeakable and full of glory.'

"The present strong cry of time commenced about the middle of July, and has spread with great rapidity and power, and is attended with a demonstration of the Spirit, such as I never witnessed when the cry was '1843.' It is now literally, 'Go ye out to meet him.' There is a leaving all, that I never dreamed could be seen. Where this cry gets hold of the heart, farmers leave their farms, with their crops standing, to go out and sound the alarm, and mechanics their shops. There is a strong crying with tears, and a consecration of all to God, such as I never witnessed. There is a confidence in this truth such as was never felt in the previous cry, in the same degree; and a weeping or melting glory in it that passes all understanding, except to those who have felt it.

"On this present truth, I through grace, dare venture all, and feel that to indulge in doubt about it would be to offend God, and bring upon myself 'swift destruction.' I am satisfied that now, 'whosoever shall seek to save his life,' where this cry has been fairly made, by indulging in an 'if it don't come,' or by a fear to venture out on this truth, 'shall lose' his life. It requires the faith that led Abraham to offer up Isaac, or Noah to build the ark, or Lot to leave Sodom, or the children of Israel to stand all night waiting for their departure out of Egypt, or for Daniel to go into the lion's den, or the three Hebrews to go into the fiery furnace. We have fancied we were going into the kingdom without such a test of faith; but I am satisfied we are not. This last truth brings such a test, and none will venture upon it but such as dare be accounted fools, [175] madmen, or anything else that Antediluvians, Sodomites, a lukewarm church, or sleeping virgins, are disposed to heap upon them. Once more would I cry, 'Escape for thy life;' look not behind you; 'remember Lot's wife.'"

N. Southard, editor of the *Midnight Cry*, September 26, 1844, says:

"Before God, whose swift, approaching judgment will bring every secret thing to light, I wish to say, that up to this hour my professed consecration to him has not been complete. If this fact makes me a hypocrite, I have been one. I have not been dead to the world. If all Christians are dead to the world, I have not been a Christian. But I now say, let Christ be all, and let me be nothing. He has a balm for every wound, for his blood cleanseth from all sin; and I, even I, can stand complete in him.

"After writing thus far, I kneeled and asked God for direction as to what I should say next. I arose and took my Bible, and opening it, read Revelation 7:9-17: 'After this I beheld, and lo, a great multitude, which no man could number, of all nations, and kindreds, and people, and tongues, stood before the throne and before the Lamb, clothed with white robes, and palms in their hands; and cried with a loud voice, saying, Salvation to our God, which sitteth upon the throne, and unto the Lamb,' etc. If this great multitude is admitted before the throne, is there anything to keep me from being there? They differ in every conceivable particular from each other, except in two. They have all washed their robes in the blood of the Lamb, and have all suffered great tribulation for his sake. Here, then, is the touchstone. Is your robe all washed clean in the blood of Christ? or have you been insulting him, by trying to [176] patch up a robe out of the filthy rags of your own righteousness? Alas! I have thought that I could rest partly upon myself and partly on Christ. I now cast myself naked and helpless upon that mercy which saved the thief on the cross, which received denying Peter, which honored Mary Magdalene as the first witness of his resurrection, and which changed a persecuting Saul into a chief apostle.

"But can I bear the second mark? Can I joyfully endure tribulation for Jesus? Not in my own strength, but his grace is sufficient for me. In that grace I believe; Lord, help mine unbelief.

"One of my besetting sins has been a desire to please those around me, instead of inquiring simply, what would the Lord have me to do, to be, and to say. I confess this before the world, but I cannot confess that I have not thought I was doing right in publishing the evidence of Christ's near coming. I have not been half enough awake to the greatness of the subject. May God forgive me in this thing, and grant me grace to be wide awake till he comes. Dear reader, are you awake? If not, it is high time to awake out of sleep."

Elder F.G. Brown, October 2, 1844, says:

"I wish to say to all my dear brethren and sisters, who with me have been waiting for the kingdom of Heaven, that I am thoroughly convinced that we are now in that portion of the parable of the ten virgins, represented by the cry at midnight, 'Behold the bridegroom cometh, go ye out to meet him.' I fully respond to the cry; my expiring lamp has been rekindled, and I am now permitted, by God's grace, to see additional light blazing from the Scriptures, and all converging to one glorious point, the advent of our blessed Lord this very month! My dear friends, I have been in an [177] awful, slumbering, sleeping state. I have been on the verge of perdition; though I have never ceased to cherish in my heart the great and leading doctrines of the Lord's coming. I thought a few weeks ago that I was in a pretty good state; awful delusion! Look out for deception! Awake, and trim your lamps, or you will be lost after all!"

Elder J. Litch, late editor of the *Advent Herald*, Boston, October, 1844, says:

"I wish to say to my dear brethren and sisters, who are looking for the coming of the Lord on the tenth day of the seventh month, but especially to those who have hesitated on the question, that the strong objections which have existed in my mind against it, are passed away, and I am now convinced that the types, together with the signs of the times, are sufficient authority for believing in the Lord's coming at that time; and henceforth I shall look to that day with the expectation of beholding the King in his beauty. I bless the name of the Lord for sending this midnight cry to arouse me to go out to meet the Bridegroom. May the Lord make us meet for the inheritance of the saints."

William Miller, Low Hampton, N.Y., October 11, 1844, says:

"I think I have never seen among our brethren such faith as is manifested in the seventh month. 'He will come," is the common expression. 'He will not tarry the second time,' is their general reply. There is a forsaking of the world, an unconcern for the wants of life, a general searching of heart, confession of sin, and a deep feeling in prayer for Christ to come. A preparation of heart to meet him seems to be the labor of their agonizing spirits. There is something in this present waking up different from anything I have ever before [178] seen. There is no great expression of joy; that is, as it were, suppressed for a future occasion, when all Heaven and earth will rejoice together with joy unspeakable and full of glory. There is no shouting; that, too, is reserved for the shout from Heaven. The singers are silent; they are waiting to join the angelic hosts, the choir from Heaven. No arguments are used or needed; all seem convinced that they have the truth. There is no clashing of sentiments; all are of one heart and of one mind. Our meetings are all occupied with prayer, and exhortation to love and obedience. The general expression is, 'Behold the bridegroom cometh, go ye out to meet him.' Amen. Even so come, Lord Jesus."

I will here give, as the closing testimony relative to the character of the seventh-month movement, one from the "Advent Shield," published January, 1845. And let it be borne in mind that the "Shield" was a standard work, of 440 pages, for all Adventists at that time, and that the following testimony from it was not published till about three months after the seventh-month movement, when Adventists had taken time to review the past, and settle, as was supposed, upon a firm, united position.

"It produced everywhere the most deep searching of heart and humiliation of soul before the God of high Heaven. It caused a weaning of affections from the things of this world, a healing of the controversies and animosities, a confession of wrongs, a breaking down before God, and penitent, broken-hearted supplications to him for pardon and acceptance. It caused self-abasement and prostration of soul, such as we never before witnessed. As God, by Joel, commanded, a rendering of hearts and not of garments, and a turning unto [179] the Lord with fasting, and weeping, and mourning. As God said by Zechariah, a spirit of grace and supplication was poured out upon his children; they looked to him whom they had pierced, there was a great mourning in the land, every family apart and their wives apart, and those who were looking for the Lord afflicted their souls before him. Such was its effect upon the children of God.

"While none could deny the possibility of the Lord's then coming, and as the fulfillment of some of the types chronologically at Christ's first advent rendered it highly probable that those which typified the second advent, would also be chronologically fulfilled, so general an awakening, and with such blessed fruits, could not but impress many minds; and those who were not convinced of the soundness of the typical argument, were led to regard it as a fulfillment of the parable of the ten virgins, in the twenty-fifth of Matthew, — as their arising to trim their lamps, after having gone forth to meet the Bridegroom, and slumbering while he tarried; so that the definite time was finally embraced by nearly all of the Advent faith. So universal a movement among those who a short time before were comparatively asleep on this question, could not be unnoticed by the world.

"The wicked, consequently, flocked to the various places of meeting, some out of idle curiosity to hear, others out of concern for their spiritual interests, and others still to scoff at solemn things. Those who believed they should so shortly stand in their Saviour's presence, and whose works corresponded with their faith, could not but feel a nearness of access to God, and sweet communion with him; and the souls of such were greatly blessed. With a realizing sense of such a nearness of the greatest of all events, as we came up to that [180] point of time, all other unnecessary cares were laid aside, and the whole soul was devoted to a preparation for the great event. God being more ready to give than we are to receive, does not permit any thus to plead in vain; and his Holy Spirit came down like copious showers upon the parched earth. It was then evident that there was faith upon the earth, such faith as is ever ready to act in accordance with what the soul believes that God has spoken; such faith as would, in obedience to a supposed command, bid all the pleasures of this world adieu, having respect to the recompense of reward. Such was a faith like that of Abraham's when, at the command of God, he went out, 'not knowing whither he went,' nor withheld his only son; and here were those all ready to join the multitude, who through faith will inherent the promises."

The Passing of the Time

The tenth day of the seventh month of the Jewish year 1844, came and passed, and left impressions upon the minds of believers not easily effaced; and although a quarter of a century has passed since that memorable period, yet that work has not lost its interest and force upon the minds of those who participated in it. Even now, when one who shared in that blessed work, and who feels its hallowed influence rekindling upon his mind — if in obedience to the injunction of the apostle when he says, "Call to remembrance the former days in which, after ye were illuminated, ye endured a great fight of afflictions, partly whilst ye were made a gazing stock, both by reproaches and afflictions, and partly whilst ye became companions of them that were so used" — shall speak of that solemn work, of that consecration [181] of all, made in full view of eternal scenes, and of that sweet peace and holy joy which filled the minds of the waiting ones, his words will not fail to touch the feelings of all who shared the blessings of that work and have held fast.

And those who participated in that movement are not the only ones who can now go back in their experience, and feast upon the faith-reviving, soul-inspiring realities of the past. Those who have since embraced the Advent faith and hope, and who have seen in the three messages, of Revelation 14, the past consecration and blessedness, the present work of preparation, and the future glory, may go back with us to the autumn of 1844, and with us share the rekindling of the heavenly illumination. Was that our Jerusalem, where we waited for, and enjoyed, the outpouring of the Holy Spirit? Then as all Christians, as well as Christ's first disciples who were present on the occasion, have looked back to the day of Pentecost with pleasure and profit, so may these who have embraced the doctrine of the Second Advent since the memorable seventh-month movement, look back to that period with all that interest those can who participated in it.

The impressions made and left upon the minds of believers were deep and lasting. However far one has since departed from God and his truth, there still remains upon the soul of the apostate traces of the work. Let him hear the subject afresh; let the simple facts be again brought before his mind, and he will feel upon this subject as he can feel upon no other. And those who took part in that work, who are far backslidden from God, yet cherish regard for the word of God and Christian experience, will yet feel deeply over this subject, and the faith of many of them will be resurrected [182] to new life. God grant that these pages may prove a blessing to many such.

The disappointment at the passing of the time was a bitter one. True believers had given up all for Christ, and had shared his presence as never before. They had, as they supposed, given their last warning to the world, and had separated themselves, more or less, from the unbelieving, scoffing multitude. And with the divine blessing upon them, they felt more like associating with their soon-expected Master and the holy angels, than with those from whom they had separated themselves. The love of Jesus filled every soul, and beamed from every face, and with inexpressible desires they prayed, "Come Lord Jesus, and come quickly." But he did not come. And now to turn again to the cares, perplexities, and dangers of life, in full view of the jeers and revilings of unbelievers who now scoffed as never before, was a terrible trial of faith and patience. When Elder Himes visited Portland, Me., a few days after the passing of the time, and stated that the brethren should prepare for another cold winter, my feelings were almost uncontrollable. I left the place of meeting and wept like a child.

But God did not forsake his people. His Spirit upon them still abode, with all who did not rashly deny and denounce the good work in the Advent movement up to that time. And with especial force and comfort did such passages as the following, to the Hebrews, come home to the minds and hearts of the tried, waiting ones: "Cast not away therefore your confidence, which hath great recompense of reward. For ye have need of patience, that, after ye have done the will of God, ye might receive the promise. For yet a little while, and He that shall come will come, and will not tarry. Now [183] the just shall live by faith; but if any man draw back, my soul shall have no pleasure in him. But we are not of them who draw back unto perdition; but of them that believe to the saving of the soul." Chap. 10:35-39. The points of interest in this portion of Scripture are -

1. Those addressed are in danger of casting away their confidence in that in which they had done right.

2. They had done the will of God, and were brought into that state of trial where patience was necessary.

3. The just at this time are to live by faith, not by doubting whether they had done the will of God, but faith, in that in which they had done the will of God.

4. Those who should not endure the trial of faith, but should cast away their confidence in the work in which they did the will of God, and draw back, would take the direct road to perdition.

But why apply all this to the subject of the second advent? Answer: Because Paul applies it there. His words, in the very center of the foregoing quotation from his epistle to the Hebrews, forbid any other application: "For yet a little while, and he that shall come will come, and will not tarry." No one will for a moment question that the second advent is the subject upon which the apostle treats. The peculiar situation of those who should be looking for the second appearing of Jesus, is the burden of his exhortation. And how wonderfully applicable to those who were sadly disappointed, tempted and tried, in the autumn of 1844, are his words. With great confidence had they proclaimed the coming of the Lord, with the assurance that they were doing the will of God. But as the time passed, they were brought into a position exceedingly trying to faith and patience. Hence the words of Paul to them, just then, and just there. "Cast not away therefore your confidence... [184]
. . . . . . Ye have need of patience . . . . . .
Ye have done the will of God." To this decision of the apostle every true Adventist, who tasted the good word of God and the powers of the world to come, in the movement of 1844, will respond, Amen.

But how fearful the words which follow: "Now the just shall live by faith; but if any man draw back my soul shall have no pleasure in him." As Adventists came up to the point of expectation in the blazing light of unsealed prophecy, and the rapidly-fulfilling signs that Christ's coming was at the doors, they walked, as it were, by sight. But now they stand with disappointed hopes, and stricken hearts, and live by faith in the sure word, and the work of God in their Second-Advent experience. With these who hold fast, God is well pleased; but in those who draw back he has no pleasure. These believe to the saving of the soul; while those who become impatient, cast away their confidence in the way God has led them, and give it up as the work of man, or of Satan, and draw back to perdition.

This and many other portions of Scripture of like import, having a direct application to the condition of believers at that time, served not only as an encouragement to them to hold fast their faith, but as a warning to them not to apostatize. And a general impression remained upon the minds of believers for some time after the disappointment, that the seventh-month movement was in the direct providence of God, and that those who had been engaged in this work had done his will.

And according to the best light they had, there was a general agreement that the seventh-month movement was the last great test, that the harvest of the earth was ripe for the sickle of the Son of man, and [185] that the door was shut. That the salvation of the soul, or perdition, hung upon the manner in which those who heard treated that solemn message, I doubt not. And this is especially clear in the case of the disappointed believers after the time passed. In holding fast and believing, there was salvation; in drawing back, the result would be perdition. The view, however, that the harvest of the earth was ripe, and that the door was shut, was soon abandoned. But although all, long since, gave up this position as incorrect, I fail to see why they should be censured for taking it upon the passing of the time. In fact, the conclusion seems very natural, and I hardly see how they could have come to any other. I will here mention some of the reasons why such a conclusion was reasonable, if not unavoidable.

1. William Miller and others had taught that the door would be shut, and that probation would close a short time before the second advent. In a letter to Elder J.V. Himes, October 6, 1844, he said: "I am strong in the opinion that the next will be the last Lord's day sinners will ever have in probation. And within ten or fifteen days from thence,

they will see Him whom they have hated and despised, to their shame and everlasting contempt."

2. And, certainly, that probation will close prior to the second advent is plainly taught in the following emphatic testimony from Revelation 22:11, 12: "He that is unjust, let him be unjust still; and he which is filthy, let him be filthy still; and he that is righteous, let him be righteous still; and he that is holy, let him be holy still. And behold I come quickly." I will only add, that the order of events here given is, first, the final decision of all men living at the close of probation, and, [186] second, then follows the advent of Him who says, "And behold I come quickly."

3. All true believers expected that probation would close as soon as the tenth day of the seventh month. And as the time of expectation drew near, their burdened spirits felt more and still more heavily the weight and responsibility of doing every duty to others. But as the point of expectation was finally reached, all this burden at once fell off. This was as true of the isolated brother or sister, in some distant part of the country, as with those in the crowded city mingling with hundreds of like faith. It was true of all. All felt that their work in warning sinners was done. No one can have a just idea of this great change, only those who participated in the movement, and came up to the time of expectation with the burden of the solemn work upon them. Jesus had not come as they expected, and why this great change had come over all was a matter of proper inquiry. And how natural the conclusion, to say the least, that probation was ended.

4. The change that had suddenly come over the ungodly seemed to strengthen the conviction that the door was shut. Although the passing of the time, removing their fears, may now be regarded as a sufficient cause for the change in them, yet at the time the fiend-like conduct of many after the tenth day passed, who but a few hours or days before had appeared penitent, gave the idea that the restraining influence of the Spirit of God had forever left them.

In view of these things it should not be a matter of surprise to any, that Adventists were agreed that the midnight cry was the last great test, that the work for the world was finished, and that the door was shut. That this was their faith, may be seen by reviewing the [187] writings of leading men in the cause, published immediately after the passing of the time.

William Miller, in a letter addressed to J.V. Himes, says:

"We have done our work in warning sinners, and in trying to awaken a formal church. God, in his providence, has shut the door; we can only stir one another up to be patient; and be diligent to make our calling and election sure. We are now living in the time specified by Malachi 3:18; also Daniel 12:10; Revelation 22:10-12. In this passage we cannot help but see that a little while before Christ should come, there would be a separation between the just and unjust, the righteous and wicked, between those who love his appearing and those who hate it. And never, since the days of the apostles, has there been such a division line drawn as was drawn about the tenth day of the seventh Jewish month. Since that time they say 'they have no confidence in us.' We have now need of patience, after we have done the will of God, that we may receive the promise."

The *Advent Herald*, for November 13, 1844, J.V. Himes, S. Bliss, and A. Hale, editors, says:

"But the alarm was everywhere made; the cry was everywhere given. And again we can see that God was with us. It was a soul-purifying work; and the children of God bowed themselves in his presence and received blessings to their souls, unprecedented in the history of the Advent cause. And yet we are disappointed; the day passed away and we are still here. And those who only looked on, and passed by, were ready to exclaim that it was all a delusion; and that now of a certainty we must relinquish all our hopes, and abandon all our expectations. We, however, do not thus feel. As great a paradox as it may be to our opponents, [188] yet we can discern in it the leadings of God's providence; and when we are reviled and censured by those to whom the world look as the Gamaliels of our age, we feel that they are only speaking of the things they understand not.

"Those who have not been in this late movement, can appreciate nothing respecting it. And we regard it as another, and a more searching test, than the first proclamation of the time. It has searched Jerusalem as with candles; and it has purged out the old leaven. It has tested the hearts of all who heard it, and awakened a love for the Lord's appearing; or it has called forth a hatred, more or less perceivable, but known to God, of his coming. It has drawn a line, and awakened sensibilities, so that those who will examine their own hearts, may know on which side of it they would have been found, had the Lord then come; whether they would have exclaimed, 'Lo! this is our God, we have waited for him and he will save us;' or whether they would have called to rocks and mountains to fall on them to hide them from the face of Him that sitteth on the throne, and from the wrath of the Lamb. God thus, as we believe, has tested his people, has tried their faith, has proved them, and seen whether they would shrink, in the hour of trial, from the position in which He might see fit to place them; and whether they would relinquish this world and rely with implicit confidence in the work of God.

"And we as much believe that we have done the will of God in thus sounding the alarm, as we believe that Jonah did when he entered into Nineveh a day's journey, and cried, saying, 'Yet forty days and Nineveh shall be overthrown.' Nineveh was not then overthrown; nor has the Lord yet wrought deliverance in the earth, [189] nor the inhabitants of the world fallen. Was Jonah a false prophet when he preached the *time* of Nineveh's destruction? No; he had only preached the preaching that God had bid him. But God had said that 'at what instant I shall speak concerning a nation and concerning a kingdom to pluck up and to pull down and to destroy it; if that nation against whom I have pronounced, turn from their evil, I will repent of the evil that I thought to do unto them.' Jeremiah 18:7, 8. 'So, the people of Nineveh believed God and proclaimed a fast, and put on sackcloth, from the greatest of them even to the least of them; and God saw their works that they turned from their evil way; and God repented of the evil that he said he would do unto them; and he did it not.' The preaching of Jonah served as a test to the inhabitants of Nineveh, and accomplished God's purposes, as much as it would have done had the city perished.

"So we believe that this last cry has been a test; and that with our views of duty, we should as much have sinned against God, had we refrained from giving that message, as Jonah did when 'he rose up to flee unto Tarshish from the presence of the Lord;' that we should as much have sinned, had we refused to give heed to it, as the Ninevites would in refusing to repent at his preaching; and that all who are angry that we have preached a time which has not been realized, are as guilty as Jonah was when he was angry and prayed the Lord to take his life from him, because God had spared that great city."

The following is from the *Advent Herald* of October 30, 1844, relative to the suspension of meetings in the Advent Tabernacle of Boston. The article from which it is taken, had previously been inserted in several of [190] the daily papers of that city. It is important, as it correctly sets forth the views and feelings of Adventists at that time. In view of such testimony, it is vain for any man to deny that it was the universal belief of Adventists, in the autumn of 1844, that their work for the world was forever done. After giving some of the reasons why they expected the Lord on the tenth day of the seventh month, the writer of the article says:

"With this expectation we were desirous to meet once more, to mingle our prayers, and to encourage one another in the last work of preparation; and for this purpose we had met at our well-known place of worship in this city. We gave no special notice of our meeting, we made no appeal to the public, and it was characterized by no exercises which were calculated to excite either the mirth or vengeance of any portion of the community.

"We were serious, we were bowed in penitence and prayer before God, or heartily affected by the mutual confessions of tried and dear friends. We had no ill-feeling to indulge toward any man; we felt that we were done with the world, and had forgiven them the many injuries they had inflicted upon us; but stale and silly slanders in reference to us were revived; the restless spirits of the community have been aroused; we could not meet in peace, and our meetings in consequence have been suspended. And we now make these remarks to disabuse the public, and with the hope that some, who would not otherwise give their attention to the calls of the present time, may lay them to heart.

"To the city authorities, who faithfully rendered their services, we are grateful, though we could not promote the objects of the meeting when such protection was needed. [191]

"We forgive our enemies. They have not injured us; and oh! that they could see how much they may have injured themselves; but we have done with them now. We expect the realization of the promise of God. He who delivered Noah and Lot; he who brought his people out of Egypt and Babylon, has promised (as we believe) to save them finally 'by his Son from Heaven.' We expect it. We have hazarded all on that expectation; and we only ask that God may give us, and all who look for him, grace to abide the issue.

"In behalf of the Adventists in Boston and vicinity,
"JOSHUA V. HIMES."

I have not a word of censure for a single soul who came to the honest conclusion that the work of warning sinners closed with the burden of the midnight cry. And more, I solemnly believe that the providence of God brought us to that position. And there the Advent hosts should have remained, patiently waiting, watching, and praying, until our true position could have been clearly seen by the light of the heavenly sanctuary.

Argument from the Types

In the providence of God, in the seventh-month movement the attention of the people was turned to the types of the law of Moses. The argument which had been given, that as the vernal types, namely, the passover, the wave sheaf, and the meat-offering, were fulfilled in their order and time in the crucifixion, the resurrection of Christ, and the descent of the Holy Spirit on the day of Pentecost, so would the autumnal types be fulfilled as to time, in the events connected with the second advent, seemed to be conclusive and satisfactory. The position taken was, that as the high [192] priest came out of the typical sanctuary on the tenth day of the seventh month and blessed the people, so Christ, our great High Priest, would on that day come out of Heaven to bless his waiting people.

But it should be borne in mind that at that time those types which point to the work in the heavenly sanctuary were not understood. In fact, no one had any definite idea of the tabernacle of God in Heaven. We now see that the two holies of the typical sanctuary, made by the direction of the Lord to Moses, with their two distinct ministrations — the daily and the yearly services, — were, in the language of Paul to the Hebrews, "patterns of things in the Heavens," "figures of the true, chapter 9. He also says of the work of the Jewish priests in chapter 8, "Who serve unto the example and shadow of heavenly things." His words mean simply this: In Heaven there is a sanctuary where Christ ministers, and that sanctuary has two holies, and two distinct ministrations, as truly as the earthly sanctuary had. If his words do not mean this, they have no meaning at all. How natural, then, the conclusion, that as the Jewish priests ministered daily in connection with the holy place of the sanctuary, and on the tenth day of the seventh month, at the close of their yearly round of service, the high priest entered the most holy place to make atonement for the cleansing of the sanctuary, so Christ ministered in connection with the holy place of the heavenly sanctuary from the time of his ascension to the ending of the 2300 days of Daniel 8, in 1844, when on the tenth day of the seventh month of that year he entered the most holy place of the heavenly tabernacle to make a special atonement for the blotting out of the sins of his people, or, which is the same thing, for the cleansing of the sanctuary. [193] "Unto two thousand three hundred days," said the angel to the prophet, "then shall the sanctuary be cleansed."

The typical sanctuary was cleansed from the sins of the people with the offering of blood. The nature of the cleansing of the heavenly sanctuary may be learned from the type. By virtue of his own blood, Christ entered the most holy to make a special atonement for the cleansing of the heavenly tabernacle. For clear and full expositions of the sanctuary and the nature of its cleansing, see works upon the subject by J. N. Andrews and U. Smith, for sale at the Review Office, Battle Creek, Mich.

With this view of the heavenly sanctuary before the reader, he can see the defect in the seventh-month theory. It now appears evident that the conclusion that Christ would come out of Heaven on that day is not justified by the premises in the case. But if Christ's ministry in the heavenly sanctuary was to last but one year, on the last day of which he would make an atonement for the cleansing of the heavenly tabernacle, according to the type, then the conclusion that he would on that day come out and bless his waiting people, would be irresistible.

But let it be remembered that "the law having a shadow of good things to come," was "not the very image of the things." In the shadow, the round of service, first in the holy place for the entire year, save one day, and second, in the most holy place on the last day of that year, was repeated each successive year. But not so in the ministry of Christ. He entered the holy place of that heavenly sanctuary at his ascension once for all. There he ministered till the time for the cleansing of the sanctuary at the close of the 2300 days [194] in the autumn of 1844. To accomplish this work, he then entered the most holy place once for all. Christ suffered upon the cross — not often — but once for all. He entered upon his work in the holy place once for all. And he cleanses the heavenly sanctuary for the sins of his people once for all. His ministry in the holy, from his ascension in the spring of A.D. 31 to the autumn of 1844, was eighteen hundred and thirteen years and six months. The period of his ministry in the most holy can no more be defined before its close, than the time of his ministry in the holy could be defined before it terminated. Therefore, however much the tenth-day atonement for the cleansing of the typical sanctuary proved that our great High Priest would enter the most holy of the heavenly tabernacle on the tenth day of the seventh month, it proved nothing to the point that he would on that day come out of the most holy place.

But just what was accomplished on the tenth day of the seventh month became a matter of discussion. Some took the rash position that the movement had not been directed by the providence of God. They cast away their confidence in that work, not having sufficient faith and patience to "wait" and "watch," until it should be explained by the light of the sanctuary and the three messages of Revelation 14, and they drew back, to say the least, toward perdition.

Others trembled for this fearful step, and felt the deepest solicitude for the welfare of the flock, and exhorted the brethren to patiently wait and watch for the coming of the Lord, in full faith that God had been in the work. Among these was William Miller. In a letter published in the *Advent Herald* for Dec. 11, 1844, he says: [195]

"DEAR BRO. HIMES: Be patient, establish your heart, for the coming of the Lord draweth nigh. For ye have need of patience, that after ye have done the will of God, ye might receive the promise. For yet a little while and he that shall come will come, and will not tarry."

The following is from the cheering pen of Eld. F.G. Brown, who was not only a man of ability, but one who drank deeply at the fountain of advent experience. He saw and felt the danger of drawing back, and wrote the following letter to encourage his brethren to hold fast and believe to the saving of the soul. It was written Nov. 11, 1844, and published in the *Advent Herald*.

"DEAR BRETHREN AND SISTERS: The great God has dealt wonderfully with us. When we were in a state of alarming blindness in relation to the coming of the great and terrible day of the Lord, he saw fit to awaken us from our death-like slumbers, to a knowledge of these things. How little of our own or man's agency was employed in this work, you know. Our prejudices, education, tastes, both intellectual and moral, were all opposed to the doctrine of the Lord's coming. We know that it was the Almighty's arm that disposed us to receive this grace. The Holy Ghost wrought it in our inmost souls, yea, incorporated it into our very being, so that it is now a part of us, and no man can take it from us. It is our hope, our joy, our all. The Bible reads it, every page is full of the Lord's immediate coming, and much from without strengthens us in the belief that the Judge standeth at the door! At present everything tries us. Well, we have heretofore had almost uninterrupted peace and exceeding great joy. True, we have had some trials formerly, but what were they in comparison with the glory to be revealed? We [196] are permitted to live in the days of the Son of man, which Jesus spake of as a desirable day. How special the honor! How unspeakable the privilege!

"And shall we be so selfish as not to be willing to endure a little trial for such a day, when all our worthy and honored predecessors have so patiently submitted to the toils and sufferings incident to their pilgrimage and to their times? Let it never be! We know that God has been with us. Perhaps never before this has he for a moment seemed to depart from us. Shall we now begin like the children of Israel to doubt, and to fear, and repine, after he has so frequently and signally shown us his hand in effecting for us one deliverance after another? Has God blessed us with sanctification, and salvation, and glory, now to rebuke and destroy us? The thought is almost blasphemous. Away with it! Have we been so long with our Lord and yet not known him? Have we read our Bibles in vain? Have we forgotten the record of his wonderful dealings unto his people in all past ages? Let us pause, and wait, and read, and pray, before we act rashly or pronounce a hasty judgment upon the ways and works of God. If we are in darkness, and see not as clearly as heretofore, let us not be impatient. We shall have light just as soon as God sees it will be for our good. Mark it, dearly beloved, our great Joshua will surely bring us unto the goodly land. I have no kind of fears of it, and I will not desert him before he does me.

"He is doing the work just right. Glory to his name! Remember, you have been sailing a long, long voyage, and you began to think yourselves pretty skillful sailors until you approached the home coast, when the Pilot coming on board, you had to relinquish the charge to him, and oh! how hard it is to commit all [197] your precious cargo and your noble vessel into his hands. You fear, you tremble, lest the gallant ship should become a wreck, and the dearly-bought freight be emptied into the ocean! But don't fear. Throw off the master, and like a good, social, relieved officer, go and take over home scenes and endearments. Cheer us, 'all's well.'

"You have finished your work, and now be patient, and you shall have the reward.

"It was necessary that our 'faith' and 'patience' should be tried before our work could be completed. We closed up our work with the world some time ago. This is my conviction. And now God has given us a little season of self-preparation, to prove us before the world. Who now will abide the test? Who is resolved to see the end of his faith, live or die? Who will go to Heaven if he has to go alone? Who will fight the battle through, though the armor-bearers faint, and fear, and fail? Who will keep his eye alone on the floating flag of his King, and, if need be, sacrifice his last drop of blood for it? Such only are worthy to be crowned, and such only will reap the glorious laurels.

"We must be in speaking distance of port. God's recent work for us proves it. We needed just such a work if Christ is coming forthwith. I bless God for such glorious manifestations of himself to his people. Don't dishonor him, questioning whether it might not have been the work of man, for he will vindicate that, and his word, too, very shortly, is my solemn belief. Do not be allured by the baits that may be flung out to draw you back from your confidence in God. The world and the nominal church know nothing at all of [198] your hope. They cannot be made to understand us. Let them alone. You have buried your name and reputation once, and now do not go to digging it up again, when all manner of evil is spoken of you, falsely, for Christ's sake. Pray for your enemies. Do look straight ahead, lest your minds again become occupied with earth — its business, cares, labors, pleasures, friends. The Bible, the Bible, is the best teacher now. Prayer, prayer, is the best helper. The next signal we have will be the final one. Oh! shall any of us be found with our lamps going out when the

Master comes? Oh! how impressive the Saviour's repeated admonition, *Watch, watch, watch*."

Many concluded that great changes took place on the tenth day of the seventh month, closely connected with the final destiny of men, but as yet there was no well-defined position as to what did take place.

Joseph Marsh, editor of the *Voice of Truth*, Nov. 7, 1844, says:

"We did believe that he would come at that time; and now, though we sorrow on account of our disappointment, yet we rejoice that we have acted according to our faith. We have had, and still have, a conscience void of offense in this matter, toward God and man. God has blessed us abundantly, and we have not a doubt but that all will soon be made to work together for the good of his dear people, and his glory.

"We cheerfully admit that we have been mistaken in the nature of the event we expected would occur on the tenth day of the seventh month; but we cannot yet admit accomplish all that the type would justify us to expect. We now believe he did."

Where are we in the fulfillment of prophecy?, soon [199] became a matter of most interesting inquiry. Some yielded to the clamors of the church and world, who called for confessions that they had been mistaken at least in the time, and among this number were several able ministers. Their fearful course greatly increased the anxiety to understand the real position. The hour was a most trying one. There seemed to be a strong inclination with many to draw back, which ripened in them into a general stampede in the direction of Egypt. Finally, not a few settled, with more or less clearness, upon a position embracing the following points:

1. That the parable of the ten virgins represented the great Advent movement, each specification illustrating a corresponding event connected with Second-Advent history.

2. That, in answer to the inquiry, Where are we? the point of time was reached, when the words of our Lord following the parable were applicable, "Watch, therefore, for ye know neither the day nor the hour wherein the Son of man cometh." Matthew 25:13.

3. That the time had come to liken, or to compare, the experience of those who were looking for the kingdom, here called the kingdom of Heaven, with an eastern marriage, and that in order to do this, both must be matters of history, showing that each specification in the parable was already fulfilled.

4. That the time when to compare Second-Advent experience with the events in the marriage was definitely pointed out by our Lord when he says, "*Then* shall the kingdom of Heaven be likened unto ten virgins." When? He had just closed a description of two kinds of servants in chapter 24, one servant giving meat to his master's household in due season, the other smiting this good and faithful servant, and in his heart saying, [200] "My Lord delayeth his coming." Just then may the events connected with Advent history be compared with the specifications of the parable. These two servants had been engaged in the same work. But by some means one begins to say in his heart, My Lord delayeth his coming, and smites his fellow. No one who wished to see, could fail to see a clear fulfillment of this illustration in the labors and general course of Advent ministers soon after the passing of the time. All came up to that time apparently a band of brothers. The time passed. Some became impatient and cast away their confidence in the work, confessed to a scoffing church and world, and because others would not confess as they had done, that a human or satanic influence had controlled them, they were ready to smite those who were strengthening the Master's household with the bread of Heaven.

The spiritual food for that time was by no means that teaching which would let them down from the position they had taken, and send them weeping and mourning back to Egypt. But meat in the due season was those expositions of God's word which showed his hand in the movement, and such cheering testimonies as are quoted in the foregoing pages in vindication of the Advent movement. How humiliating and painful the fact that Satan is permitted to bring the spiritual warfare within the Second-Advent ranks.

5. That in the sense of the parable the Bridegroom had come. Come where? Answer, To the marriage. Was the marriage of the Lamb to take place in this world at the second appearing of Christ? The Bridegroom had

not come. But if the marriage of the Lamb was to take place in Heaven, the position might be correct. And right here the charge of our Lord to the [201] waiting ones comes in with peculiar force: "Let your loins be girded about, and your lights burn, and ye yourselves like unto men that wait for their Lord when he will return from the wedding." Luke 12:35, 36. If our Lord at his second appearing returns from the wedding, then the marriage of the Lamb must take place in Heaven prior to his return. Therefore, the coming of the bridegroom in the parable illustrated some change in the position and work of our great High Priest in Heaven in reference to the marriage of the Lamb.

In a letter to the *Voice of Truth* for Feb. 19, 1845, William Miller says:

"I presume, Bro. Marsh, you have seen Brn. Hale and Turner's *Advent Mirror*, printed in Boston, Jan., 1845, concerning the marriage, in the parable of the virgins. I do believe in the main they are right — that cannot be the personal coming of Christ. Why, say you? Read Luke 12:36: 'And ye yourselves like unto men that wait for their Lord, when he shall return from the wedding, that when he cometh and knocketh, they may open to him immediately.' You see his coming, for which we look, is after the wedding.

"Has Christ come in the sense spoken of, Matthew 25:10? I think he has.

"I know many of my brethren whom I highly esteem, will, and do, disagree with me on this matter. I would advise them not to have any hardness. Remember what James says, v. 9: 'Grudge not one against another, brethren, lest ye be condemned: behold the Judge standeth before the door.' It would seem that in this very time when we have need of patience, the apostle, by the inspiration of the divine [202] Spirit, foresaw that there would be danger of grudging, or grieving one another, and warns us not to do it, lest ye be condemned: for 'the Judge standeth before the door!'

"Let the dear brethren see to it, that we give meat in due season. Let no one say in his heart, My Lord delayeth his coming, and begin to beat and bruise, and grudge against his fellow-servant. He that seeks to save his life now by conformity to the world, or worldly men, will lose it; and he that loses his life now for the truth's sake, will find eternal life."

6. That the established view, that in the marriage of the Lamb the church is the bride of Christ, was among the errors of past times. By investigation it was clearly seen that there were two things which the Scriptures of the Old and New Testaments illustrate by marriage. First, the union of God's people in all past ages, as well as at the present time, with their Lord. Second, Christ's reception of the throne of David, which is in the New Jerusalem. But union of believers with their Lord has existed since the days of Adam, and cannot be regarded as the marriage of the Lamb. It is supposed that Isaiah 54:5, speaks of the church when he says, "Thy Maker is thine husband;" but Paul, in Galatians 4, applies this prophecy to the New Jerusalem.

Says John, speaking of Christ, "He that hath the bride is the bridegroom." John 3:29. That Christ is here represented in his relation to his followers by a bridegroom, and his followers by a bride, is true; but that he and they are here called the bridegroom and bride, is not true. No one believes that the event called the marriage of the Lamb took place eighteen hundred years since. [203]

Paul, in writing to the church, 2 Corinthians 11:2, says, "I have espoused you to one husband, that I may present you a chaste virgin to Christ." But does this prove that the marriage of the Lamb took place in Corinth? Or, did Paul only wish to represent by marriage, the union which he had effected, through the gospel, between Christ and the church at Corinth?

He also says, Ephesians 5:23, "For the husband is the head of the wife, even as Christ is the head of the church." But please turn and read from verse 22, and it will be seen that Paul's subject is the relation and duty of man and wife to each other. This is illustrated and enforced by the relation of Christ and the church. Those who suppose that Paul is here defining who the Lamb's wife is, are greatly mistaken. That is not his subject. He commences, "Wives, submit yourselves unto your husbands." Verse 22. It is, "Husbands, love your wives." Verse 25. It is, indeed, an excellent subject, but has nothing to do in determining what the bride is.

The marriage of the Lamb does not cover the entire period of probation, in which believers are united to their Lord, from Adam to the close of probation. It is one event, to take place at one point of time, and that is just prior to the resurrection of the just.

Then what is the bride in the marriage of the Lamb? Said the angel to John, "Come hither, I will show thee the bride, the Lamb's wife." Revelation 21:9. Did the angel show John the church? Let John testify. "And he carried me away in the Spirit to a great and high mountain, and showed me that great city, the holy Jerusalem, descending out of Heaven from God." Verse 10.

The New Jerusalem is also represented as the mother. "But Jerusalem which is above is free, which is the [204] mother of us all." Galatians 4:26 Christ is represented (Isaiah 9:6,) as the "everlasting Father" of his people; the New Jerusalem, the mother, and the subjects of the first resurrection, the children. And, beyond all doubt, the resurrection of the just is represented by birth. How appropriate, then, is the view that the marriage of the Lamb takes place in Heaven before the Lord comes, and before the children of the great family of Heaven are brought forth at the resurrection of the just.

Let those who are disposed to cling to the old view that the church is the bride, and that the marriage is after Christ comes, and the saints are caught up to Heaven, answer the following questions:

1. Who are illustrated by the man found at the marriage, Matthew 22, not having on the wedding garment?

2. Will any be caught up by mistake, to be bound hand and foot, and be cast down to the earth again?

3. If the church is the wife, who are they that are called to the marriage as guests?

4. Jerusalem above is the mother of the children of promise; but if the church is the Lamb's wife, who are the children?

5. That the door was shut. The clear light from the heavenly sanctuary that a door, or ministration, was opened at the close of the 2300 days, while another was closed at that time, had not yet been seen. And in the absence of light in reference to the shut and open door of the heavenly sanctuary, the reader can hardly see how those who held fast their Advent

experience, as illustrated by the parable of the ten virgins, could fail to come to the conclusion that probation for sinners had closed.

But light on the subject soon came, and then it was [205] seen that although Christ closed one ministration at the termination of the 2300 days, he had opened another in the most holy place, and still presented his blood before the Father for sinners. As the high priest, in the type, on the tenth day of the seventh month, entered the most holy place, and offered blood for the sins of the people, before the ark of the testament and the mercy-seat, so Christ, at the close of the 2300 days, came before the ark of God and the mercy-seat to plead his blood in behalf of sinners. Mark this: The great Redeemer then approached the mercy-seat in behalf of sinners. Was the door of mercy closed? This is an unscriptural expression, but, if I may be allowed to use it, may I not say that in the fullest sense of the expression the door of mercy was opened on the tenth day of the seventh month, 1844?

Beside the ark of God containing the ten precepts of his holy law, over which was the mercy-seat, did the trusting ones now behold their merciful High Priest. They had stood in harmony with the whole Advent host at the passing of the time, then represented as "the church in Philadelphia;" meaning brotherly love. And with what inexpressible sweetness did the following words addressed to that church come home to their stricken hearts: "These things saith he that is holy, he that is true, he that hath the key of David, he that openeth, and no man shutteth; and shutteth, and no man openeth. I know thy works. Behold, I have set before thee an open door, and no man can shut it." Revelation 3:7, 8.

Adventists were agreed that the seven churches of Revelation 2 and 3, symbolized seven states of the Christian church, covering the entire period from the first advent of Christ to his second appearing, and that the sixth [206] state addressed represented those who with one united voice proclaimed the coming of Jesus, in the autumn of 1844. This church was about to enter upon a period of great trial. And they were to find relief from it, so far as ascertaining their true position is concerned, by light from the heavenly sanctuary. After the light should come, then would also come the battle upon the shut and open door. Here are seen the connecting link between the work of God in the past Advent movement, in connection with the claims of the Sabbath of the fourth commandment, these men, especially those who had given up their Advent experience, felt called upon to oppose. And their opposition, as a general thing, was most violent, bitter, and wicked.

The shut and open door of the heavenly sanctuary constituted the strong point upon which the matter turned. If we were right on the subject of the cleansing of the sanctuary, then the door or ministration of the holy place was shut, and the door or ministration of the most holy place was opened, the 2300 days had ended, the preaching of time was correct, and the entire movement was right. But let our opponents show that we were in error upon the sanctuary question, that Christ had not entered the most holy place to cleanse the sanctuary, then the 2300 days had not ended, the preaching of the time was an error, and the entire movement was wrong. And, again, if the door or ministration of the most holy place was opened, and the faith of the waiting ones was to view Jesus standing before the mercy-seat and the ark of the ten commandments in Heaven, how forcible the arguments for the [207] perpetuity and claims of the entire law of God, the fourth precept not excepted. The hand of the Lord was with those who took a firm position that the great Advent movement had been in his direct providence, and that the time had come for the Sabbath reform, and many embraced these views. Then it was that our opponents arose in the spirit of persecution, manifesting the wrath of the dragon against those who kept the commandments of God, and labored to open the door that had been shut, and to shut that door which had been opened, and thus put an end to the matter. Hence the strong expressions quoted above — "He that openeth and no *man* shutteth, and shutteth and no *man* openeth." "Behold I have set before thee an open door, and no *man* can shut it." Nothing can be plainer than that man, or a set of men, near the close of the history of the church, would war against the truth of God in reference to the shut and open door.

And to this day those who retain the spirit of war upon those who keep the commandments of God, make the belief in the shut and open door odious, and charge it all upon Seventh-day Adventists. Many of them, however, are not unaware of the injustice of this. Some of this people did believe in the shut door, in common with the Adventists generally, soon after the passing of the time. Some of us held fast this position longer than those did who gave up their Advent experience, and drew back in the direction of perdition. And God be thanked that we did hold fast to that position till the matter was explained by light from the heavenly sanctuary.

And it may be worthy of notice that although the belief in, and abandonment of, the shut-door position has been general, there have been two distinct and opposite [208] ways of getting out of it. One class did this by casting away their confidence in the Advent movement, by confessions to those who had opposed and had scoffed at them, and by ascribing the powerful work of the Holy Spirit to human or satanic influences. These got out of the position on the side of perdition.

Another class heeded the many exhortations of Christ and his apostles, applicable to their position, with its trials, dangers, and duties — Watch — Be ye therefore patient — Cast not many therefore your confidence — For ye have need of patience — Hold fast. They waited, watched, and prayed, till light came, and they by faith in the word saw the open door of the heavenly sanctuary, and Jesus there pleading his precious blood before the ark of the most holy place.

But what was that ark? It was the ark of God's testimony, the ten commandments. Reader, please follow these trusting, waiting ones, as they by faith enter the heavenly sanctuary. They take you into the holy place and show you "the candlestick, and the table, and the shewbread," and other articles of furniture. Then they lead you into the most holy where stands Jesus, clad in priestly garments, before the mercy-seat which is upon, and but the cover of, the ark containing the law of God. They lift the cover and bid you look into the sacred ark, and there you behold the ten commandments, a copy of which God gave to Moses. Yes, dear reader, there, safe from the wrath of man and the rage of demons, beside his own holiness, are the ten precepts of God's holy law.

The waiting, watching, praying ones, embraced the fourth precept of that law, and with fresh courage took their onward course to the golden gates of the city of God, cheered by the closing benediction of the Son of [209] God: "Blessed are they that do his commandments, that they may have right to the tree of life, and may enter in through the gates into the city." Thus they came out of the position of the shut door on the side of loyalty to the God of high Heaven, the tree of life, and the eternal city of the redeemed. The reader will not fail to see the difference between their course and getting out of the shut door on the side of perdition. God pity the apostate.

The Seventh Angel

The seventh angel, the last of the seven trumpet angels, had been supposed to be the same as the "last trump," which will awake the righteous dead. But many among the Adventists were about this time taking a different view of the subject. The six former trumpet angels were symbols, and each had occupied a period of time, during which a series of events took place. Why not the seventh be a symbol covering a period of time, during which a series of events might also transpire?

But the scenes connected with the last trump mentioned by the apostle, are represented as transpiring "in a moment, in the twinkling of an eye." Not so with the events under the sounding of the seventh angel," is the testimony of Revelation 10:7. As this entire chapter has a direct bearing upon the subject of the great Advent movement as symbolized by the three messages of Revelation 14, I will here give it with a few brief remarks of application.

"And I saw another mighty angel come down from Heaven, clothed with a cloud; and a rainbow was upon his head, and his face was as it were the sun, and his [210] feet as pillars of fire. And he had in his hand a little book open: and he set right foot upon the sea, and his left foot on the earth, and cried with a loud voice, as when a lion roareth: and when he had cried, seven thunders uttered their voices. And the angel which I saw stand upon the sea and upon the earth, lifted up his hand to Heaven, and sware by him that liveth forever and ever, who created Heaven, and the things that therein are, and the earth, and the things which are therein, that there should be time no longer." Verses 1-6.

I will briefly call attention to the following points in the above quotation:

1. The angel, in a most solemn manner, swore that there should be time no longer. This does not mean that with the oath of the angel, time as measured by days, months and years, would cease; for the next verse

speaks of the "days" of the voice of the seventh angel. And even from the second advent of Christ and the resurrection of the just, a thousand years are marked as reaching to the resurrection of the just. In fact, while the earth and the sun and moon shall endure and continue their revolutions, so long will there be days, months and years. And there is no scripture evidence that these bodies will ever cease to exist. The oath of the angel, therefore, must refer to prophetic time.

2. The angel holds in his hand, as he swears upon the subject of time, a little book open. It may be inferred from this language, that this book was at some time closed up. This was true of the book of Daniel. "But thou, O Daniel, shut up the words and seal the book, even to the time of the end; many shall run to and fro, and knowledge shall be increased." Daniel 12:4 It was to be sealed only to the time of the end, when it [211] was to be opened, knowledge of the subject of which it treats should be increased, and many run to and fro in the Scriptures and obtain knowledge upon the subject. If this open book in the hand of the angel represents the unsealed book of Daniel, how forcible the application of his solemn oath to the manner in which the close of prophetic time was proclaimed in 1844.

The oath of this angel must be regarded as a symbol of a most solemn and positive message proclaimed by the servants of God. His right foot upon the earth, and his left upon the sea, represent its extent, and shows that it was to be borne to the people by sea and by land. The prophet continues:

"But in the days of the voice of the seventh angel, when he shall begin to sound, the mystery of God shall be finished, as he had declared to his servants, the prophets." Verse 7.

Why introduce the sounding of the seventh angel thus, unless his sounding commenced with the termination of the prophetic time? He is to continue his sounding a period of days, probably prophetic, meaning years, and in the beginning of his sounding, or during the first portion of the period of his sounding, the mystery of God is to be finished. This mystery is the gospel considered with especial reference to the means by which its blessings are secured to the nations of the earth. It is something which, before the apostles' days, even from the foundation of the world, was not made known as it was then revealed. Romans 16:25, 26;

Ephesians 3:3-5. It was known that the woman's seed should bruise the serpent's head, and that in Abraham and his seed should all the nations of the earth be blessed; but how this was to be accomplished was not understood till more fully revealed at the first advent of the Saviour, and set forth [212] by the preaching of his apostles. Before this it was not seen that when the Redeemer should be manifested to the world, all walls of partition shall be broken down, all distinctions be obliterated, and a Jew and Gentile, male and female, bond and free, be on equal terms and in equal measure blessed in him. Hence Paul presents as the distinguishing feature of the mystery of God, the fact "that the Gentiles should be fellow-heirs, and of the same body, and partakers of the promise in Christ by the gospel," and that in Christ all might be gathered together in one. Ephesians 3:6; 1:9, 10. Hence we more fully define the mystery of God to mean the great plan of salvation, as it centres in the work of Christ, and is revealed in the New Testament. See also Ephesians 6:19; Colossians 4:3; and Galatians 1:11, 12, compared with Ephesians 3:3.

The finishing of the mystery of God is the completion of the great plan of salvation in connection with Christ's ministry in the heavenly sanctuary. In the type the yearly round of service was finished on the tenth day of the seventh month. In the antitype Christ entered the most holy place of the heavenly sanctuary at the end of the 2300 days, to finish the great plan of salvation. The mystery of God was to be finished, as he had declared by his servants, the prophets; and the cleansing of the sanctuary spoken of by the prophet Daniel, is only another expression signifying the same thing as the finishing of the mystery of God. Hence the seventh angel began to sound at the close of the 2300 days, in 1844, when the cleansing of the sanctuary, or the finishing of the mystery of God, commenced.

A series of events to occur under the sounding of the seventh angel is mentioned in chapter 11. After the announcement, in verses 15-17, of his sounding, during which period all earthly kingdoms are to pass into the [213] hands of the King of kings, an event which interests both earth and Heaven, and calls for the grateful thanks of the good of both worlds, this series is given as follows:

1. "And the nations were angry." This is supposed to have reference to the political commotions and wars of the nations, which the prophets of God have described as marking the closing hours of probation.

2. "And thy wrath is come." This has reference to the seven last plagues, which will be poured out immediately following the ministry of Christ in the heavenly sanctuary.

3. "And the time of the dead, that they should be judged," This is not the investigative Judgment of the wicked dead. We are therefore carried forward in this third event to the time of Christ's appearing in the clouds of heaven, and the resurrection of the just, when he and they will sit in Judgment on the cases of the wicked during the one thousand years.

4. "And that thou shouldst give reward unto thy servants, the prophets, and to the saints, and them that fear thy name, small and great." It is true that all these receive immortality at the second coming of Christ, at the commencement of this great Judgment period; but their reward embraces the promised inheritance, the new earth, which will not appear till the close of the one thousand years. "Blessed are the meek for they shall inherit the earth." Then, at the close of the one thousand years, will the prophets, the saints, and all who fear the name of God, both small and great, receive their full reward.

5. "And shouldst destroy them which destroy the [214] earth." This is also the period of the final destruction of God's enemies, who have taken part in destroying (corrupting, margin,) the earth. And here closes the sounding of the seventh angel, or the third woe. The prophet still continues:

"And the voice which I heard from Heaven spake unto me again, and said, Go, and take the book which is open in the hand of the angel which standeth upon the sea and upon the earth. And I went unto the angel, and said unto him, Give me the little book. And he said unto me, Take it, and eat it up; and it shall make thy belly bitter, but it shall be in thy mouth sweet as honey. And I took the little book out of the angel's hand, and ate it up; and it was in my mouth sweet as honey; and as soon as I had eaten it my belly was bitter." Verses 8-10.

In this highly-figurative portion of the prophecy, John, in receiving the little book from the hand of the angel, represents those who received the doctrine of the coming and kingdom of Christ, as proclaimed in connection with the time, based upon the prophecy of Daniel. His eating the little book, and enjoying its sweetness, represents the holy delight with which they feasted upon the gospel of the coming kingdom. In the symbol, the little book in the mouth of John was as sweet as honey. "What is sweeter than honey?" And what could feast the consecrated soul, imbued with the love of Jesus, as the news of his soon return in glory, with all the holy angels, to redeem those who loved and looked for his appearing?

But in the symbol there is a change from the sweetness of honey to bitterness. This represents the change from the joy of bright hope to the painful sadness of disappointment, experienced by believers at the passing [215] of the time. The hope and faith had been to them an anchor in the storm, a shield in the fight, and their exceeding joy all the day long; and as they drew near the point of expectation, their hopes grew brighter, their faith stronger, and their joys were complete. The time passed; and only those who felt it can form any idea of the bitterness of that disappointment. Probably there never has been a time since the crucifixion, that the high expectations and bright hopes of the disciples of Jesus, have been so completely crushed as at the passing of the time in 1844. And the feelings of the many thousands of disappointed ones were like those expressed by Mary: "They have taken away the Lord out of the sepulchre, and we know not where they have laid him."

A good degree of relief, however, very soon came in the well-defined position that there was a time of waiting for the Lord, and trial of faith, after just such a disappointment as believers had experienced. And with it came also the general impression that our work, in bearing testimony to the world, was finished. The solemn announcement of the hour of God's Judgment, in the first message of Revelation 14, had been made. The stirring testimony in reference to the condition of those who rejected this message, and still clung to a corrupted Christianity, symbolized by the second message, had been borne. Everywhere among believers had been heard the solemn cry, "Babylon is fallen, is fallen." "Come out of her my people." And these messages were clearly seen to be in the past.

But when was the third message to be given? This is one of the series, all of which are to be given in the history of God's people in this mortal state. This is as distinctly marked in the prophetic sketch of Revelation 14, as the first and second messages are. And although [216] the disappointed ones felt for a time that their work in warning the world was done, yet God designed to roll upon them again the burden of his work, and they go forth and proclaim the third message. This work, dear reader, is most clearly pointed out in the remaining verse of the chapter upon which I have been commenting: "And he said unto me, Thou must prophesy again before many peoples and nations and tongues and kings."

To prophesy sometimes means simply to teach, as in 1 Corinthians 11:4, 5; 14:3, 24; Matthew 7:22. In the first and second messages the prophecies had been opened to the people, and they had been taught the solemn and stirring truths relating to the Judgment. Believers had come up to the time of expectation with a testimony for the people, and the burden of the work upon them. The time passed, and with it also passed from them the burden of the work, and they suddenly found themselves destitute of any message for the people. They felt that their work was done for the world. In that position they should have waited until the great truths connected with the third message were seen by the light of the heavenly sanctuary, and the Spirit of God impressed them with the new work before them, to proclaim the third message, expressed by the prophetic words, "Thou must prophesy [teach the people] again." This brings me to consider briefly the three messages of Revelation 14.

The First Message

"And I saw another angel fly in the midst of heaven, having the everlasting gospel to preach unto them that dwell on the earth, and to every nation, and kindred, and tongue, and people, saying with a loud voice, Fear God, and give glory to him; for the hour of his Judgment [217] is come; and worship him that made heaven and earth, and the sea, and the fountains of waters." Revelation 14:6, 7.

This is called the first angel, because it is the first of the series. See verse 9. John calls it "another angel," from the fact that he had previously seen an angel flying in the midst of heaven.

This proclamation is one of pre-eminent importance. It is not a mere local judgment, but one that concerns all the inhabitants of the earth. Hence it has reference to the final Judgment scene. It is the same gospel that Paul preached that is here styled the "everlasting gospel." But the great truth uttered by this angel would not have been a truth if uttered by Paul, for he lived at the commencement of the gospel dispensation, and this proclamation relates to its closing scenes. It seems to be the same as "this gospel of the kingdom," that our Lord presents in Matthew 24:14, as the sign of the end of this dispensation, and which was to be preached in all the world for a witness unto all nations before the end should come.

The truth on this point is well expressed in the following language of the late Mr. Bliss, editor of the *Advent Herald*, December 14, 1850:

"As an indication of the approach of the end, there was, however, to be seen another angel flying through the midst of heaven, having the everlasting gospel to preach unto them that dwell on the earth, and to every nation, and kindred, and tongue, and people. Revelation 14:6. The burden of this angel was to be the same gospel which had been before proclaimed; but connected with it was the additional motive of the proximity of the kingdom, 'saying with a loud voice, Fear God, and give [218] glory to him; for the hour of his Judgment is come; and worship him that made heaven and earth, and the sea, and the fountains of waters.' Verse 7. No mere preaching of the gospel without announcing its proximity, could fulfill this message."

In harmony with this testimony from the editor of the *Herald*, I will here give another from a tract on prophecy, published by J.V. Himes about the same time, which also speaks of the character of the message and the time of its application. The title of the tract is "Our Specific Work."

"the proclamation of an everlasting gospel, 'The hour of his Judgment is come,' Revelation 14:6, 7, is the leading Advent proclamation.

"The facts summed up are these: John, looking into the distant future, gazing upon the theatre of the final conflict, sees a messenger, a minister of an everlasting gospel, fly through mid-heaven, with a special, elevated, joyous, public, proclamation, requiring haste and extraordinary energy in its delivery. The proclamation contains a fact, and a command founded upon that fact. 1. The fact: 'The hour of his Judgment is come.' 2. The command: 'Fear God,' etc. These are the elements of this special commission. The work of this symbol agent is thus clearly defined; no terms more specific.

"Does this messenger symbolize a class of teachers? Such has been the general understanding of expositors. Mr. Wesley and Dr. Benson so interpret the passage. On this point there is great unanimity. It is plain from the fact that it is said to preach. That class of people is modern. Mr. Wesley and Dr. Benson make this messenger symbolize the Protestant reformers in the days of Luther. With their view agree a mass of expositors. This commission, however, cannot be Luther's. [219]

"That body must exist somewhere, and, in its character and in the nature of its work, it must agree with the symbol messenger. They must agree as face to face in a mirror. Can such a body be found? The proclamation above stated has been heard. The world can bear testimony to this. The cry, 'The hour of his Judgment is come,' sounded through all Christendom. The multitudes heard, and scoffed, or trembled. By what body of believers was this proclamation made? Not by those who taught that that Judgment was a thousand years in the future. No church which holds to the doctrine of a spiritual reign can be that body, as the elements above stated. Such a body now existing can be found alone among those who constituted the Advent believers in Europe and America."

In proof that this message has not been fulfilled in the history of the church in ages past, I offer the following reasons:

1. No proclamation of the hour of God's Judgment come, has ever been made in any past age.

2. If such a proclamation had been made many centuries in the past, as some contend, it would have been a false one.

3. The prophecies on which such a proclamation to men in a state of probation must be based, were closed up and sealed to the time of the end.

4. The Scriptures plainly locate the message of warning respecting the Judgment in a brief space immediately preceding the advent of our Lord; thus directly contradicting the view that locates these messages in past ages.

We now offer proof in support of the foregoing propositions. If they are sustained, they establish the fact [220] that the present generation is that one to which the angels' messages are addressed. We earnestly invite all who wish the truth, to weigh this part of the argument with especial care.

1. Has the proclamation of the hour of God's Judgment come, been made in any past age? If such a proclamation has never been made in past centuries, there is an end to controversy on this part of the subject. No persons have ever been able to show any such proclamation in the past. The apostles did not make such a proclamation. On the contrary, they plainly inform us that the day of the Lord was not then at hand. Martin Luther did not make this proclamation; for he thought the Judgment about three hundred years in the future. And finally, the history of the church presents no such proclamation in the past. Had the first angel preached to every nation, and kindred, and tongue, and people, that the hour of God's Judgment had come, the publicity of such a proclamation would be a sufficient guaranty that the history of the world would contain some record of the fact. Its total silence respecting such a proclamation, is ample proof that it never was made, and should put to silence those who make such an affirmation.

2. We are on firm ground, also, when we say that had such a proclamation been made to the world in past ages, it would have been a false proclamation. Four reasons sustain this statement. 1. There is no part of the Bible on which such a message, centuries in the past, could have been based. Hence had such a proclamation been made, it would have been without scriptural foundation, and consequently not from Heaven, 2. It would have been in direct opposition to those scriptures which locate the Judgment, and the warning [221] respecting its approach, in the period of the last generation. The scriptures which sustain these two reasons we shall presently cite. 3. The history of the world amply evinces that the hour of God's Judgment had not come ages in the past. 4. Nor would it be true of past ages, if limited to Babylon. For Revelation 18:8-10, clearly shows that the hour of Babylon's Judgment is yet in the future. It is certain, therefore, that the angel with the proclamation respecting the hour of God's Judgment, has not given it at a time when it would be not only destitute of scriptural support, but would absolutely contradict their plain testimony.

3. The prophecies which give us the time of the Judgment, and which present the succession of events leading down to that great crisis, were closed up and sealed till the time of the end. We refer particularly to the prophecies of Daniel. See chap. 8:17, 26; 12:4, 9. Hence it is evident that God reserves the warning to that generation which alone needs it. Noah's warning respecting the flood, was alone applicable to those who should witness it; thus also the warning respecting the Judgment is alone applicable to that generation which lives in the last days.

4. The Bible locates these messages in the period which immediately precedes the second advent, and plainly warns us against the proclamation of the Judgment at hand prior to that time. Here we join issue with our opponents. Instead of finding that the apostles gave this proclamation, as some teach, we shall find indubitable evidence that they located this warning far in the future, and that they admonished the church to heed none that should precede a given time. If we recur to the book of Acts, we shall find Paul preaching before Felix, of the Judgment to come; and before the Athenians, [222] that God hath appointed a day in which he will judge the world in righteousness by Jesus Christ. Acts 24, 25; 17:31 But that book

nowhere intimates that Christ was immediately coming to Judgment. Peter points his hearers to the future, saying, that the heavens which had then received Christ, must retain him until the times of restitution. Acts 3:21.

The first epistle to the Thessalonians may seem to teach that the apostles expected the coming of Christ to Judgment in their day. Indeed, it is evident that such an idea was received from it by the Thessalonian church. Hence it was, that in his second epistle to them, Paul found it necessary to speak explicitly on the point. He tells them that the coming of Christ to the Judgment could not take place until the great apostasy; and as the result of that apostasy, that the Man of Sin should be revealed, showing himself that he is God, or that is worshiped. That this mystery of iniquity is the great Romish apostasy, none but a Papist will deny.

Paul reminds the Thessalonians that he had told them of these things when he was yet with them. And where could Paul have learned this fact, which he had thus stated to them? He was accustomed to reason from the Scriptures, and not to deal in assertion. Hence it is very evident that he refers to the prophecy of Daniel, which in its seventh chapter has given the successive events which intervened between its time and the Judgment. In this series of events it has with wonderful precision described the power to which Paul has referred as the Man of Sin. No Protestant will deny the identity of Daniel's little horn and Paul's Man of Sin. And as Daniel has brought it into a series of events which ends with the Judgment and the setting up of the everlasting [223] kingdom, it was an easy matter for Paul to tell where in this series of events he stood, and whether the Judgment was its next event or not. The apostle, therefore, plainly tells him that that day was not at hand. For the Man of Sin, the little horn, must arise and perform his predicted work, and when that should be accomplished, the coming of Christ should transpire, to consume "that Wicked" with its brightness.

Now when was the little horn to arise? Daniel was told that it should arise after the ten horns upon the fourth beast; or, in other words, after the fourth empire should be divided into ten kingdoms, which was accomplished about five hundred years after Christ. The Judgment therefore could not come prior to that time. But how long was this little horn to have power to wear out the saints? Daniel informs us that it should be for "a time and times, and the dividing of time." How long is this period? Revelation 12 shows that it is 1260 prophetic days, or years. Verses 6, 14. It follows therefore that the apostle carries the mind forward five hundred years to the development of the Man of Sin, and thence 1260 years for his triumph, before the Judgement could be preached as an event immediately impending. Whoever will carefully read Daniel 7, will get the original of Paul's argument in 2 Thessalonians 2, and will not fail to see the force of his statement.

The papal supremacy began 538, and ended in 1798 with the overthrow of the Pope's temporal power. The warning of Paul against a false proclamation respecting the Judgment at hand, therefore, expires at that time, and not before. For we have then reached the point of time where the last important event in Daniel 7, before the Judgment has transpired. An angel from Heaven preaching the hour of God's Judgment come, many [224] years in the past, would be giving a different gospel from that preached by Paul. Those who locate the angel of Revelation 14:6, 7, in past ages, virtually place upon his head the anathema of Paul in Galatians 1:8.

And what is of very deep interest, the point of time at which Paul's warning expires is the commencement of the time of the end — the very point to which the visions of Daniel were closed up and sealed. Compare chapter 11:33, 35; 7:25, and the fact that the 1260 years' persecution of the saints terminates with the commencement of the time of the end, will appear obvious. How gloriously does this view of the subject make the truth of God shine out! For the warning of the apostle against a false proclamation of the Judgment at hand, expires at the very point where the seal is taken from those prophecies which show when the Judgment sits. And it is respecting this period, the time of the end, that it is said, Many shall run to and fro, and knowledge [on the very subject which was before concealed] shall be increased. Then the time of the end is the period in which the Judgment-hour cry, and the subsequent messages are to be given. Daniel 8:17, 26; 12:4, 9.

Another important argument on this point is found in what our Lord has said relative to the signs of his second advent. The church were to understand when his coming was at hand, by the fulfillment of certain promised tokens. Until these should be seen, they were not authorized to look for the immediate advent of the Lord. But when the signs which our Lord promised began to appear, his church might then know that his coming to judge the quick and the dead was at hand. It is an interesting fact that Christ has marked the time in which these signs were to begin to appear. Consequently [225] the messages in question could not be delivered prior to that time. "Immediately after the tribulation of those days shall the sun be darkened, and the moon shall not give her light, and the stars shall fall from heaven, and the powers of the heavens shall be shaken." Matthew 24:29. "But in those days, after the tribulation, the sun shall be darkened, and the moon shall not give her light, and the stars of heaven shall be shaken." Mark 13:24, 25. We think there can be no mistake that in these scriptures our Lord refers to the papal tribulation of Daniel the prophet. The signs of his second coming were to commence "*in* those days," but "*after* that tribulation." In other words, the 1260 prophetic days should not be quite over, but their tribulation should be ended, when the sun should be darkened. The sun was darkened in 1780, and the tribulation of those days was then past, but the days did not expire till 1798. Thus we have the signs of our Lord's immediate advent just opening upon us, as we come down to the time of the end, the period when the vision should be unsealed, and many run to and fro with the word of warning to a perishing world.

The extent of this proclamation is worthy of notice. An English writer, Mourant Brock, thus remarks: "It is not merely in Great Britain that the expectation of the near return of the Redeemer is entertained, and the voice of warning raised, but also in America, India, and on the continent of Europe. In America about three hundred ministers of the word are thus preaching 'this gospel of the kingdom;" whilst in this country, about seven hundred of the church of England are raising the same cry." — *Advent Tracts*, Vol 2, p. 135.

Dr. Joseph Wolfe traveled in Arabia Felix, through [226] the region inhabited by the descendants of Hobab, Moses' father-in-law. In Yemen he saw a book which he mentions thus:

"The Arabs of this place have a book called Seera, which treats of the second coming of Christ, and his reign in glory!'

"In Yemen he spent six days with the Rechabites. 'They drink no wine, plant no vineyards, sow no seed, live in tents, and remember the words of Jonadab, the son of Rechab. With them were children of Israel, of the tribe of Dan, who reside near Terim in Hatramawt, who expect, in common with the children of Rechab, the speedy arrival of the Messiah in the clouds of heaven.'" — *Wolfe's Mission to Bokhara.*

"In Wirtemberg there is a Christian colony numbering hundreds, who look for the speedy advent of Christ; also another of like belief on the shores of the Caspian; the Molokaners, a large body of Dissenters from the Russian Greek church, residing on the shores of the Baltic — a very pious people, of whom it is said, 'taking the Bible alone for their creed, the *norm* of their faith is simply the Holy Scriptures' — are characterized by the 'expectation of Christ's immediate and visible reign upon earth.' In Russia the doctrine of Christ's coming and reign is preached to some extent, and received by many of the lower class. It has been extensively agitated in Germany, particularly in the south part among the Moravians. In Norway, charts and books on the Advent have been circulated extensively, and the doctrine received by many. Among the Tartars in Tartary, there prevails an expectation of Christ's advent about this time. English and American publications on this doctrine have been sent to Holland, Germany, India, Ireland, Constantinople, Rome, and to nearly [227] every missionary station on the globe. At the Turks Islands, it has been received to some extent among the Wesleyans. Mr. Fox, a Scottish missionary to the Teloogoo people, was a believer in Christ's soon coming. James McGregor Bertram, a Scottish missionary of the Baptist order at St. Helena, has sounded the cry extensively on that island, making many converts and premillennialists; he has also preached it at South Africa, at the missionary stations there. David N. Lord informs us that a large proportion of the missionaries who have gone from Great Britain to make known the gospel to the heathen, and who are now laboring in Asia and Africa, are Millennarians; and Joseph Wolfe, D.D., according to his journals, between the years 1821 and 1845, proclaimed the Lord's speedy advent in Palestine, Egypt, on the shores of the Red Sea, Mesopotamia, the Crimea, Persia, Georgia, throughout the Ottoman Empire, in Greece, Arabia, Turkistan, Bokhara, Afghanistan, Cashmere, Hindostan, Thibet, in Holland, Scotland and Ireland, at Constantinople, Jerusalem, St. Helena, also on shipboard in the Mediterranean, and at New York city, to all denominations. He declares he has preached among Jews, Turks, Mohammedans, Parsees, Hindoos, Chaldeans, Yesedes, Syrians, Sabeans, to Pachas, Shieks, Shahs, the kings of Organtsh and Bokhara, the queen of Greece, etc. And of his extraordinary labors the *Investigator* says: 'No individual has, perhaps, given greater publicity to the doctrine of the second coming of the Lord Jesus Christ, than has this well-known missionary to the world. Wherever he goes, he proclaims the approaching advent of the Messiah in glory.'" — *Voice of the Church*, pp. 342-344.

The following, from the pen of the editor of the [228] *Voice of Truth* for January, 1845, fairly represents the position of all American Adventists at that time:

"We are doubtless near that auspicious hour when the harvest of the earth will be reaped, as described in Revelation 14:14-16. The history of God's people in this mortal state, as given in that chapter, before being glorified, is nearly complete. The everlasting gospel, as described in verses 6 and 7, has been preached unto every nation, kindred, tongue, and people; saying with a loud voice, Fear God, and give glory to him; for the hour of his Judgment is come, and worship him that made heaven, and earth, and the sea, and the fountains of waters. No case can be more clearly demonstrated with facts than that this message has been borne to every nation and tongue under heaven, within a few past years, in the preaching of the coming of Christ in 1843, or near at hand. Through the medium of lectures and publications the sound has gone into all the earth, and the word unto the ends of the world."

But those were disappointed who expected the Lord would come in 1843 and in 1844. This fact, with many, is sufficient reason for rejecting all the testimony in the case. To them the position that the Advent movement was in fulfillment of prophecy, when at the same time those who took part in the movement were sorely disappointed, is an absurdity.

We acknowledge the disappointment, but cannot acknowledge that this furnishes a just reason for denying the hand of God in that work. It is a fact that God's people have fulfilled prophecy, and at the same time been disappointed in their hopes. This was the case with the disciples and the shouting multitude on the occasion of our Lord meekly riding into Jerusalem, when they cried, "Hosannah to the Son of David: Blessed is he that cometh [229] in the name of the Lord; Hosannah in the highest." The prophet of God had said, "Rejoice greatly, O daughter of Zion; shout, O daughter of Jerusalem: behold, thy King cometh unto thee: he is just, and having salvation; lowly, and riding upon an ass, and upon a colt the foal of an ass." Zechariah 9:9. And his words must be fulfilled. That which inspired the shouts of the disciples was the expectation that their Master would then ascend to the throne of David and reign among them. But in this they were disappointed. In a few days their hopes died, as he expired upon the cross. Did they fulfill prophecy? No one will deny that they did. Were their expectations which moved them to fulfill the prophecy realized? They were utterly disappointed.

And while those were disappointed in every particular, Adventists, in 1844, were right in three of the four leading points of the Advent faith. These points were, first, the manner and object of Christ's second advent; second, the application of the prophetic symbols of the book of Daniel; third, prophetic time; and fourth, the event to take place at the end of the prophetic periods. In respect to the first three points, the Adventists of 1844 were right. As to the fourth, they were mistaken. The angel did not tell Daniel that Christ would come at the end of the 2300 days. His words to the prophet are: "Unto two thousand and three hundred days, then shall the sanctuary be cleansed." The subject of the cleansing of the sanctuary of Daniel 8:14, is now understood, and seen to be quite another thing than the second coming of Jesus Christ in the clouds of heaven, to redeem his people and destroy his enemies by the fires of the last day.

Disappointment by no means proves that God has no [230] hand in the guidance of his people. It should lead them to correct their errors, but it should not lead them to cast away their confidence in God. It was because the children of Israel were disappointed in the wilderness that they so often denied divine guidance. They are set forth as an admonition to us, that we should not fall after the same example of unbelief.

But it must be apparent to every student of the Scriptures, that the angel who proclaims the hour of God's Judgment, does not give the latest message of mercy. Revelation 14, presents two other and later proclamations, before the close of human probation. This fact alone is sufficient to prove that the coming of the Lord does not take place at the close of the first angel's proclamation.

The Second Message

"And there followed another angel, saying, Babylon is fallen, is fallen, that great city, because she made all nations drink of the wine of the wrath of her fornication."

This angel is spoken of as the second, because the one following it is, in the language of inspiration itself, called the third. In commenting upon language so highly symbolic, the first point is to determine the meaning of the symbol introduced.

1. What, then, is the Babylon of this message? It is here simply called "that great city." But it is elsewhere spoken of in the book of Revelation in a manner which cannot fail to lead to a correct solution of this question. In Revelation 17:18, this same city is called a woman. "And the woman which thou sawest is that great city, which reigneth over the kings of the earth." [231] Now a woman is always in the Scriptures, when used as a symbol, taken to present religious organizations, the true church being represented by a virtuous woman, as in chapter 12, and the false by a corrupt woman, as in the text before us, and many other places. Babylon is something distinct from the civil powers of the earth; for with her the kings of the earth form unlawful connections. It is the place where the people of God as a body are, for they are a certain time called away from her communion. These considerations show that we are not to look to any literal city for the Babylon of the Apocalypse, nor to any civil powers, but to ecclesiastical or church organizations. Is, then, any particular church, to the exclusion of all others, designated by the term Babylon? It would not be consistent to suppose this; for 1. The term Babylon, from Babel, where God confounded the language of men, signifies mixture, confusion. In the sense in which we have shown it to be used in the book of Revelation, it must denote conflicting and discordant religious creeds and systems. But this would not be applicable to any one religious denomination, as each of these denominations is more or less a unit. 2. The people of God who

are called out of Babylon, are not as a body connected with any single denomination. Hence we must understand by the term all the false and corrupted systems of Christianity. That the Romish and Greek churches are included in these, few will be disposed to deny; while the Protestant churches, alas! more or less identified with war, for a long time the bulwark of American slavery, fatally conformed to the world, and guilty of the long catalogue of sins charged by Paul upon professed Christians in the last days, 2 Timothy 3:1-5, must be reckoned as a member of the family. In this branch of the family we find [232] that mixture and confusion in the multiplicity of sects and creeds which most fitly answers to the import of the term.

2. What is the fall of Babylon? Evidently a moral fall. In Revelation 18:1-5, where a second and subsequent announcement of this event seems to be given, we read, "Babylon the great is fallen, is fallen, and is become the habitation of devils, and the hold of every foul spirit, and a cage of every unclean and hateful bird." That is, as the result of her fall she had sunk to this deplorable condition. Having fallen, her iniquities rapidly increased, her sins reached unto Heaven, and God's people are called out. Verses, 4, 5. Hence this fall is a moral one. The absurdity of applying this to Rome or any other literal city, where but few, if any, of the people of God are, and out of which they could not be called after its fall or destruction, must be very apparent. The harmony of applying it to a religious body which can apostatize and become corrupt, and from which the people of God can be subsequently called out, is equally clear, and the necessity for such an application no less evident. No other is at all admissible.

The cause of the fall of Babylon is said to be because she "made all nations drink of the wine of the wrath of her fornication." Her fornication was her unlawful connection with the kings of the earth. The wine of this is that with which the church has intoxicated the nations of the earth. There is but one thing to which this can refer, and that is, false doctrine. This harlot, in consequence of her unlawful union with the powers of earth, has corrupted the pure truths of the Bible, and with the wine of her false doctrine has intoxicated the nations. As a few of the gross errors [233] which she has caused the masses to receive as Bible truth, we mention the following: 1. That the soul is immortal. 2. That sprinkling and pouring are baptism. 3. That Sunday is the Sabbath. 4. That there are to be a thousand years of peace and prosperity before the coming of the Lord. 5. That the saints' inheritance is not the earth made new, but an immaterial, intangible region beyond the bounds of time and space. 6. That the second advent is to be understood spiritually, and that it takes place at the destruction of Jerusalem, or that it takes place at conversion or at death. 7. That it is right and scriptural to hold human beings in bondage; and 8. That it is of no consequence, if we may judge from their practice, to come out and be separate from the world. Most of these pernicious errors Protestant sects have themselves originated, showing conclusively that they are but the daughters of the great apostasy.

We have seen that Babylon is composed of several divisions; and we know that the name of the whole is frequently applied to any one of its parts. Hence the name Babylon may be applied to any one of these divisions. Consequently when it is announced that Babylon is fallen, it is not necessary to understand that as a whole it experienced a moral change for the worse. It would be true if such change took place in any one of its great branches. The cry, Babylon is fallen, being given subsequent to the first message, is evidence that the fall took place at that time.

The truths connected with the proclamation of the first angel were calculated to correct many of the fundamental errors of Babylon, and open the way for the [234] reception of the whole truth in place of her false doctrines. That these errors were honestly held by the different churches, is not to be questioned. But after light has been given to a person sufficient to enable him to discard an error, he becomes guilty for longer retaining it. So when Babylon, through the proclamation of the first message, was called upon to correct her errors, and redeem her influence over the people, and refused to do so, she then became guilty of willfully refusing the truth, and making the nations intoxicated with her false teaching. Just as the people of God when they are called out after her fall, become guilty by longer retaining their connection with her. Hence the proclamation of the fall of Babylon comes in after the first message, stating the consequence of her rejection of that message. That message has already been located in the present generation; and Revelation 18 shows that Babylon's fall must take place in the last days, as it is just previous to her final destruction. But as we look over apostate Christendom, we see that the Romish and Greek churches are no more corrupt, either in doctrine or practice, than they have been for ages past. No marked change for the worse has taken place in those bodies within the present generation, nor is there scarcely room for them to become worse than they have already for centuries been. We therefore look to the religious bodies composing the great Protestant family for the fulfillment of the announcement made in the second message, especially in our own country, where the first message was more definitely proclaimed. The inquiry now arises, has there been any moral declension in these bodies within the memory of the generation now living? Did any such change take place with them about the time of the first message, and have they since been filling [235] up their cup of iniquity, as represented in Revelation 18? If so, we have the place for an unmistakable application of the second message.

But that we may not seem to judge these denominations ourselves, as we might be accused of not rendering impartial judgment, we will let their own members speak, and on their testimony will let the question rest. To show that we are not alone in ranking the popular Protestant sects as a part of Babylon, we offer the following. If they themselves claim it, we are not disposed to dispute it.

Mr. William Kinkade, in his "Bible Doctrine," p. 294, says:

"I also think Christ has a true church on earth, but its members are scattered among the various denominations, and are all more or less under the influence of Mystery Babylon and her daughters."

Mr. Hopkins, in a treatise on the millennium, says:

"There is no reason to consider the antichristian spirit and practices confined to that which is now called the Church of Rome. The Protestant churches have much of antichrist in them, and are far from being wholly reformed from her corruptions and wickedness."

Mr. Simpson, in his "Plea for Religion," says:

"For though the Pope and Church of Rome is at the head of the grand 1260 years' delusion, yet all other churches, of whatever denomination, whether established or tolerated, which partake of the same spirit, or have instituted doctrines or ceremonies inimical to the pure and unadulterated gospel of Christ, shall sooner or later share in the fate of that immense fabric of human ordinances; and that Protestant churches should imitate the Church of Rome, in this worst part of its conduct, can never be sufficiently bewailed." [236]

Alexander Campbell says:

"The worshiping establishments now in operation throughout Christendom, increased and cemented by their respective voluminous confessions of faith, and their ecclesiastical constitutions, are not churches of Jesus Christ, but the legitimate daughters of that mother of harlots, the Church of Rome."

Lorenzo Dow says of the Romish Church:

"If she be a mother, who are the daughters? It must be the corrupt, national, established churches that came out of her." *Dow's Life*, p. 542.

In the Religious Encyclopedia, (Art. Antichrist), we read:

"The writer of the book of Revelation tells us he heard a voice from Heaven, saying, 'Come of her, my people, that ye partake not of her sins, and receive not of her plagues.' If such persons are to be found in the 'mother of harlots,' with much less hesitation may it be inferred that they are connected with her unchaste daughters, those national churches which are founded upon what are called Protestant principles."

In the spring and summer of 1844, a distant message was proclaimed, setting forth the fallen condition of the churches, which resulted in calling from them fifty thousand believers in the immediate coming of Christ. And the testimonies from the very churches they had left could but convince them that they had entertained correct views of the fallen state of the churches, and had done the will of God in separating from them.

The *Christian Palladium* for May 15, 1844, speaks in the following mournful strains: "In every direction we hear the dolorous sound, wafting upon every breeze of heaven, chilling as the blast from the icebergs of the north — settling like an incubus on the breasts of the [237] timid, and drinking up the energies of the weak; that lukewarmness, division, anarchy and desolation are distressing the borders of Zion."

The *Religious Telescope*, of 1844, uses the following language: "We have never witnessed such a general declension of religion as at the present. Truly the church should awake and search into the cause of this affliction; for an affliction every one that loves Zion must view it. When we call to mind how 'few and far between' cases of true conversion are, and the almost unparalleled impenitence and hardness of sinners, we almost involuntarily exclaim, 'Has God forgotten to be gracious? or is the door of mercy closed?'"

These testimonies only are offered out of much of like import that might be quoted, as they are specimens of the whole. But it may be said that our views of the moral fall and spiritual death of the churches are shown to be incorrect by the great revivals of 1858. Of the fruit of these revivals let the leading Congregational and Baptist papers of Boston bear testimony. Says the *Congregationalist* for November 19, 1858:

"The revival piety of our churches is not such that one can confidently infer, from its mere existence, its legitimate, practical fruits. It ought, for example, to be as certain, after such a shower of grace, that the treasuries of our benevolent societies would be filled, as it is after a plentiful rain, that the streams will swell in their channels. But the managers of our societies are bewailing the feebleness of the sympathy and aid of the churches.

"There is another and sadder illustration of the same general truth. The *Watchman and Reflector* recently stated that there had never been among the Baptists so lamentable a spread of church dissension as prevails at present. [238] And the sad fact is mentioned that this sin infects the very churches which shared most largely in the late revival. And the still more melancholy fact is added, that these alienations date back their origin, in most cases, to the very midst of that scene of awakening. Even a glance at the weekly journals of our own denomination, will evince that the evil is by no means confined to the Baptists. Our own columns have, perhaps, never borne so humiliating a record of contentious, and ecclesiastical litigation as during the last few months."

A Presbyterian pastor, of Belfast, Ireland, uses the following language respecting the recent revivals in this country: "The determination to crush all ministers who say a word against their national sin [slavery], the determination to suffocate and suppress the plain teachings of Scripture, can be persisted in and carried out at the very time these New York Christians are expecting the religious world to hail their revivals. Until the wretchedly-degraded churches of America do the work of God in their own land, they have no spiritual vitality to communicate to others; their revivals are in the religious world what their flaunted cries of liberty, intermingled with the groans of the slave, are in the political." *New York Independent, December*, 1859.

During the time of the great Irish revival of the past year [1859] the General Assembly of the Presbyterian church of Ireland, held its session in Belfast. Says the Belfast *News-Letter* of September 30: "Here in this venerable body of ministers and elders, we find two ministers openly giving each other the lie, and the whole General Assembly turned into a scene of confusion bordering upon a riot."

These sad facts need no comment. In Ireland the ministers of the gospel are unable to meet in General [239] Assembly without a riot among themselves; in America prayers for the enslaved were not allowed in the revival meetings. No wonder that fruit of genuine piety is difficult to be found.

How unlike what God designed that his people should be, has this great city become! The church of Christ was to be the light of the world, a city set upon a hill, which could not be hid. Matthew 5:14-16. But instead of this, his professed people have united with the world and joined affinity with it. This unlawful union of the church and the world (James 4:4,) has resulted in her rejection by God; for how can the God of truth and holiness recognize as his people, those who in addition to their departure from their Lord, have rejected with scorn the tidings of his speedy coming?

The following extract is from an address before the Theological School, Cambridge, Mass.:

"I think no man can go with his thoughts about him into one of our churches without feeling that what hold the public worship had on men is gone or going. It has lost its grasp on the affections of the good, and the fear of the bad. It is already beginning to indicate character and religion to withdraw from religious meetings. I have heard a devout person, who prized the Sabbath, say in bitterness of heart, 'On Sunday it seems wicked to go to church.' And the motive that holds the best there is now only a hope, and a waiting."

Prof. S.C. Bartlett, of Chicago, in the New York *Independent*, says:

"Religion now is in a different position from Methodism then. To a certain extent it is a very reputable thing. Christianity is, in our day, something of a success. Men 'speak well of it.' Ex-presidents and statesmen have been willing to round off their career with a [240] recognition of its claims. And the popularity of religion tends vastly to increase the number of those who would secure its benefits without squarely meeting its duties. The church courts the world, and the world caresses the church. The line of separation between the godly and the irreligious fades out into a kind of penumbra, and zealous men on both sides are toiling to obliterate all difference between their modes of action and enjoyment."

For further testimony from their own lips respecting the state of the churches, their covetousness, pride in church buildings, operatic singing in their worship, their religious gambling, their endorsement of dancing, their zeal for worldly pleasure, and their pride and fashion, we refer the reader to the works entitled "The Three Messages," and "The State of the Churches," for sale at the Review Office, Battle Creek, Mich.

The Third Message

"And the third angel followed them, saying with a loud voice, If any man worship the beast and his image, and receive his mark in his forehead, or in his hand, the same shall drink of the wine of the wrath of God, which is poured out without mixture into the cup of his indignation; and he shall be tormented with fire and brimstone in the presence of the holy angels, and in the presence of the Lamb; and the smoke of their torment ascendeth up forever and ever; and they have no rest day nor night, who worship the beast and his image, and whosoever receiveth the mark of his name. Here is the patience of the saints; here are they that keep the commandments of God and the faith of Jesus." Revelation 14:9-12. [241]

This is the most solemn warning that the Bible contains. As the pen of inspiration has recorded this language for our instruction, it will be wise for us to listen and obey. It is certain that church history presents no testimony that this message has been heard in the past. And the fact that the first and second angels of this series apply to the present generation, most clearly establishes the point that this message does not belong to past ages. Said J.V. Himes, in 1847:

"But the fourteenth chapter [of Rev.] presents an astounding cry, yet to be made, as a warning to mankind in that hour of strong temptation. Verses 9-11. A denunciation of wrath so dreadful cannot be found in the book of God, besides this. Does it not imply a strong temptation, to inquire so terrific an admonition?"

It is proper that I should here notice three symbols employed in this message, namely, the beast, his image and his mark, and call attention to four other distinct points embraced by it. These are, the patience of the saints, the commandments of God, the faith of Jesus, and the penalty threatened.

1. The Beast. The familiar manner in which the Beast, the Image, and the Mark, are introduced in this message, shows that they are symbols which are elsewhere explained in the prophetic word; for when a symbol

is first introduced into prophecy, specifications and particulars are given sufficient to lead the humble seeker after truth to an understanding of it. We find no such particulars in this message respecting the symbols here introduced, and therefore look for them in other portions of the book of Revelation. In chapter 13:1, and onward, we find a power introduced under the symbol and name of "a beast." The time and manner of its use is given, its characteristics are pointed out, [242] its work is described, the time of its duration is stated, and the termination of its career is foretold. That this is the beast mentioned in the third message is certain; for it is the only symbol in the book of Revelation which bears the unqualified title of "the beast." In verse 11 of chapter 13, another beast is introduced, but after being once named as another beast, it is ever after designated by the pronoun he. This other beast makes an image to the first beast, and causes all to receive the mark of that beast. No other image or mark as pertaining to any beast are anywhere introduced; hence these are the ones referred to in the third message. Therefore the symbols before us are all described in chapter 13.

We now inquire, What power is represented by the beast? To learn this, we go still further back, to chapter 12, where we find a power symbolized by a great red dragon, which is the one next preceding the beast of chapter 13. The seven heads and ten horns upon both of these symbols, show that they represent two phases of the same power. By universal consent of Protestant expositors, the great red dragon is considered a representative of Pagan Rome. The next phase presented by Rome after the Pagan form was the Papal. Rome Papal succeeded Rome Pagan. The dragon gave his seat, power, and great authority to the beast. Hence the beast can represent none other but Papal Rome.

This is further shown by the identity that exists between this beast and the little horn of Daniel 7:8, 19-26, which Protestant commentators all agree is a symbol of the Papacy. If the reader will compare carefully the verses referred to in Daniel 7, with Revelation 13:1-10, he will see, 1. That both these powers are blasphemous powers, speaking great words and blasphemies against [243] God. 2. That they both make war with the saints, and prevail against, or overcome them. 3. That they both have a mouth speaking great things. 4. That they both succeed the Pagan form of the Roman empire. 5. That they both continue a time, times, and dividing of time or 1260 years. 6. That both at the end of the specified period lose their dominion. Now here are points that prove identity; for when we have in prophecy two symbols, as in this instance, representing powers that come upon the stage of action at the same time, occupy the same territory, maintain the same character, do the same work, exist the same length of time, and at the same time, and at the end of that time meet the same fate, those symbols represent the same identical power. Now all these particulars do apply alike to the little horn of Daniel 7, and the beast of Revelation 13, conclusively showing that they both represent the same power. No more need here be said to show that the beast is the Papacy. Those who wish to pursue the argument more at length, will find it presented in works published at the Review Office.

2. The image. This is the image of the beast we have just been considering. An image is a representation, similitude, copy or likeness, of any person or thing. As the beast is the Papal church, a church having civil power to carry out its decrees, and execute whatever penalty it might affix to the crime of heresy, an image of this beast must be an ecclesiastical organization, possessing the same essential features and established upon the same basis. Do we anywhere see any room for, or any indications of, a movement of this kind? The power that forms the image, is the second beast of Revelation 13, called another beast having two horns like a lamb. Any inquiry respecting the image, properly calls for a previous examination of this two-horned beast symbol; [244] but for this we have not space in the present work. A few propositions only can here be laid down; and perhaps this is all that is in the present case essential, as they will be found abundantly proved in other works. 1. The two-horned beast is a symbol of the United States of America. 2. Its two horns represent the two leading principles of this government, Republicanism and Protestantism. 3. It occupies the right territory to answer to the prophecy; for as it is another beast, it must be located outside of the territory occupied by the first beast and its ten horns. 4. It was seen coming up at the right time, the time when the first beast went into captivity, in 1798. This nation was then

beginning to attract the notice of the world as a rapidly-developing and rising power. 5. It bears the right form of government, which, according to the prophecy, must be republican, not monarchical. 6. It is performing the work assigned it in the prophecy. In short, it most admirably fits every part of the prophetic description.

The formation of the image is yet future; but if we are right in the application of the two-horned beast, we are to look for it in our own country; and within a very short time; as the career of all earthly governments is soon to close in the ushering in of the day of the Lord. Let us then notice how the way is prepared and preparing for this last great act of the two-horned beast. Under the mild influence of one of the lamb-like horns, the Protestant principle that all have liberty to worship God according to the dictates of their own consciences, which the government has thus far guaranteed to all its subjects, churches have multiplied in the land. But these churches have rejected light and truth, and as a body have met with a moral fall. A catalogue of twenty immoral features, with no good ones, is the photograph [245] which Paul gives in 2 Timothy 3:1-5, of the popular churches of these last days. But many of the people of God are yet to be found in connection with these churches, and are yet to be called out. Revelation 18:4. And when this shall be accomplished, and the good have all left the nominal churches, when the saving influence of such is all withdrawn from their communion, then we shall have most fitting material for the formation of an image to the beast; for they will then be ready for any acts of persecution and oppression against the people of God, which Satan can induce those to enter upon who are led captive by him at will. And where could we more naturally look for an image to the mother of harlots, than to the daughters? We may be sure that the child will develop into a perfect image of its mother. Then let these fallen churches, from whom the good have all departed, and the grace of God is withdrawn, be formed into an ecclesiastical organization, and let the government grant it power (which of course it will not have till the government does grant it) to enforce its dogmas under the pains and penalties of the civil law, and what do we have? An exact image to the first beast, a church clothed with power to enforce its doctrines upon dissenters with fire and sword. That the churches in the condition to which these are fast tending, will be ready for such a work, history and analogy abundantly prove. And here would be an organization, separate from the government, constituting no part of it, yet created by it, and forming a most perfect counterpart to the prophecy of the image of the beast.

And now we ask, Do we see any indications of a movement of this kind? We answer, Yes, as the following extracts out of many that might be given will [246] show. Let it be remembered that first it is "said" to them that dwell on the earth, the people of the nation, that they should make an image to the beast. The question must first be agitated, and the movement be recommended, before the public mind will be prepared for decisive action in the matter.

Dr. Lyman Beecher, as quoted by Lorenzo Dow, said:

"There is a state of society to be formed by an extended combination of institutions, religions, civil and literary, which never exists without the co-operation of an educated ministry."

Rev. Charles Beecher, in his sermon at the dedication of the Second Presbyterian church, Fort Wayne, Indiana, February 22, 1846, said:

"Thus are the ministry of the evangelical Protestant denominations, not only formed all the way up, under a tremendous pressure of merely human fear, but they live, and move, and breathe, in a state of things radically corrupt, and appealing every hour to every baser element of their nature to hush up the truth, and bow the knee to the power of apostasy. Was not this the way things went with Rome? Are we not living her life over again? And what do we see just ahead? Another General Council! A world's convention! Evangelical alliance, and universal creed!"

In a speech delivered in New York, Mr. Havens said:

"For my own part, I wait to see the day when a Luther shall spring up in this country who shall found a great American Catholic Church, instead of a great Roman Catholic Church; and who shall teach men that they can be good Catholics without professing allegiance to a Pontiff on the other side of the Atlantic."

The *Northwestern Christian Advocate*, of December 10, 1862, of the President's message says: [247]

"The Chief Magistrate sees in the dogmas of the quiet past, nothing equal to the stormy present. He sees that history must be made. He sees further, that the Union may be saved, if Christianity and statesmanship may join hands."

There are movements already inaugurated to form a great union of the popular churches. Rev. J. S. Smart (Methodist), in a published sermon on the "political duties of Christian men and ministers," says:

"I claim that we have, and ought to have, just as much concern in the government of this country as any other men.... We are the mass of the people. Virtue in this country is not weak; her ranks are strong in numbers, and invincible from the righteousness of her cause. Invincible if united! Let not her ranks be broken by party names."

In a speech delivered in New York city, on "The Coming Conflict," February, 1866, the speaker said:

"The time is coming when an attempt will be made to engraft a religion upon the laws of the country, and make adherence to a certain form of religion absolutely necessary for an applicant for office."

An association has just been formed for the purpose of securing the adoption of certain measures for the amending of the National Constitution, so that it shall speak out the religious views of the majority, and, especially to enforce Sunday-keeping under the popular name of "Christian Sabbath." It is called the "National Association," and its officers are a long array of Reverends, D.D.'s Honorables, Esquires, etc. In their address they say:

"Men of high standing, in every walk of life, of every section of the country, and of every shade of political [248] sentiment and religious belief, have concurred in the measure."

In their appeal they most earnestly request every lover of his country to join in forming auxiliary associations, circulate documents, attend conventions, sign the memorial to Congress, etc., etc.

In their plea for an amended Constitution, they ask the people to "consider that God is not once named in our National Constitution. There is nothing in it which requires an 'oath of God,' as the Bible styles it (which, after all, is the great bond both of loyalty in the citizen and of fidelity in the magistrate); nothing which requires the observance of the day of rest and of worship, or which respects its sanctity. If we do not have the mails carried and the post offices open on Sunday, it is because we happen to have a Postmaster-General who respects the day. If our Supreme Courts are not held, and if Congress does not sit on that day, it is custom, and not law, that makes it so. Nothing in the Constitution gives Sunday quiet to the custom house, the navy yard, the barracks, or any of the departments of government.

"Consider that they fairly express the mind of the great body of the American people. This is a Christian people. These amendments agree with the faith, the feelings, and the forms of every Christian church or sect. The Catholic and the Protestant, the Unitarian and the Trinitarian, profess and approve all that is here proposed. Why should their wishes not become law? Why should not the Constitution be made to suit and to represent a constituency so overwhelmingly in the majority? .... This great majority is becoming daily more conscious not only of their rights but of their power. Their number [249] grows, and their column becomes more solid. They have quietly opposed infidelity, until it has, at least, become politically unpopular. They have asserted the rights of man and the rights of the government, until the nation's faith has become measurably fixed and declared on these points. And now that the close of the war gives us occasion to amend our Constitution, that it may clearly and fully represent the mind of the people on these points, they feel that it should also be so amended as to recognize the rights of God in man and in government. Is it anything but due to their long patience that they be at length allowed to speak out the great facts and principles which give to all government its dignity, stability, and beneficence?"

We offer these extracts simply to show the tendency of the popular agitation on this subject. It indicates what is in the hearts of leading ones in the popular churches, and what they are waiting to do, as soon as they shall have the power. It is corroborative evidence that the application we make of the two-horned beast, and the image, is correct.

3. The mark and worship of the beast. The two-horned beast causes men to worship the first beast and receive his mark. The worship and mark are alike enforced by the two-horned beast. It is this worship and mark against which the third angel warns us. It becomes, therefore, a matter of solemn moment to inquire what is meant by these expressions, since the message levels against these things, whatever they are, a denunciation more terrific than any other threatening that can be found in the word of God. The sin must be one which is most presumptuous and Heaven-daring. What is it? Many are ready to assert that we never [250] can know, and accuse us of prying into secret things, when we raise the question. But is this possible? If we cannot know what the mark and worship are, we are liable to receive the one, and perform the other, without knowing it. We then become subject to the terrible punishment threatened. But would God ever punish a person thus for sins which he did not know he was committing? Never. It would be contrary to the principles on which he has thus far dealt with mankind, and contrary to the justice of his own nature. And a special message, that of the third angel, is sent out to warn men, not against something they are never to know anything about, but against a plain and open act of disloyalty to God, which the two-horned beast is to require of them, and to which if they yield, they must drink of the unmingled wrath of God. We return to the inquiry, What is the mark of the beast?

The beast, as we have seen, is the Papacy. The two-horned beast which is to enforce the mark is our own government. What is the mark of the Papacy which this nation is to enforce? It must be something on which they occupy common ground, and in which both are equally interested. The mark of any power must be something to distinguish the adherents of that power. This none can dispute. And that which distinguishes the adherents of any power, must be some law, requirement, or institution of that power. It can be nothing else. The mark of the beast, then, must be some requirement, of course of a religious nature, which the Papacy has instituted, and to which it claims obedience from its followers, as a token of its right to legislate in religious matters. This is an unavoidable conclusion from the foregoing principles, which must be admitted as sound. [251]

Again, the beast has been shown to be identical with the little horn of Daniel 7, and of that power it is said that he should "think to change times and laws." What laws are these which the Papacy should think to change, but not have power to change? It must be divine laws, the laws of God; for all human laws may be changed by earthly powers. This power is again brought to view under the title of the "Man of Sin;" 2 Thessalonians 2:3; and of him it is said that he "exalteth himself above all that is called God." How could he do this? There is one way, and only one, in which it could be done, and that is, to change the law of God by putting in place of some of its requirements an enactment of his own, and demanding obedience to that change, to the violation of the law of God.

In all these testimonies, the evidence tends with wonderful harmony to one conclusion, namely, that the Papacy was to promulgate some religious enactment, which would involve a change of the law of God, and obedience to which would stand as an acknowledgment of its supremacy in religious things. If we can find a Papal enactment of such a nature, this surely must be the mark of the beast. It may now facilitate our investigations of this subject to appeal directly to the Romish church for information. Among its claims and institutions do we find anything of this kind? We do; and it may surprise some Protestants to learn that it is the institution of Sunday in place of the Sabbath of the fourth commandment. Hear what that church claims on the subject of the change of the Sabbath:

"Q. Have you any other way of proving that the *Church has power* to institute festivals of precept?

"A. Had she not such power, she could not have done that in which all modern religionists agree with [252] her; — she could not have *substituted the observance of Sunday*, the first day of the week, for the observance of Saturday, the seventh day, a change for which there is no scriptural authority." — *Doct. Catechism.*

"Q. How prove you that the church *hath power* to command feasts and holy days?

"A. *By the very act of changing the Sabbath into Sunday*, which Protestants allow of; and, therefore, they fondly contradict themselves, by keeping Sunday strictly, and breaking most other feasts commanded by the same church.

"Q. How prove you that?

"A. Because by keeping Sunday, they *acknowledge the Church's power* to ordain feasts, etc."—*Abridgment of Chris. Doc.*, pp. 57-59.

These extracts are from standard Roman Catholic works, and clearly set forth the claim of that church. When a person is charged with a crime and confesses it, that is usually considered sufficient to settle the matter and preclude the necessity of any further investigation. The prophecy declared that the little horn should think to change times and laws; and here the Papacy claims to have accomplished this very work; and we must admit the claim or give up the prophecy as a failure; for no other fulfillment can be shown. What need have we of further evidence? Notice, also, how admirably this work of the Papacy answers to all the prophecies touching it. 1. It is a change of the law of God, such as the little horn was to accomplish; for the fourth commandment requires the observance of the seventh day as a memorial of creation, while this requires the observance of the first day for another reason. 2. It is a work by which it sets itself up above God, as the Man of Sin was to do; for it places its [253] institution in place of that of Jehovah, and demands obedience to it on its own authority in preference to the requirement of God. 3. It involves on the part of those who understandingly yield to it, that worship which the beast, Revelation 13:8, was to receive from those that dwell on the earth. 4. It is in striking contrast with the commandments of God, which those are found keeping, Revelation 14:12, who refuse the mark and worship of the beast. 5. It is claimed as a token of the authority of the church to ordain religious institutions, just such as the mark of the beast must be intended to show; for, in so many words, the "*very act* of changing the Sabbath into Sunday," is claimed by that church as proof of its power to command feasts and holy days; and the observance of this institution is considered by them as an *acknowledgment* of such power. 6. Protestants have brought this error from the Romish church, and though they rest it on different ground, are equally tenacious of the institution, and equally zealous for its preservation. As above quoted from the address of the "National Association" for amending the Constitution, Catholic and Protestant are alike interested in this matter; and the Protestant will, of course, be ready to join the Catholic in upholding that which is to him equally dear.

Here, then, we have an institution of the Papacy which admirably answers to every specification of the prophecy, and which singularly enough, this nation, though Protestant, is taking steps to make a national institution, and will soon be ready to enforce by the civil arm. For proof that Sunday-keeping has no foundation in the Scriptures, but is an institution of the Papacy, as Romanists claim, see History of the Sabbath, and other works, published at the Review Office. [254]

If, then, the keeping of a counterfeit Sabbath, and one so long and generally observed as the first day of the week, constitute the mark of the beast, the question will doubtless arise in many minds, if the good of the past ages who have lived in the observance of this institution, have borne the mark of the beast, and rendered worship to that antichristian power; and if the many Christians of the present time who are still keeping the first day, are worshiping the beast, and wearing his mark. By those who wish to raise a blind prejudice against the views of S.D. Adventists, we are uniformly represented as so teaching. But it is purely a misrepresentation. We do not so teach; nor does such a conclusion follow from our premises. It has already been noticed that the mark and worship of the beast are both enforced by the two-horned beast. Now, in view of this fact, there can be no worship nor reception of the mark, such as is contemplated in the prophecy, till it is enforced by this power. The great majority of Protestants who have kept the first day of the week as the Sabbath, although it is an institution of the Papacy, have not had the remotest idea that it had any connection whatever with that false system of worship. Have such been worshiping the beast, while they have been keeping Sunday without a thought of that power, honestly supposing they were keeping a Bible institution? By no means. Have they had the mark of the beast? Not at all. The denunciation of the third message is against those who knowingly keep Sunday as an institution of the beast. It speaks of those who are enlightened in the matter, and of those alone. And for a person thus enlightened, knowing what God requires and what the beast requires, to basely yield to the requirements of the beast, to avoid persecution, turning away [255] in a cowardly manner from what he knows God requires, from motives of worldly interest,— this is what makes his sin so presumptuous and Heaven-daring in the sight of God; this is what calls forth the terrible threatening uttered by the third angel. But the good of past ages have not kept the day with any such understanding of the matter, nor from any such motives.

Just so with the mass of Protestants now living. But the third message is sent forth to warn us in reference to an issue yet future. The people of God are coming up to translation. They must be freed from Papal errors. The truth is to be agitated; and the antagonism between the requirements of God and those of antichristian powers, is to be set in a clearly-defined light before the people. The issue is to be met understandingly, the two-horned beast demanding from its subjects the reception of the mark, and the performance of the worship of the first beast, on pain of death, and God commanding us to refuse the mark and worship of the beast, and keep his commandment, on pain of drinking his unmingled wrath. With this issue before them, those who yield to his requirements instead of the requirements of God, will worship the beast and receive his mark. Thus seeking to save their lives by avoiding the wrath of earthly powers, they will lose them by becoming exposed to the wrath of God. Till this issue is upon the people, under the enactment of civil law, we accuse no one of worshiping the beast or receiving his mark. And the third message is sent forth to warn men to put away their errors and receive the truth, that they may be prepared to stand when this fiery ordeal shall come, and, at last, having gotten the victory over the beast, his image, his mark, and the number of his name, to sing the victor's song upon the sea of glass. [256]

4. The patience of the saints. The chronology of the third message is distinctly marked as being the period of "the patience of the saints" which follows the proclamation of the two former messages. "Here is the patience of the saints: here are they that keep the commandments of God, and the faith of Jesus." Verse 12. And this period of the saints' patience is marked by a most important fact, namely, the keeping of the

commandments of God and the faith of Jesus. We have seen that the first angel's message refers to the solemn proclamation of the immediate second advent, consequently the period of patience here brought to view must be the same as that which in many scriptures is located immediately preceding the second advent. A few texts must suffice as examples.

"Cast not away therefore your confidence, which hath great recompense of reward. For ye have need of patience; that, after ye have done the will of God, ye might receive the promise. For yet a little while, and He that shall come will come, and will not tarry. Now the just shall live by faith; but if any man draw back, my soul shall have no pleasure in him. But we are not of them who draw back unto perdition, but of them that believe to the saving of the soul." Hebrews 10:35-39.

"Be patient therefore, brethren, unto the coming of the Lord. Behold, the husbandman waiteth for the precious fruit of the earth, and hath long patience for it, until he receive the early and latter rain. Be ye also patient, stablish your hearts: for the coming of the Lord draweth nigh. Grudge not one against another, brethren, lest ye be condemned: behold the Judge standeth before the door. Take, my brethren, the prophets, who have spoken in the name of the Lord, [257] for an example of suffering affliction, and of patience." James 5:7-10.

"Because thou hast kept the word of my patience, I also will keep thee from the hour of temptation, which shall come upon all the world, to try them that dwell upon the earth. Behold, I come quickly: hold that fast which thou hast, that no man take thy crown." Revelation 3:10, 11.

"And it shall be said in that day, Lo, this is our God; we have waited for him, and he will save us: this is the Lord; we have waited for him, we will be glad and rejoice in his salvation." Isaiah 25:9.

5. The commandments of God. The period of the saints' patience is distinguished by the fact that they are keeping the commandments of God, and the faith of Jesus. It should be distinctly noticed that the commandments here brought to view, are not the commandments of Christ. There may be a certain sense in which all the precepts of the Saviour may be called the commandments of God; that is, if viewed as proceeding from the sovereign authority of the Father; but when the commandments of

God are spoken of in distinction from the testimony or faith of Jesus, there is but one thing to which reference can be made, namely, the commandments which God gave in person, the ten commandments. See John 15:10. "If ye keep my commandments ye shall abide in my love; even as I have kept my Father's commandments, and abide in his love." And thus we find the law of God which he proclaimed in person referred to in the New Testament as "the commandments of God," or as "the commandments."

"And he said unto him, Why callest thou me good? there is none good but one, that is, God: but if thou wilt enter into life, keep the commandments. He saith [258] unto him, Which? Jesus said, Thou shalt do no murder, Thou shalt not commit adultery, Thou shalt not steal, Thou shalt not bear false witness, Honor thy father and thy mother, and Thou shalt love thy neighbor as thyself." Matthew 19:17-19.

"And they returned and prepared spices and ointment; and rested the Sabbath day, according to the commandment." Luke 23:56.

"Think not that I am come to destroy the law or the prophets: I am not come to destroy, but to fulfill. For verily I say unto you, Till heaven and earth pass, one jot or one title shall in no wise pass from the law, till all be fulfilled. Whosoever therefore shall break one of these least commandments, and shall teach men so, he shall be called the least in the kingdom of Heaven: but whosoever shall do and teach them, the same shall be called great in the kingdom of Heaven." Matthew 5:17-19.

"Honor thy father and thy mother (which is the first commandment with promise), that it may be well with thee, and thou mayest live long on the earth." Ephesians 6:2, 3.

"But he answered and said unto them, Why do ye also transgress the commandment of God by your tradition? For God commanded, saying, Honor thy father and mother: and he that curseth father or mother, let him die the death. But ye say, Whosoever shall say to his father or his mother, It is a gift, by whatsoever thou mightest be profited by me; and honor not his father or his mother, he shall be free. Thus have ye made the commandment of God of none effect by your tradition." Matthew 15:3-6.

"What shall we say then? Is the law sin? God forbid. Nay, I had not known sin, but by the law; for [259] I had not known lust, except the law had said, Thou shalt not covet." Romans 7:7.

6. The faith of Jesus. This term is used in distinction from the commandments of God. It does not refer to a particular degree or kind of faith which the Saviour exercised in the performance of his miracles; for it appears that he wrought these by the power which he had already received from his Father. Matthew 8:2, 3; Mark 1:40, 41; Luke 5:23, 24. The world itself was made by him. John 1. He had ample power, therefore, to perform every miracle which he wrought. There is but one other thing to which this term can refer, namely, the precepts and doctrines of our Lord as recorded in the New Testament. Thus "the faith of the gospel" (Philippians 1:27) must refer to the precepts and doctrines of the gospel. The faith to which a multitude of the priests were obedient (Acts 6:7), which was committed to the apostles for the obedience of all nations (Romans 1:5), which Paul testifies that he had kept (2 Timothy 4:7), and which is to be earnestly maintained, as once delivered to the saints (Jude 3), must refer, we think, to the precepts and doctrines of the everlasting gospel. That the faith of Jesus is used in this sense in Revelation 2:13, we think cannot be denied. "Thou holdest fast my name," says Jesus, "and hast not denied my faith." That this is the sense in which it is used in Revelation 14:12, is further evident from the fact that it is spoken of as kept in the same manner that the commandments of God are kept.

"Here are they that keep the commandments of God [the Father], and the faith of Jesus" [the Son]. This excludes alike the blind Jew, who makes his boast in the law and rejects Jesus, and also the Christian who [260] professes faith in Christ while he breaks the commandments of God. It embraces Christian commandment-keepers only.

7. The penalty threatened. The fearful penalty connected with the warning of the third angel consists of two things: 1. The wine of the wrath of God, poured out without mixture into the cup of his indignation. 2. The torment with fire and brimstone in the presence of the holy angels, and of the Lamb. Let us carefully consider each in order.

What is the wine of the wrath of God? The next chapter clearly explains this point. "And I saw another sign in heaven, great and marvelous, seven angels having the seven last plagues; for in them is filled up the wrath of God. And one of the four beasts gave unto the seven angels seven golden vials, full of the wrath of God, who liveth forever and ever." Revelation 15:1, 7. It follows therefore that the wine of the wrath of God is the seven last plagues. This fact will be further apparent as we proceed to show that these plagues are future. That the plagues pertain to the future, we think can be established beyond controversy.

1. The wrath of God as threatened by the third angel, is poured out in the seven last plagues; for the first plague is inflicted on the very class that the third angel threatens. Compare Revelation 14:9, 10; 16:1, 2. This fact proves that the plagues must be future when the third angel's message is given; and it also proves the identity of the wrath of God without mixture, and the seven last plagues.

2. We have shown that the plagues, and the wrath of God without mixture, are the same. And wrath without mixture must be wrath with nothing else; that is, wrath without mercy. God has not yet visited the [261] earth with unmixed wrath; nor can he while our great High Priest ministers in the heavenly sanctuary, and stays the wrath of God by his intercession for sinful men. When the plagues are poured out, mercy has given place to vengeance.

3. Hence it is that the seven angels are represented as receiving the vials of the wrath of God, the seven last plagues, after the opening of the temple of God in Heaven. If we turn to Revelation 11:15-19, we shall find that the opening of the temple in Heaven is an event that transpires under the sounding of the seventh angel. And that account concludes with a brief statement of the events of the seventh vial or last plague. Now if we turn to chapter 15:5-8, 16:1-21, we shall read an expanded view of the facts stated in chapter 11:15-19, and shall find that the two accounts conclude in the same manner, namely, with the events of the last plague. These scriptures show that the seven angels do not receive the vials of the wrath of God to pour out upon the earth until the temple in Heaven is opened. That temple is opened under the voice of the seventh angel. The

third woe is by reason of the voice of the seventh angel. Chap. 8:13; 9:12; 11:14. The seven plagues are poured out under the sounding of that angel, hence the plagues are future, and constitute the third woe.

The foregoing reasons establish the fact that the plagues are future. We see no reason why they will not be similar in character to those poured out on Egypt, while their consequences will be far more terrific and dreadful. May God count us worthy to escape the things coming on the earth, and to stand before the Son of man. The seven last plagues are poured out on the living wicked; but the second part of the penalty [262] affixed to the warning of the third angel, is not afflicted until the end of the thousand years, when all the wicked are raised and suffer it together. This part of the penalty I will now consider.

"He shall be tormented with fire and brimstone in the presence of the holy angels, and in the presence of the Lamb; and the smoke of their torment ascendeth up forever and ever," etc. The final perdition of ungodly men, in the lake of fire, is without doubt the subject of these awful words. That we may rightly understand this text, we call attention to several important facts.

1. The punishment of the wicked will be inflicted upon them on this earth; for the final conflagration of our globe is to constitute the lake of fire in which they are rewarded, each according to his works.

"Behold the righteous shall be recompensed in the earth; much more the wicked and the sinner." Proverbs 11:31.

"But the heavens and the earth which are now, by the same word are kept in store, reserved unto fire against the day of Judgment and perdition of ungodly men." 2 Peter 3:7.

"But the fearful and unbelieving, and the abominable, and murderers, and whoremongers, and sorcerers, and idolators, and all liars, shall have their part in the lake which burneth with fire and brimstone: which is the second death." Revelation 21:8.

"For behold the day cometh that shall burn as an oven; and all the proud, yea, and all that do wickedly, shall be stubble; and the day that cometh shall burn them up, saith the Lord of hosts, that it shall leave them neither root nor branch." Malachi 4:1.

"And when the thousand years are expired, Satan [263] shall be loosed out of his prison, and shall go out to deceive the nations which are in the four quarters of the earth, Gog and Magog, to gather them together to battle: the number of whom is as the sand of the sea. And they went up on the breadth of the earth, and compassed the camp of the saints about, and the beloved city: and fire came down from God out of Heaven and devoured them." Revelation 20:7-9.

2. The prophet Isaiah (chapter 34) describes the final conflagration of our globe in language which is a complete parallel to that of the third angel in describing the punishment of the wicked. Those who contend that Isaiah refers only to ancient Idumea, must admit that the period of time described in this strong language, must finally come to an end. And those who admit that Isaiah, in the language we are about to quote, refers to the conflagration of our earth, will find in what follows ample proof that that scene will finally close.

"For it is the day of the Lord's vengeance, and the year of recompenses for the controversy of Zion. And the streams thereof shall be turned into pitch, and the dust thereof into brimstone, and the land thereof shall become burning pitch. It shall not be quenched night nor day; the smoke thereof shall go up for ever; from generation to generation it shall lie waste; none shall pass through it for ever and ever." Chap. 34:8-10.

3. But this terrific scene of final conflagration is not to last throughout unlimited duration. For the earth having been burned, and all its elements melted, new heavens and new earth are to follow, as the present earth succeeded to that which was destroyed by water. And in the earth thus made new the righteous are to be recompensed.

"But the day of the Lord will come as a thief in the [264] night; in which the heavens shall pass away with a great noise, and the elements shall melt with fervent heat, the earth also; and the works that are therein shall be burnt up. Seeing then that all these things shall be dissolved, what manner of persons ought ye to be in all holy conversation and godliness; looking for and hasting unto the coming of the day of God, wherein the heavens, being on fire, shall be dissolved, and the elements shall melt with fervent heat? Nevertheless we, according to his promise, look for new heavens and a new earth, wherein dwelleth righteousness." 2 Peter 3:10-13. "And I saw a new heaven and a new earth; for the first heaven and the first earth were passed away; and there was no more sea." Revelation 21:1.

4. Thus however dreadful and long-continued the punishment of the wicked will be (for each is to be punished according to his deserts), that punishment will finally result in the utter destruction of all transgressors. All the wicked will God destroy. Psalm 145:20. They shall die the second death. Revelation 21:8; Romans 6:23; Ezekiel 18:4, 20. They shall perish, being consumed into smoke. Psalm 37:10, 20, 38. They shall be punished with everlasting destruction, being burned up in unquenchable fire. 2 Thessalonians 1:9; Matthew 3:12. And thus having been consumed, root and branch, they shall be as though they had not been. Malachi 4:1; Obadiah 16.

Rise and Progress the Third Message

The position of all Adventists after the passing of the time, was at best a very trying one, and the work for a time moved slowly, attended with much opposition. To "hold fast the beginning of their confidence" [265] in the great movement, in the face of a scoffing world and church, and amid violent opposition from those who were drawing back from the faith, was a severe trial of faith and patience. And the numbers who had the moral courage, and shared sufficiently in the grace of God, to do this, were found to be small.

Those who cowardly yielded to the clamors of opponents to confess that they had been in error on the time, occupied the unhappy position of wearing the Advent name after giving up as error the very means which had made them Adventists. While those who apostatized so far as to give up the Advent faith, hope, and name, for a place in some one of the nominal churches, were destined to be regarded as vacillating, and ever feel the sting of remorse for so great a weakness as embracing the "blessed hope." Those who wished to renounce the Advent faith, and free themselves from the reproach suffered by those who adhered to it, might find a degree of relief for the present in confessing their way back into the church. But of those who have been imbued with the spirit of the Advent faith and hope, and have tasted the heavenly gift, and have been partakers of the Holy Ghost, and have tasted the good word of God, and the powers of the world to come, and have apostatized, there are few who can again enjoy the insipid piety of the popular churches. In fact such persons are very unhappy and dissatisfied with their position and relations in religious matters, unless their apostasy has been so sinful as to obliterate from the soul all traces of Christian experience, and they be given over to the sensual pleasures of this life. May God pity this unhappy class, and may they again stand with those who are looking for the blessed hope. [266]

But the position of those who discard the great movement which made them Adventists, and yet cherish some of the leading views of William Miller, and rejoice in the Advent name, is more inconsistent, and their course far more sinful in the sight of God, than that of those who made an entire surrender of both position and name. What a position in the sight of God, angels and men! They bless the Advent faith, hope and name, and curse the very means which has made them what they profess to be! These may hold the doctrines of the personal coming of Christ the literal resurrection of the dead, and life and immortality alone through Christ to be given at the resurrection of the just, but while failing to acknowledge the hand of God in the Advent movement in the past, and standing opposed to the third angel's message of the present, have no well-defined position as to the plan of God in warning the world and proving his people preparatory to the coming of the Son of man. And it is because of the ignorance of the people as to the true position, and because there is no real cross in what these men do teach, that they have influence. Some of them speak of Millerism and Miller, as they would of Mormonism and the notorious Smith, and yet claim to be Adventists. But if the hand of God has been with those who have borne the Advent name at any time, it was during the great time movement of 1843 and 1844. More recent time movements and operations of various kinds, by those who regard that grand movement as an error of Millerism, compare with it about the same as a rushlight compares with the noonday sun.

And these men will speak proudly of their Advent faith, and bless the Advent name, while they curse the great Advent movement, which has brought the Advent [267] doctrine before the present generation. The sin against the Holy Ghost, which had no forgiveness in the days of Christ, was to attribute the work of the Spirit, in the miracles of Jesus, to Satan. How much less, think you, is the sin of those who deny the work of the Spirit of God in the Advent movement, and attribute the power which attended that work to human and satanic influences? I do not say that all Adventists, besides Seventh-day Adventists, take the foregoing positions.

Most of them, however, do; and the candid reader who regards the view of the great Advent movement taken in these pages with favor, will not fail to see both the glaring inconsistencies and the sinfulness of the positions taken by these professed Adventists.

But the true position is free from such absurdities, and is harmonious in itself. It honors God, vindicates his word, and sustains Christian experience. It explains the past, definitely points out present duty, and lights up the glorious future. It presents a connected system of truth, the most beautiful in all its parts, that the mind of man ever contemplated.

The period of the third message dates from the disappointment in 1844, and from that time to the present the development of its great truths has been progressive. Immediately after the passing of the time, not a few took a firm stand that the first and second messages were in the past, that the midnight cry had been given, that the 2300 days had ended, and that we had reached the patient waiting, watching time. But it was not until the subject of the cleansing of the sanctuary was brought out in 1846, that the termination of the 2300 days became one of the clearest points in the entire system of Second-Advent truth. This established us in the fulfillment of the first and second messages in the past, opened [268] before us the ark of God containing the ten precepts of his holy law in the most holy place of the heavenly sanctuary, and called our attention to the third message, with its solemn warning to flee the worship of the beast and his image, and in its stead keep the commandments of God and the faith of Jesus. How forcible the closing words of the third angel: "Here is the patience of the saints, here are they that keep the commandments of God and the faith of Jesus." And how natural the conclusion that the Sabbath reform should come in right here.

Introduction of the Sabbath

As early as 1844, sister Preston, a Seventh-day Baptist, who was a believer in the soon coming of Christ, introduced the Sabbath to the Adventists of Washington, N.H., and made a good impression. With the help of the publications of her people, and the blessing of God, about forty embraced the Sabbath. The truth on this subject reached other points in New Hampshire. About that time Elder T.M. Preble embraced the Sabbath, and began to teach it. He called the attention of Adventists to the question, by a pamphlet on the subject, dated February 13, 1845. After showing the claims of the Bible Sabbath, and the fact that it was changed to Sunday by the Papacy, he said; "Thus we see Daniel 7:25, fulfilled, the little horn changing times and laws. Therefore it appears to me that all who keep the first day for the Sabbath, are the Pope's Sunday-keepers, and God's Sabbath breakers." But Elder Preble, not seeing the Sabbath reform under the message of the third angel, and that in the ripening of the harvest of the earth, the Sabbath was to be a test, continued [269] his ministerial labors in connection with those who bitterly opposed it. He soon lost his interest in the subject, and has since become one of its bitterest opposers. The same is true of Elder J.B. Cook, and a few other Advent ministers, who at a later point of time, embraced the Sabbath and abandoned it. Elder Preble had, however, called the attention of Adventists to this subject, and several in different parts of New England embraced the Sabbath, whose interest in it did not prove as transient as his had been.

In 1845, Elder Joseph Bates, then of Fairhaven, Mass., began to teach the Sabbath of the Bible, and several in Massachusetts, and Maine, embraced it as the fruit of his labors. He wrote and circulated gratuitously a small work upon the subject. By reading this little pamphlet, I was established upon the Sabbath, and began to teach it. This little work reached several in Connecticut, and with Bro. Bates' personal labors, brought over to the Sabbath a number in western New York and different parts of New England.

But these were generally the poor of this world, and the very few among them who had means, did not realize that on them rested the responsibility of sending the truth to others. Hence the cause moved slowly.

In the autumn of 1847, Bro. Bates sat down to write a work of more than one hundred pages, with only a York shilling at his command. And I was chopping cord-wood for my daily bread for the support of my little family, where I could earn but fifty cents a day. We two were alone in publicly teaching the Sabbath. Under such circumstances we could do but little in the cause. I state these things to show the reader the humble manner in which this cause commenced, and the sacrifices then made to spread the truth. [270]

I well remember when Bro. Bates felt deeply impressed with the duty to labor in Vermont, and, being destitute of means, resolved to start on foot from Fairhaven, Mass. A natural sister of Mrs. W. had come from Maine to Fairhaven, to perform the duties of the kitchen for one dollar a week, and in this way raise means to spread the truth. On learning Bro. Bates' intention to perform the long journey on foot, she went to her employer and asked for five dollars, which she obtained and gave to Bro. Bates to help him on his way to Vermont. God greatly blessed the mission, as many witnesses, who still observe the Sabbath, can testify. Let not those brethren and sisters who take but little interest in spreading the truth, blush at this simple narrative. He who notices the sparrows, saw this act of self-sacrifice, and set his seal of approbation. It was written in the books from which all are to be judged according to their deeds. And did not the angels who rejoice much over one repenting sinner, rejoice over this simple means of sending the light of present truth among the Green Mountains of Vermont? That sister will receive her reward. I write not these things to shame the wealthy believer, who is burying himself up in his wealth and his cares, and losing his interest in the cause, and his hold on Heaven; but I design to state facts that you may be led to seek that spirit of sacrifice, which those who were first in this cause evinced, that you may walk in that humble path of obedience in which they walked, and enjoy the blessing of entire consecration, which then rested upon them.

First Conference of Believers

In the spring of 1848, in company with Bro. Bates, Mrs. W. and self attended a conference of believers, at [271] Rocky Hill, Conn. This was the first general meeting held by Seventh-day Adventists. In point of numbers and influence, it marked a new era in the cause; and yet we all numbered less than thirty. The brethren were much encouraged, and Bro. Bates began to labor more extensively as the way opened before him.

Mrs. White's Experience

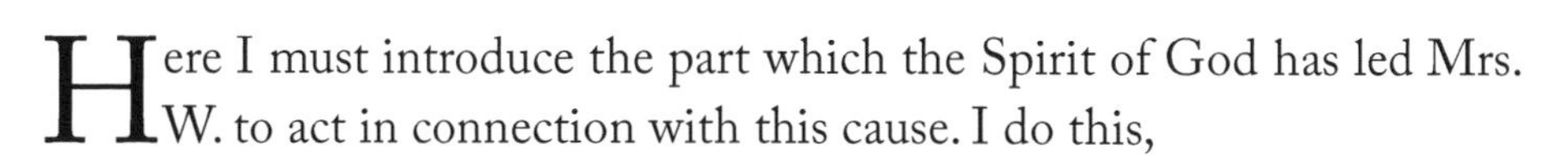

Here I must introduce the part which the Spirit of God has led Mrs. W. to act in connection with this cause. I do this,

1. Because her experience and labors have been closely connected with its rise and progress.

2. Because of the spirit of prejudice and enmity existing against her calling and labors. This is manifested by those who are ignorant of the facts in the case, or if not wholly ignorant, are led by a spirit of frenzied persecution. The bearing which this has upon the cause is a sufficient reason for laying the facts as they are before the public.

3. Because of the importance of her work, in connection with this cause, as will be seen in the following pages.

It was but a few weeks after the passing of the time, in 1844, that she had her first vision. The circumstances of this manifestation are briefly stated by Mrs. W. as follows: "I visited sister H., one of our Advent sisters, whose heart was knit with mine. In the morning we bowed at the family altar. It was not an exciting occasion. There were but five of us present, all females. While praying, the power of God came upon me, as I never had felt it before. I was surrounded with light, and was rising higher and higher from the [272] earth," etc. (*Spir. Gifts*, vol. ii,p.30.) Her condition in vision may be described as follows:

1. She is utterly unconscious of everything transpiring around her, as has been proved by the most rigid tests, but views herself as removed from this world, and in the presence of heavenly beings.

2. She does not breathe. During the entire period of her continuance in vision, which has at different times ranged from fifteen minutes to three hours, there is no breath, as has been repeatedly proved by pressing upon the chest, and by closing the mouth and nostrils.

3. Immediately on entering vision, her muscles become rigid, and joints fixed, so far as any external force can influence them. At the same time her movements and gestures, which are frequent, are free and graceful, and cannot be hindered nor controlled by the strongest person.

4. On coming out of vision, whether in the day-time or a well-lighted room at night, all is total darkness. Her power to distinguish even the most brilliant objects, held within a few inches of the eyes, returns but gradually, sometimes not being fully established for three hours. This has continued for the past twenty years; yet her eyesight is not in the least impaired, few persons having better than she now possesses.

She has probably had, during the past twenty-three years, between one and two hundred visions. These have been given under almost every variety of circumstance, yet maintaining a wonderful similarity; the most apparent change being, that of late years they have grown less frequent, but more comprehensive. She has been taken off in vision most frequently when bowed in prayer. Several times, while earnestly addressing the congregation, unexpectedly to herself and to all around [273] her, she has been instantly prostrated in vision. This was the case June 12, 1868, in the presence of not less than two hundred Sabbath-keepers, in the house of worship, in Battle Creek, Mich. On receiving baptism at my hands, at an early period of her experience, as I raised her up out of the water, immediately she was in vision. Several times, when prostrated by sickness, she has been relieved in answer to the prayer of faith, and taken off in vision. At such times her restoration to usual health has been wonderful. At another time, when walking with friends, in conversation upon the glories of the kingdom of God, as she was passing through the gate before her father's house, the Spirit of God came upon her, and she was instantly taken off in vision. And what may be important to those who think the visions the result of mesmerism, she has a number of times been taken off in vision, when in prayer alone in the grove or in the closet.

It may be well to speak as to the effect of the visions upon her constitution and strength. When she had her first vision, she was an emaciated invalid, given up by her friends and physicians to die of consumption. She then weighed but eighty pounds. Her nervous condition was such that she could not write, and was dependent on one sitting near her at the table to even pour her drink from the cup to the saucer. And notwithstanding her anxieties and mental agonies, in consequence of her duty to bring her views before the public, her labors in public speaking, and in church matters generally, her wearisome travels, and home labors and cares, her health and physical and mental strength have improved from the day she had her first vision.

As to the character of the visions, I only wish to state [274] at present that this may be learned by reading the several volumes of "Spiritual Gifts," for sale at the Review Office. As to their fruits, and the nature of the opposition they have met, I shall speak more fully hereafter.

Second General Conference

In the summer of 1848, we received an invitation to hold a Conference with the few friends in Western New York. I was destitute of means, and with feeble health entered the hay-field to earn the sum necessary to bear our expenses to that meeting. I took a large job of mowing, and when fainting beneath the noonday sun, I would bow before God in my swath, call upon him for strength, rise freshened, and mow on again. In five weeks I earned enough to bear our expenses to the conference. Bro. Bates joined us at this meeting. The notice had been given to all in the Empire State who were in sympathy with our views, and there was a general rally; yet there were not more than forty present.

And what confusion of sentiment among this few! A spirit of discussion and contention for points not important prevailed, so that we who had come so far could hardly have chance to give our message, and the meeting would have proved a failure, and the good brethren would have separated in confusion and trial, had not the Lord worked in a special manner. His Spirit rested upon Mrs. W., and she was taken off in vision. The entire congregation believed that it was the work of God, and were deeply affected. She related what she had seen, which was given to correct some errors among them, and in melting strains exhorted them to leave their errors, and those points on which they had differed, and unite on the important truths of the third [275] message. And on that good evening the brethren sacrificed their Babel of sentiments and united on the truth. And what was the result? Harmony began to prevail, and many came flocking to the standard of truth.

The fruit of this vision was good. It could not have been the work of an enemy, according to the test given by our Lord, in Matthew 7:15-20: "Beware of false prophets, which come to you in sheep's clothing, but inwardly they are ravening wolves. Ye shall know them by their fruits. Do men gather grapes of thorns, or figs of thistles? Even so every good tree bringeth forth good fruit; but a corrupt tree bringeth forth evil fruit. A good tree cannot bring forth evil fruit, neither can a corrupt tree bring forth good fruit. Every tree that bringeth not forth good fruit is hewn down, and cast into the fire. Wherefore, by their fruits ye shall know them."

The Opposition

By the spring of 1849 the subject of the Sabbath began to attract considerable notice from Advent believers, who, seeing that the first day of the week could not be sustained by divine authority, were falling back to the position of no Sabbath in the Christian dispensation. And it may be worthy of notice, that this is the result everywhere the Sabbath question is discussed. The reason why the regular Baptists have taken this position more generally than any other denomination, may be because of their relation to the Seventh-day Baptists, who have more or less brought the subject to their notice. As an illustration of this point, when William E. Arnold, of Rochester, N.Y., in 1844, stated to Elder Joseph Marsh his convictions of duty to observe the [276] seventh day as the Sabbath, Elder Marsh replied that the first day of the week, as the Sabbath for Christians, was clearly proved from the word of God, and the unvarying practice of the Christian church. Mr. Arnold invited him to give the subject especial attention. He promised to do so and report the next Sunday. His report was simply this: That he had examined the subject, and had become satisfied that the Sabbath was Jewish, and that there was none for Christians.

The change from the first day to no Sabbath cannot be regarded in any better light than a change from bad to worse, and it is a matter of grief that thousands, finding themselves utterly unable to sustain the observance of first-day, take refuge from the pointed arrows of truth in this comparatively strong hold of unbelief. The masses are ignorant of the facts relative to the first day of the week. They think the New Testament abounds with direct testimony that it is sacred time. Elder Joseph Bates asserted in a grove, in Connecticut, in 1849, that there was not one text in the New Testament which taught a change of the Sabbath from the seventh to the first day of the week. An intelligent-appearing gentleman interrupted by saying, "There are more than twenty." "Well," said Bro. Bates, "will you please give us one?" The gentleman replied, "I can give you twenty." Bro. B. urged, "If you can give twenty, you can certainly give one. We wait for one; only give us one text." The gentleman was silent; and Bro. B. went on with his subject.

It is a fact the first day of the week is mentioned in the New Testament only eight times, and is not in a single instance spoken of as a sacred day. Inspiration gives it the simple title of first day of the week. See [277] Matthew 28:1; Mark 16:2, 9; Luke 24:1; John 20:1, 19; Acts 20:7; 1 Corinthians 16:2.

It is also a fact that inspiration in the New Testament gives the seventh day of the week the sacred title of Sabbath, fifty-nine times, and in every instance refers to the day on which God rested, and which he sanctified and blessed. See Matthew 12:1, 2, 5, 8, 10, 11, 12; 24:20; 28:1; Mark 1:21; 2:23, 24, 27, 28; 3:2, 4; 6:2; 15:42; 16:1; Luke 4:16, 31; 6:1, 2, 5, 6, 7, 9; 13:10, 14, 15, 16; 14:1, 3, 5; 23:54, 56; John 5:9, 10, 16, 18; 7:22, 23; 9:14, 16; 19:31; Acts 1:12; 13:14, 27, 42, 44; 5:21; 16:13; 17:2; 18:4.

Those who examine the subject are generally compelled to admit that there is no inspired testimony favoring a change of the day. Some, however, cling to the idea that the change is sustained by the example of Christ and the apostles. As far as the example of our Lord is concerned, they can refer us to but two instances of his meeting his disciples on the first day of the week. The first occasion was when he appeared to them on the evening of the day of his resurrection; and they were astonished to learn that he had risen from the dead. The second was eight days after this, and hence could not be upon the first day of the week; and neither of these meetings, so far as we have any proof, were from previous appointment, or designed for religious worship.

And there is no evidence that the apostles regarded the first day of the week as a day of worship. There is no record of a single instance of their holding a meeting in the daytime of the first day of the week. It is true that Paul met with his brethren, at Troas, on a first-day evening to break bread. That meeting continued all night on the first day of the week. The night is the [278] first half of the twenty-four hour day. Therefore that meeting was held on what we call Saturday night. The next morning, Sunday, Paul started on his long journey to Jerusalem, and spent the last half of that day in traveling on foot, and sailing with his brethren toward

Mitylene. Thus we have apostolic example for regarding the first day as a proper day for secular business.

Neither can 1 Corinthians 16:2, serve the cause of first-day observance. This text does not refer to a single element of the Sabbath. Holy time, rest from labor, and public assembling for divine worship, are not intimated therein. Justin Edwards, in his Notes on the New Testament, comments on this text thus: "Lay by him in store; at home. That there be no gatherings; that their gifts might be ready when the apostle should come."

With this now contrast New Testament testimony relative to the Sabbath. Our Lord recognized the existence of the Sabbath at the destruction of Jerusalem, A.D. 70, as verily as the seasons of the year. "And pray ye that your flight be not in the winter neither on the Sabbath day." He refers to a definite day. Not one day in seven and no day in particular, but the day of the Sabbath. In Mark 2:27, he says, The Sabbath was made for man.

In Luke 23:56, is the record of the disciples' resting the Sabbath day according to the commandment. This act of resting on the Sabbath was after the crucifixion, and the record of it was made by inspiration nearly thirty years later still.

The book of Acts shows what the apostles did. Which day of the week did they observe as the Sabbath? The writer of the book of Acts records instances of the apostles' holding meetings upon the Sabbath. On one occasion [279] when Paul had been addressing a mixed assembly, "the Gentiles besought that these words might be preached to them, the next Sabbath," showing that it was understood even by the Gentiles, that the Sabbath was Paul's regular day of worship. Acts 13:42. And the next Sabbath day came almost the whole city together, to hear the word of God. Verse 44.

At another time Paul and Timotheus, on the Sabbath, went out of the city of Philippi to a place "by the river side, where prayer was wont to be made," and held a public meeting. Lydia believed, and was baptized, and her household. But was the Sabbath Paul's regular preaching day? Was this his manner? Let chapter 17:2, answer. "And Paul, as his manner was, went in unto them, and three Sabbath days reasoned with them out of the Scriptures."

Chapter 18:1-11, contains important testimony on this subject. Paul at Corinth abode with Aquila and Priscilla, and worked with them at tent making. "And he reasoned in the synagogue every Sabbath, and persuaded the Jews and the Greeks." Verse 4. How long did he remain at Corinth? "And he continued there a year and six months, teaching the word of God among them." Verse 11. Here is apostolic example for seventy-eight successive Sabbaths. And it will be seen by verses 5-8, that the apostle occupied the synagogue a part of these Sabbaths, until the Jews opposed and blasphemed, then he went into the house of Justus, where he preached the remaining portion. Here, dear reader, is apostolic example in harmony with the divine precept, showing its application and force in the present dispensation.

The cross of Sabbath-keeping in the face of decided opposition, when its friends were few, was very great. [280] Thousands became convinced that apostolic example was in harmony with the fourth precept of the decalogue; but the numbers who had the moral courage to act up to their convictions, were found to be comparatively few. And no sooner was a by-path opened around this cross by way of no-Sabbath, than multitudes eagerly pressed into it. Some of those who taught the Sabbath abolished labored to obliterate all distinction between typical institutions and moral principles, and to show that everything in the form of law recorded in the Old Testament was abolished. Others could not go so far, but took the position that the seventh-day Sabbath was of the same nature as the feast days of the typical system, and expired with them. These could not see any reason why the precepts of the decalogue, excepting the fourth, should be abolished. In their nature they are adapted to man, throughout all dispensations of his fallen condition. They exactly meet his wants. He cannot dispense with them. Why, then, should the crucifixion of the Saviour of sinners do them away? These could see how typical institutions, pointing to the death of Christ, could cease at the cross, but could not understand how moral precepts, applicable to the entire period of man's fallen state, could be effected by the death of the Son of God.

The mistaken view that the Sabbath was typical, had long been held by the churches; hence this class could more easily receive the idea that when Paul says, "Let no man therefore judge you in meat or in drink, or in respect of a holy day, or of the new moon, or of the sabbath days, which are a shadow of things to come," Colossians 2:16, 17, he includes the Sabbath of the Lord. The apostle here speaks of sabbath days, or sabbaths. Leviticus 23, shows seven Jewish sabbaths, to be celebrated [281] at their appointed times, "besides the Sabbaths of the Lord." See verses 37 and 38. Here the distinction between the two kinds of sabbaths is seen. Paul refers to those which are classed with meat, drink, new moon, etc., and not to the Sabbath which the Lawgiver has wisely associated with nine moral precepts. The "Sabbath Manual," by Justin Edwards, speaks with clearness and ability upon this point, and also in reference to the days spoken of in Romans 14:

"Under the Jewish dispensation were incorporated two kinds of laws. One was founded on obligations growing out of the nature of men, and their relations to God and one another; obligations binding before they were written, and which will continue to be binding upon all who shall know them, to the end of time. Such are the laws which were written by the finger of God on the tables of stone, and are called moral laws.

"The other kind, called ceremonial laws, related to various outward observances, which were not obligatory till they were commanded, and then were binding only on the Jews till the death of Christ.

"There were also two kinds of Sabbaths, or days of rest. One was a day of weekly rest; and the command to keep it holy was placed by the Lawgiver in the midst of the moral laws. It was called, by way of eminence, 'The Sabbath.' The command to keep the other sabbaths was placed by the Lawgiver among the ceremonial laws, because it was like them, as the command to keep the weekly Sabbath was like the laws with which it was associated. One class were fundamental, permanent, universal, moral laws; the other class were local, temporary, ceremonial laws. One had their origin in the nature and relations of man; the other in the peculiar [282] circumstances in which, for a time, a peculiar people were placed. One would be binding in all ages, upon all who should know them; and the other would be binding only upon the Jews till the death of the Messiah.

"The Jews, at the coming of Christ, being in a state of great spiritual darkness and grievous apostasy from God, did not well understand the nature and objects of their laws. Often they overlooked the spirit, and were superstitiously devoted to the forms. Some, after they embraced the gospel, thought that the ceremonial as well as the moral laws were binding; others, more enlightened, thought that they were not. This led to contentions among them. Paul, in the fourteenth chapter of Romans, presented such considerations as were adapted to lead them, in this matter, to a right decision.

"'One man,' he says, 'esteemeth one day above another. Another esteemeth every day alike. Let every man be fully persuaded in his own mind. He that regardeth the day, regardeth it unto the Lord; and he that regardeth not the day, to the Lord he doth not regard it.' Both mean to honor God, and he will accept them. But what day does he speak of? 'The Sabbath' of the fourth commandment, associated by God inseparably with the moral laws? Read the connection. What is it? Is it, one man believeth he must worship Jehovah; another, who is weak, worshipeth idols? One believeth that he must not commit murder, adultery or theft, and another thinks he may? Were those the laws about which they were contending, and with which were connected the days that he speaks of? No; about those laws there was no dispute.

"But 'One believeth that he may eat all things,' (which are nourishing, whether allowed in the ceremonial [283] law, which regulateth such things, or not); 'another, who is weak, eateth herbs. Let not him that eateth despise him that eateth not; and let not him which eateth not, judge him that eateth, for God hath received him.' Those were not the laws about which they were contending, and with regard to which the apostle was giving them instruction. It was not the moral, but the ceremonial laws; and the days spoken of were those which were connected, not with the former, but with the latter.

"So, in the second chapter of Colossians, "Let no man judge you in meat or in drink, or in respect of a holy day, or of the new moon, or of the sabbaths. The sabbaths spoken of are not the Sabbath associated with, Thou shalt not commit murder, or adultery, or theft; but the sabbaths associated with meats and drinks, and new moons, which were indeed shadows of things to come. But to take what he said about those sabbaths which were associated by God with the ceremonial laws, and which the apostle himself, in this very discourse, associates with them, and apply it, as some have done, to 'The Sabbath' which God associated with moral laws, is wrong." pp. 133,136.

All types point forward to something connected with the work of redemption. They have no other design than this. Hence no type would ever have been introduced had not man fallen and needed a redemption. They all originate, therefore, this side of the fall. But the Sabbath was instituted before the fall, before man needed redemption, and before anything was, or could have been, reasonably given to foreshadow that work. All the types that were ever instituted had no meaning except as they recognized the work of Christ in redemption; but the seventh-day Sabbath was from creation a [284] holy day, and all the facts to which the fourth commandment points would have been just as true as they are now if Christ had never died. While the types, among which were the typical sabbaths of the Jews, recognized man's guilt, and signified God's willingness to save, the seventh-day Sabbath would have occupied the same place it now occupies, and ever has occupied, even if man had never sinned. The typical sabbaths were shadows of things to come; the seventh-day Sabbath was and is a memorial of things past. The two classes of sabbaths point in opposite directions, and hence cannot be classed together. The one pointed forward to redemption; the other points back to creation. "For in six days the Lord made heaven and earth, the sea, and all that in them is, and rested the seventh day; wherefore the Lord blessed the Sabbath day and hallowed it." The seventh-day Sabbath therefore is not a type, if reason and revelation may decide this question.

William Miller's views respecting the perpetuity of the Sabbath, and its distinction from the sabbaths of the Jews, is also worthy of notice.

"I say, and I believe I am supported by the Bible, that the moral law was never given to the Jews as a people exclusively, but they were for a season the keepers of it in charge. And through them the law, oracles and testimony have been handed down to us. See Paul's clear reasoning in Romans 2:3, 4, on that point. Then, says the objector, we are under the same obligation to keep the sabbaths of weeks, months and years that the Jews were. No, sir; you will observe that these were not included in the decalogue.... Only one kind of Sabbaths was given to Adam, and only one remains for us. See Hosea 2:11. 'I will cause all her mirth to cease, her feast days, her new moons, and her sabbaths, [285] and all her solemn feasts.' All the Jewish sabbaths did cease, when Christ nailed them to his cross. Colossians 2:14-17. 'Blotting out the hand-writing of ordinances that was against us, which was contrary to us, and took it out of the way, nailing it to his cross; and having spoiled principalities and powers, he made a show of them openly, triumphing over them in it. Let no man therefore judge you in meat, or in drink, or in respect of a holy day, or of the new moon, or of the sabbath days, which are a shadow of things to come; but the body is of Christ.' These were properly called Jewish sabbaths. Hosea says, 'her sabbaths.' But the Sabbath of which we are speaking, God calls 'my Sabbath.' Here is clear distinction between the creation Sabbath and the ceremonial. The one is perpetual; the others were merely shadows of good things to come, and are limited in Christ." — *Miller's Life and Views*, pp. 161, 162.

Here let it be distinctly understood that those who hold that no change has taken place in the law of God, excepting in the fourth precept, have no right whatever to appeal to those texts usually quoted to prove the abolition of the entire code.

Those who took the extreme position that all ten of the commandments were abolished, relied with great confidence on what the apostle has said respecting the two ministrations. 2 Corinthians 3. These seemed to overlook the fact that a law is one thing, and the ministration of that law quite another thing. Paul is here contrasting two ministrations of the same law. He is contrasting the ministration of the law of God under Moses, (which was a ministration of condemnation and death,) with the ministration of the same law under Christ (which is the ministration of the Spirit). It is the ministration [286] of death that is done away, to give place to the more glorious ministration of God's law, called the ministration of the Spirit. But we would inquire, Why should all ten of the commandments of God be slain at the cross, even if it were necessary to abolish the fourth? All agree that nine are good, yea, indispensable for the Christian dispensation. Was it an oversight in the Lawgiver in placing the Sabbath in the midst of nine moral precepts? And did he have to slay the whole ten in order to get rid of the Sabbath? But if all ten were abolished at the cross, how is it that nine are still binding? "Why," says the objector, "nine of them were re-enacted during Christ's ministry, before the ten were abolished at his death!

If it be said that the apostles re-enacted nine of the commandments for the gospel after their Lord ascended and the Holy Spirit was poured out upon them, we reply that according to this view there was a space between the abolition of the ten, at the cross, and the re-enactment of the nine; a space when there was no law, consequently no transgression, and men might blaspheme, murder, etc., and not commit sin! But if the objector takes the ground that the nine commandments were re-enacted at the cross at the time when he thinks the ten were abolished, then we shall understand him that Heaven aimed a blow that killed all ten of the commandments, and that the same blow, at the same moment, brought nine of them to life again! And all this to get rid of the Sabbath which Christ says was made for man.

By many it was assumed, 1. That Christ was the Christian's lawgiver, and 2. That he has given in person [287] and by his inspired apostles, a complete code of laws for the present dispensation. It was then asserted that as the law of the Sabbath was not repeated in the New Testament, the seventh-day Sabbath is not binding upon Christians. Deuteronomy 18:15-18, was offered as proof that Christ was our lawgiver, but it may be seen that the text teaches the reverse. "The Lord thy God will raise up unto thee a prophet from the midst of thee, of thy brethren, like unto me; unto him ye shall hearken.... And the Lord said unto me, They have well spoken that which they have spoken. I will raise them up a prophet from among their brethren, like unto thee, and will put my words in his mouth, and he shall speak unto them all that I shall command him."

Peter, speaking of Christ, says: "For Moses truly said unto the fathers, A prophet shall the Lord your God raise up unto you, of your brethren, like unto me; him shall ye hear in all things whatsoever he shall say unto you." Acts 3:22.

Christ, as a prophet, or teacher, was like Moses. We now inquire, Did Moses legislate? Did he make laws for the people? He did not. Moses received words from the mouth of God and spake them to the people. There is no record that he ever assumed the position of an independent lawgiver; while the inspired word furnishes facts quite the reverse. In the case of the man who gathered sticks on the Sabbath, (Numbers 15:32-36,) Moses did not presume to decide his case, but left that for the great Lawgiver. "And they put him in ward, because it was not declared what should be done unto him. And the Lord said unto Moses, the man shall be surely put to death." See also Numbers 27:5-7; Leviticus 24:11-14. [288]

That Christ, as a prophet, or teacher, was like Moses, we have the united testimony of Moses, (Deuteronomy 18:15,) the Lord, (verse 18,) and Peter, (Acts 3:22,) therefore he was not an independent lawgiver. Says the eternal Father, when speaking of his Son, "He shall speak unto them all that I shall command him." Jesus testifies of himself on this subject, and his testimony agrees with that of his Father. Mark well the following declarations of the Son of God:

"Jesus answered them, and said, My doctrine is not mine, but his that sent me." Chap. 7:16.

"For I have not spoken of myself; but the Father which sent me, he gave me a commandment what I should say, and what I should speak. And I know that his commandment is life everlasting: whatsoever I speak therefore, even as the Father said unto me, so I speak." Chap. 12:49, 50.

"He that loveth me not, keepeth not my sayings; and the word which ye hear is not mine, but the Father's which sent me." Chap. 14:24.

By these testimonies from the Father and Son, we learn that it was not the work of our Lord Jesus Christ to legislate; but he received the doctrines which he taught, from the mouth of the Father, and spake them to the people. In this respect, as a prophet, or teacher, he was like Moses. In both cases the Father is the lawgiver.

The transfiguration is referred to as proof that Christ is the lawgiver in the gospel age. It is said that the presence of both Moses and Christ, (the teachers of both [289] dispensations,) and Moses' being placed upon the background by the voice from Heaven, saying, "This is my beloved Son, in whom I am well pleased, hear him," shows that Christ is the lawgiver of the present age, and that his teachings take the place of the law of God. But a very important personage is overlooked by those who take this position. It is the Father. He also appears at the mount of transfiguration. His voice is heard as the highest authority — "This is my beloved Son, hear him." However much the glory of Christ excelled that of Moses, it did not eclipse the glory of the Author of the ten commandments. The great God spoke the ten precepts of his holy law in the hearing of all the people. He did not leave them with Moses to write and deliver to the people. Neither was it the work of the Son of God to deliver them, or any portion of them, the second time for the men of the present dispensation. Under circumstances of awful grandeur, the great Lawgiver spoke the ten commandments directly to the people, and wrote them in the tables of stone. Christ quotes several of them at different times to enforce the doctrines he taught. He treats them as the law of his Father, and affirms their immutability.

If it be said that the apostles in their writings have given a code of laws for the gospel age, we reply, that this view makes twelve lawgivers, whereas James says, "There is one lawgiver."

See the commission to the eleven: "Go ye therefore and teach all nations, baptizing them in the name of the Father, and of the Son, and of the Holy Ghost; teaching them to observe all things whatsoever I have commanded you." Matthew 28:19, 20. Christ taught the apostles what he had received of the Father, and this they were to teach men to observe. Notice also the [290] work of the Holy Spirit, and from whom it proceeds. "But the Comforter, which is the Holy Ghost, whom the Father will send in my name, he shall teach you all things, and bring all things to your remembrance, whatsoever I have said unto you." John 14:26. "And I will pray the Father, and he shall give you another Comforter, that he may abide with you forever." Verse 16. The Holy Spirit came from the Father, and one object for which it was sent, was to call to the disciples' memory the words of divine truth which the Son had received of the Father, and had spoken to them.

It is God, the great Lawgiver, that speaks to his people in both dispensations: "God, who at sundry times and in divers manners spake in time past unto the fathers by the prophets, hath in these last days spoken unto us by his Son." Hebrews 1:1, 2.

A Paper Started

The subject of the Sabbath was growing clearer, and up to this time the foregoing positions were being presented to small congregations, by Bro. Bates and myself. Opposition was waxing stronger, and the battle was increasing. Burdened with a sense of duty to enter the field in defense of truth, in July, 1849, I issued the first number of a little sheet called *The Present Truth*, from which I give the following extract to show the spirit of that time:

"It is through the truth that souls are sanctified and made ready to enter the everlasting kingdom. Obedience to the truth will kill us to this world, that we may be made alive, by faith in Jesus. "Sanctify them through thy truth; thy word is truth.' John 17:17. This was the prayer of Jesus. 'I have no greater [291] joy than to hear that my children walk in truth.' 3 John 4.

"Error darkens and fetters the mind, but the truth brings with it freedom, and gives light and life. True charity, or love, 'rejoiceth in the truth.' 1 Corinthians 13:6. 'Thy law is truth.' Psalm 119:142. David describing the day of slaughter, when the pestilence shall walk in darkness, and destruction waste at noonday, so that 'a thousand shall fall at thy side and ten thousand at thy right hand,' says: 'He shall cover thee with his feathers, and under his wings shalt thou trust; his truth shall be thy shield and buckler.' Psalm 91:4.

"The storm is coming. War, famine and pestilence are already in the field of slaughter. Now is the time, the only time to seek a shelter in the truth of the living God. In Peter's time there was present truth, or truth applicable to that present time. The church have ever had a present truth. The present truth now, is that which shows present duty, and the right position for us who are about to witness the time of trouble such as never was. Present truth must be oft repeated, even to those who are established in it. This was needful in the apostles' day, and it certainly is no less important for us, who are living just before the close of time.

"For months I have felt burdened with the duty of writing and publishing the present truth for the scattered flock; but the way has not been opened for me to commence the work until now. I tremble at the word of the Lord, and the importance of this time. What is done to spread the truth must be done quickly. The four angels are holding the angry nations in check but a few days, until the saints are sealed; then the nations will rush, like the rushing of many waters. Then it will be too late to spread before precious souls the present, [292] saving, living truths of the Holy Bible. My spirit is drawn out after the scattered remnant. May God help them to receive the truth, and be established in it."

A few numbers of this little sheet had been published which, with Bro. Bates' publications, were a great help in the cause. Then the few that taught the truth traveled on foot, in second-class cars, or on steamboat decks, for want of means. The testimony they bore was pointed. God worked with them mightily; and the cheering news of conversions to the truth were coming in on every hand. Several brethren sold possessions, and handed out their means, to advance the cause. Young men and women could then give up their wages to help preachers from place to place, and to publish books for gratuitous distribution. All seemed to give cheerfully, and God abundantly blessed the cheerful giver. Ministers and people then felt for souls, and labored for them as though the coming of the day of God was an absorbing reality. But in those days of prosperity to the cause, there were trials; and these gradually arose in consequence of a disposition to draw off from the great truths connected with the third message, to points of no vital importance. It was impossible to make some see that present truth really was *present* truth, and not future truth, and that the word, as a lamp, shines brightest where we stand, and not so plainly on the path in the distance. Hence the order of events a thousand years in the future, or just before or after the coming of the Lord, was all-absorbing theme with some.

The Review and Herald

In 1850 I commenced publishing the *Review and Herald* at Paris, Me. As friends were few and generally [293] poor, we chose this country location to save expense. By this time several preachers had united in the proclamation of the present truth, and our hearts were often cheered by their success. But those were days of poverty, deprivation, toil and anguish of spirit. We labored ardently to bring some to a knowledge of the truth, divided our scanty purse with them, and at the same time were suffering for the comforts of life. With feeble health we traveled from town to town, and from State to State, preaching the word and holding conferences; and at the same time issuing the *Review* once in two or three weeks.

About this time Bro. J. N. Andrews commenced his labors, which was no small reinforcement. Faithfully has this dear brother labored in the cause, which is now blessed with his clear expositions of Bible truth in our most important publications.

The first number of the second volume of the *Review*, was issued at Saratoga Springs, N.Y., August 5, 1851. Up to this time we had no permanent home, but had traveled as the way opened, then stopped to write and publish where brethren made us welcome. Our two little boys were from us, and six hundred miles from each other.

In March, 1852, the *Review* was established at Rochester, N.Y. The friends of the cause raised seven or eight hundred dollars to purchase press and printing material with which to issue it. This was a new and important era in the progress of the cause. Here commenced Bro. Andrews' letters to O. R. L. Crosier, which not only exposed the weakness of the no-Sabbath heresy, but the deceitful manner in which some handled the word of God. Success attended the cause east and west. Bro. Waggoner raised up witnesses for the truth in [294] many places in Wisconsin. The labors of Brn. Cornell and Cranson were greatly blessed in Michigan. Bro. Bates was having his usual success in different States and the Canadas, through which he so rapidly passed, and other brethren in the State of New York, and in New England, were reporting success. I cannot better represent the state of things that followed, than by quoting from the *Review*, vol. xi, p. 77, which I give under the appropriate head of a

Purifying Process

"It is evident, however, that with the increase of numbers there was not a corresponding increase in consecration and in the graces of the Spirit. The truth was being more clearly brought out, and many were embracing it, and at the same time the standard of consecration, self-denial and sacrifice, was being lowered among us as a people. There was a great increase of numbers. The scripture evidences of our position were the themes of public lectures, and close, practical preaching was too much neglected, and most Sabbath-keepers became quite satisfied with the form without the power. Hypocrites crowded into the ranks. Men destitute of principle, and having a seared conscience, professed the Sabbath. And the spirit of the world prevailed in the body.

"Church discipline was urged through the *Review*, which was very disagreeable to some in the ranks who wished to have their own way, and hated reproof and instruction. They chose to be teachers, when they should have been learners. They went out to teach the truth without being sent of the Lord, or approbated by the church, and sowed the seeds of discontent, disunion and death wherever they went. Some of them were [295] labored with and reproved. Others did not receive as much approbation and attention as they desired. And not a few were rebuked of the Lord for their unchristian, reckless course. This aroused their jealousy and anger, and finally they started a sheet of slander at Jackson, Mich., which met the feelings of all those who were ready to be inspired with jealousy and a feeling of hatred and revenge toward those who had reproved them for their wrongs, and they all poured forth their feelings of bitterness and wrath into this sheet.

"This was a cause of great grief to many dear brethren, and it appeared for the time that the precious cause was being injured. But this sheet was manifesting hearts and purifying the body. It was evident to all decent people that those who would go with such a sheet were not fit to go with the saints. We will mention some of the leading men in this faction, and their position when last heard from. W ----n, rejected by his party for crime, and a town charge; B-----o, their editor, fined $25 for presenting a pistol, and threatening to shoot a scholar in school; C ----e, run out as a preacher, and fishing on the lakes; C -----n, in a clothing store; L -----s, a Spiritualist. R -----l and H ------s had denounced B -----o and the publishers of their sheet as hypocrites, and were standing alone. It seems that as soon as these restless spirits went out from the body by themselves, they immediately went to biting and devouring one another, until not one of the eighteen messengers of which they once boasted as being with them, is now bearing a public testimony, and there is not one place of regular meeting, to our knowledge, among them east or west.

"The true friends of the cause have been led by these things to see the necessity of bearing a bold and independent [296] testimony for the truth, and for the gifts of the Holy Spirit. And that gift which was so despised by the faction, never was prized by the body as now. The faction has crumbled and disappeared, and the body has risen in union and strength. And where one destitute of moral worth has left the ranks, four of real worth have joined the ranks of Sabbath-keepers. At the time of the disaffection, when the effort was to break down the *Review*, the church property at the Office was only $700; since, it has increased to $5,000. Then there were but about one thousand paying subscribers, now there are nearly two thousand, besides quite a free list.

"We mourn our lukewarm condition. We have nothing to boast of. But thanks be to God who has given the truth the victory thus far through our Lord Jesus Christ. The truth will triumph. Though those who now profess it be laid aside for their unfaithfulness, God can raise up a faithful army to fight his battles, and wear the victor's crown. But those who have stood the storms of the past will not fall away now. Though many who have not the truth in them sufficient to move them cheerfully to action, may be shaken out, and left behind, yet the faithful ones who have toiled on, groaning, sighing and crying for salvation and deliverance, will go through to the city of God, and share the everlasting rest."

Tent Meetings

Tent operations, as an effective method of spreading the truth, were commenced among us in the summer of 1854. The first meeting of the kind was held in Battle Creek, Mich., June 10 and 11, of that year. These meetings called out large congregations, and gave greater [297] publicity to our views, by means of the oral lectures, and of our publications, which had been greatly multiplied, and were eagerly called for. Since that time tent meetings have been held with great success in New England, New York, Pennsylvania, Ohio, Michigan, Illinois, Wisconsin, Iowa, and Minnesota.

Removal to Michigan

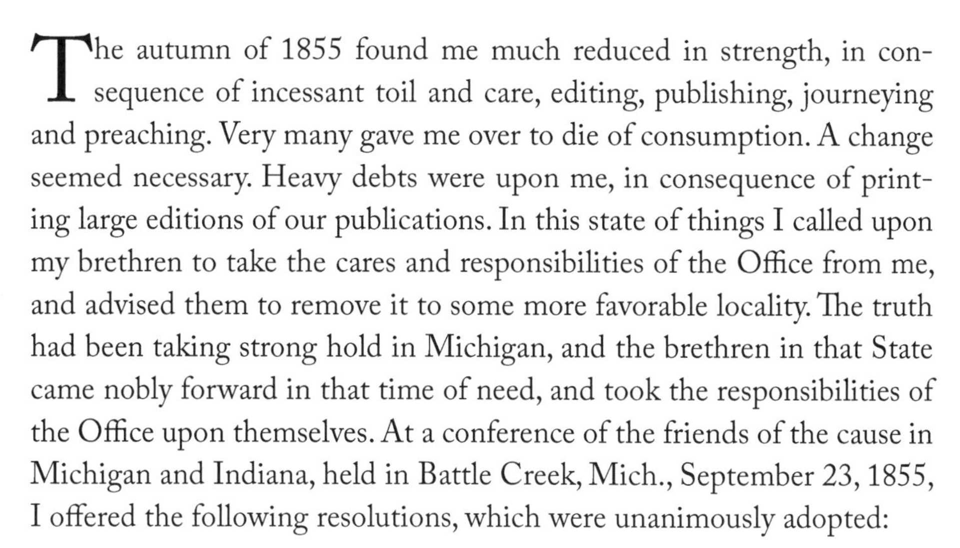

The autumn of 1855 found me much reduced in strength, in consequence of incessant toil and care, editing, publishing, journeying and preaching. Very many gave me over to die of consumption. A change seemed necessary. Heavy debts were upon me, in consequence of printing large editions of our publications. In this state of things I called upon my brethren to take the cares and responsibilities of the Office from me, and advised them to remove it to some more favorable locality. The truth had been taking strong hold in Michigan, and the brethren in that State came nobly forward in that time of need, and took the responsibilities of the Office upon themselves. At a conference of the friends of the cause in Michigan and Indiana, held in Battle Creek, Mich., September 23, 1855, I offered the following resolutions, which were unanimously adopted:

"1. That the Advent Review Office still remain the property of the church.

"2. That the Advent Review Office be removed to Battle Creek, Mich.

"3. That a financial committee of three be chosen, whose duty it shall be to move the Office, and publish the *Advent Review*.

"4. That D.R. Palmer, of Jackson, Henry Lyon and [298] Cyrenius Smith, of Battle Creek, be that Committee."

A building was immediately erected, and steps taken for the removal of the Office.

A General Conference was held at Battle Creek, November 16, 1855, which sanctioned the doings of the conference of September 23, 1855, and elected Uriah Smith resident editor of the *Review*. The last paper published in Rochester, N.Y., was dated October 30, 1855, and its publication was resumed in Battle Creek, December 4, following. The expenses of the new building, and the removal of the Office, were promptly met, and soon the publishing department was in a prosperous condition.

Power Press

The business at the Office increased so rapidly that the hand press soon became entirely inadequate for the work. An appeal was again made to the friends of the cause, this time for means sufficient to purchase a power press. The brethren immediately responded. An Adams' New Patent Power Press was purchased, and the *Review* of July 30, 1857, was the first number printed upon it. A steam engine was soon obtained to run the press. The entire cost of press, engine, and fixtures, was twenty-five hundred dollars, which was soon met by the donations of the brethren.

Publishing Association

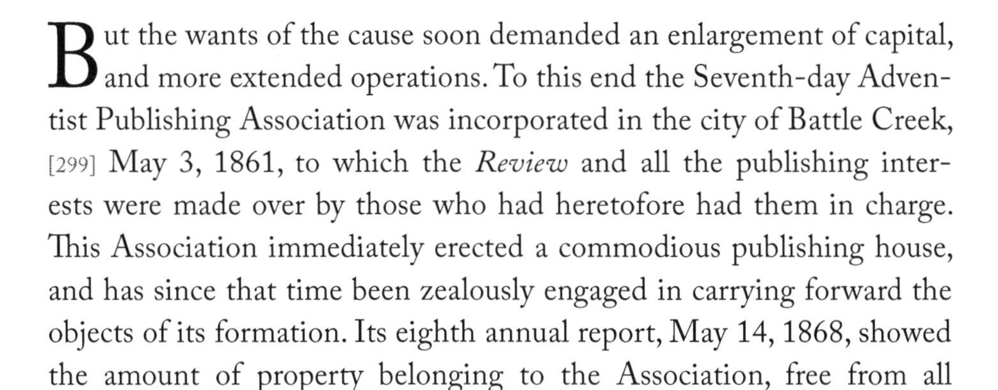

But the wants of the cause soon demanded an enlargement of capital, and more extended operations. To this end the Seventh-day Adventist Publishing Association was incorporated in the city of Battle Creek, [299] May 3, 1861, to which the *Review* and all the publishing interests were made over by those who had heretofore had them in charge. This Association immediately erected a commodious publishing house, and has since that time been zealously engaged in carrying forward the objects of its formation. Its eighth annual report, May 14, 1868, showed the amount of property belonging to the Association, free from all incumbrance, to be $35,996.59.

Organization

The subject of church order had been from time to time set forth in the *Review* since 1850, and the necessity of some simple form of organization had been quite fully discussed. The positions taken upon the subject of Babylon, the burden of the second message, had led many of our people to stand in great fear of organization, however simple. Babylon signifies confusion. God did not design to bring his people out of the confusion of Babylon into the greater confusion of no order nor discipline. This would only be making a bad matter worse. His object in bringing them out from the churches was to discipline and unite them for the last great battle of truth under the third message. It was not ambition to build up a denomination that suggested organization, but the sheer necessities of the case. For a time, the subject of organization waded heavily. But the importance of united action, and some simple form of organization by which we could legally hold our places of worship, and property necessary to efficiently conduct the publishing department, being earnestly plead by those who saw and felt the wants of the cause, our people generally soon overcame their fears, and [300] united fully in the work. It has proved a success.

In our church organization, the General Conference, composed of delegates from the different State Conferences, is our highest authority. This Conference chooses annually, besides the usual officers, a committee of three who have the oversight of the work throughout the entire field.

Next to this are our several State Conferences, composed of the ministers and delegates from all the churches, in their respective States. These Conferences also have a committee of three to take the oversight of the work in their several States during the Conference year.

Next to these stand individual churches, associated together under the following simple covenant: "We, the undersigned, hereby associate ourselves together as a church, taking the name Seventh-day Adventists, covenanting to keep the commandments of God, and faith of Jesus." The officers of the church are local elders, deacons, and clerk.

Systematic Benevolence

In the early stage of the cause, our people had no system upon which to act in the support of ministers. Those who were disposed to give anything, gave what they chose. For a time our ministers were quite well sustained, by a few liberal souls, while the majority excused themselves from doing anything. Ere long, it became evident that these liberal ones were becoming weary of this inequality, and they began to withhold their support. Hence, in the winter of 1858-9, some of our most efficient laborers were contemplating leaving [301] the gospel-field to labor with their hands for the support of their families.

In this state of things, feeling that something must be done, I finally prepared an address on the subject of Systematic benevolence, for the church in Battle Creek. This address was adopted, and published in the *Review* of Feb. 3, 1859, as an appeal from that church to the churches and brethren in Michigan. This system is based on 1 Corinthians 16:2: "Upon the first day of the week, let every one of you lay by him in store, as God hath prospered him, that there be no gatherings when I come," and, as now matured, suggests to all believers who are enjoying common prosperity, 1. That they give at the rate of two cents each week upon every one hundred dollars worth of property which they possess. 2. That they give a personal donation, each week, of from one to twenty-five cents, or more, according to their ability. The object of this second suggestion is to embrace those who have ability to earn, but have little or no property. The necessity and equality of the system are plead before all; yet all are left to assess their own property, and give, in the love and fear of God, according to their prosperity. Widows, the aged, and the infirm, who are in straitened circumstances, are excused. It is not a system of compulsion, but, as carried out among us, is Systematic Benevolence. While all are entreated to act their part in this work, with feelings of cheerful benevolence, none are compelled.

For a time this system received considerable opposition; but when fully explained, it was seen to be a perfect system of equality. The poor who had but a very few hundred dollars, were called upon by this system for so trifling a sum that they were the last to object to it; and the wealthy were certainly able to pay [302] the small percentage from their abundance. This system is generally adopted by our people everywhere, and affords a liberal support to our ministers, leaving them free to devote themselves entirely to the work of the ministry.

Glance at the Past

As we look back upon the Advent movement, with its joyful expectations and bitter disappointments, its prosperity and adversity, its triumphant victories and its trials, it appears just like the work of God in separating a people from the world, to purify, make white, and try, and thus make them ready for the coming of their Lord. Have Adventists been disappointed? So were the Israelites, in not immediately entering Canaan, and the disciples, as Jesus died upon the cross. Have the faith and patience of Adventists been tried? So were the faith and patience of the Israelites tried in their term of forty years' wandering in the wilderness. And that of the disciples was severely tested in the unexpected death of their beloved Teacher. Have but comparatively few of the once happy expectants of the King of glory held fast their faith and hope? And have many cast away their confidence in this work and drawn back to perdition? Caleb and Joshua alone, of the six hundred thousand male adults that left Egypt, entered the goodly land. And what of the chosen twelve in the hour of our Lord's apprehension? "Then all the disciples forsook him and fled." Matthew 26:56.

God has never been able to make anything very great or very good of man. It has been his plan to prove his people in every age, to test their faith and patience. This has been for the good of man and the glory of his [303] name. It was necessary that such noble characters as Noah, Abraham, Job, and Daniel, should suffer the severest tests. And how unlike the work of God in all past time, had the many thousands of Adventists triumphantly entered the kingdom at the point of expectation, with hardly a single trial. "Blessed is the man that endureth temptation; for when he is tried, he shall receive the crown of life." James 1:12. This is God's plan. First the cross and the trial, then the crown of unfading glory. As I "call to remembrance the former days," touching the Advent movement, and see its adaptation to the wants of the people, and God's great plan of saving men, my soul says, "He hath done all things well."

It was necessary, in order that the first message should arouse the people and separate those who should receive it from the spirit of the world, that it should not only relate to the fearful realities of the Judgment, but also to the period when it might be expected. "Fear God, and give glory to him, for the hour of his Judgment is come." The proclamation of the time was a part of God's plan. This brought the coming of the Lord very near. This was right. This was necessary to move the people. And when the time passed, instead of calling the attention of believers to some period in the future to which they might look for the coming of the Lord, the Spirit of God sweetly and powerfully applied to their consecrated minds and hearts, such passages as, "Cast not away, therefore, your confidence, which hath great recompense of reward. For ye have need of patience, that, after ye have done the will of God, ye might receive the promise. For yet a little while, and He that shall come will come, and will not tarry." [304]

How long this little while would be, no one knew. It was not best that any one should know when it would terminate. And more, it was God's plan that this should be known; but that they should move along through the period of the patience of the saints, Revelation 14:12, up to the coming of the Lord, ever keeping that event just before them. Those who have taught the three messages the past twenty years, have all the way presented the coming of Christ at hand. This has been as God designed. And those who would murmur at God's ministers for this, murmur against the providence of God.

It is painful to hear those who have their faces set toward Egypt, complain that the message was not properly preached to them. The coming of the Lord was presented too near. And that if they had understood the matter, they should have laid their plans for the future differently, and now their property might be double its present value. These murmur against the direct providence of God. The coming of the Lord was brought very near in 1844, to rid men of the love of this world, that they might share the love of the Father, and seek a preparation for the coming of his Son.

They cannot have both. "If any man love the world, the love of the Father is not in him." 1 John 2:15. And it was designed that the coming of Christ should be viewed near by believers, every step of the way from the disappointment in 1844 to the gates of the golden city, to keep them from the love of this world.

An energetic Advent minister, on visiting the believers at Roxbury, Mass., being asked, "What is your message now, Bro. B.?" answered, "Come out of her my people." Soon after the passing of the time he visited [305] that people again, and in reply to the inquiry, "What is your message now, Bro. B.?" made the apt and appropriate reply, "*Stay* out of her my people." So Heaven designed that the coming of Christ should be brought very near to tear from men the love of this world, and that in their faith they should ever hold his coming just before them all the way till faith should be lost in the blazing glories of the coming of the Son of man. If we keep the coming of Jesus ever near, and live consistently with such a faith, keeping the commandments of God and the faith of Jesus, we may be saved. But remove the coming of the Lord to the distant future, become imbued with the love and spirit of this world, and remain in such a state, and perdition is certain. Let the painful history of the past relative to those who have said in their hearts, "My Lord delayeth his coming," have apostatized and have been scattered to the world and to Satan, be a warning to all to be ever "looking for and hasting unto the coming of the day of God."

When the warning voice of the first angel was first heard, it found the nominal churches asleep upon the subject of the second advent, dreaming of the world's conversion. But the truth was clear, and, in the hands of devoted men, was powerful. Every where the message was proclaimed it produced general conviction. The Scriptures were searched as never before; a great revolution in religious belief took place in a few short years; and at least fifty thousand in America alone, became decided believers. The prophetic times in connection with that message served their purpose, and terminated with that message. The second and third are not time messages. That aroused men in view of the [306] fast approaching Judgment. These tell them what they must do to be saved. And it has been Satan's grand object to institute numerous time movements among certain Adventists since 1844, to contravene this work of preparation. The passing of each time has weakened the faith of believers, and has caused unbelievers to look upon Adventists with increasing disgust. And confusion and irreligion have resulted from these spurious time movements everywhere they have reached.

The title page of this work calls attention to the great Advent movement as illustrated by the three angels of Revelation 14. The truth and work of God in this movement, commencing with the labors of William Miller, and reaching to the close of probation, is illustrated by these three angels. The first was a time message, and related to the Judgment. The second described the condition of corrupted Christianity. The third is a solemn warning relative to what men may not do, and what they must do, in order to be saved at the coming of Christ. These angels illustrate the three great divisions of the genuine movement. They do not illustrate the numerous time movements which have appeared since 1844; therefore, to say the very least, these movements were not from Heaven.

Seventh-day Adventists hold fast the great Advent movement, hence have use for the messages. They explain them in their sermons, treat upon them in their books, and give them a place with the other prophetic symbols upon their charts. They cannot spare these links in the golden chain of truth, that connect the past with the present and future, and show a beautiful harmony in the great whole.

Timeists, and in fact all Adventists who do not acknowledge the special providence of God in the work [307] of William Miller and his associates, in 1843 and 1844, have no use for the three angels' messages. They do not introduce them into their sermons and printed expositions of prophecy, unless it be to oppose us. They find no place for them among the other prophetic symbols upon their charts. Indeed, they treat them with all that neglect that would be justifiable, were they a wicked interpolation by men who sought to corrupt the sacred Scriptures. And no reason can be given why these men should pursue their fanatical course in relation to definite time, and other fancies not symbolized by the three angels, and therefore no part of the great movement, and resist the truth of God for this time, unless it be that in consequence of not receiving and retaining the love of the truth of the fulfillment of prophecy in the Advent movement, God has given them over to strong delusions. I repeat it. The three messages symbolize the three parts of the genuine movement. That which has appeared not symbolized by the three angels, though it be branded "Adventism," is spurious.

Again, the sanctuary was the heart of the typical system. It was the repository of the ark of God, in which ark his law was deposited. By this law the people had the knowledge of sin. It was also the place where they, in figure, found pardon for their sins through the offerings there made. This entire system, with its great center, the sanctuary, was but the shadow of the realities of the present system of salvation. The shadow was on earth; the reality is in Heaven. The facts are stated by the apostle in few words: "We have such an High Priest, who is set on the right hand of the throne of the Majesty in the heavens; a minister of the sanctuary, and of the true tabernacle, which the Lord pitched, and not man." Hebrews 8:1, 2. The sanctuary of the new [308] which is in Heaven, is the great heart of the plan of redemption. There Christ offers his blood for the sins of men. In the real tabernacle there are two holies, if there were two in the shadow. In the holiest is the ark of God, containing the ten precepts of his law, if they were in the holiest of the shadow. Here is a theme worthy the attention of all Christians. And it is one in which they should feel the deepest interest, as each has a case of eternal consequence pending there.

The work of cleansing this sanctuary, at the close of the 2300 days, is a subject which should materially interest all Adventists. It pertains to the confession, pardon, and blotting out of sins. A correct and intelligent faith sees the adorable Redeemer in the most holy of the true tabernacle, offering his blood before the mercy seat for the sins of those who have broken the law of God beneath it in the ark. True faith reaches within the second vail, where Jesus and the ark of God are seen. There, by the law we have the knowledge of sin, and through the blood of Jesus we may find pardon, and share eternal redemption. The subject of the cleansing of this sanctuary, then, is now of most thrilling interest, especially to all Adventists. It is the key to the great Advent movement, making all plain. Without it the movement is inexplicable.

Seventh-day Adventists dwell upon this subject with great delight. It opens to them the ark of God, in which is seen the ten precepts of his law. They keep them. It presents Jesus before the mercy-seat, ready to plead the cause of sinners, who in the spirit of penitence and confession, go to him for help. They love and seek to obey him, so that it is said of them, "Here are they keep the commandments of God, and the faith of Jesus." They treat upon the subject of the [309] sanctuary in their sermons and books, and find a place for it among the symbols of prophecy upon their charts. Seventh-day Adventists cannot spare the subject of the sanctuary, as it is the great center around which all revealed truth relative to salvation clusters, and contributes more toward defining their present position, than any other.

But nominal Adventists treat the subject as one of no interest or importance to them. Having in their own hearts abolished the ten commandments, they have no use for the ark of God, and cast it aside as an antiquated and unfashionable piece of furniture. Their sermons, and their printed essays and expositions, do not refer to the cleansing of the heavenly sanctuary, unless it be to oppose the views of Seventh-day Adventists, and ridicule them, and ignorantly and contemptuously talk of Heaven being dirty, and needing cleansing. And as in the case of the three angels, you do not find the sanctuary represented upon their prophetic charts.

But these we value above all earthly good, and make them prominent in all our religious teachings, because the truth of God for this time, or present truth, is in them. And for this reason those who "call evil good, and good evil; that put darkness for light, and light for darkness; that put bitter for sweet, and sweet for bitter," cast this subject from them, as unworthy of their notice, unless it be to oppose, denounce and ridicule.

The Tongue of Slander

During the rise and progress of the third message, the tongue of slander has not been silent. Men will use the best arguments they have. When unable from [310] the Bible to meet the positions of those who teach unpopular truth, some will resort to slander as the next best argument. The case is sometimes felt to be urgent and even desperate. Truth is mighty. The people will hear, and some will obey. These are frequently the best members of the various religious bodies. Efforts at argument from the Bible, in opposition, fail to silence the voice of truth, and in some cases turn the minds of many of the people to the truth. Something must be done. And it is painful to record, that in many cases professed ministers of Jesus Christ deal in smut and blacking, and stoop to invent and repeat the vilest slanders to prejudice the people against those who plead for the truth of God.

"There are hundreds of ministers in the United States who, if disturbed in their quiet possession of the ears of the people, by the proclamation of the unpopular truths of the third message in their vicinity, would take delight in repeating the old threadbare falsehoods concerning ascension robes, and the like, to cut off the influence of the servant of God.

"In almost every place where our ministers give discourses upon the second coming of Christ, and the necessary preparation for that event, they have to labor against the prejudices of the people, caused by reports of the inconsistencies of Adventists; one of which is, that at a point of expectation in the past, many of them did prepare robes of white linen, and put them on ready to ascend and meet their coming Lord.

"While all sane persons, who have any knowledge of what the holy Scriptures do teach of the necessary preparation to meet the Lord as he shall descend from Heaven, will agree that to prepare a literal white robe made of cloth as a fitting preparation for the transit [311] from earth to Heaven, from mortality to immortality, must be an indication of downright insanity, none will see in such an act evidences of criminality.

"But I do not believe that anything of the kind ever occurred. I have been actively engaged in the proclamation of the doctrine of the second advent for more than twenty-five years, and have traveled and preached in Maine, New Hampshire, Vermont, Massachusetts, Connecticut, Rhode Island, New York, Ohio, Michigan, Illinois, Wisconsin, Iowa, and Canada, and have not met a person who has seen an Adventist thus attired, or one that was able to give better proofs that anything of the kind ever did occur than vague reports. I have never found the place where the thing occurred. It was always in the next town, county, or State.

"Again, reports in relation to this matter, and slanders of a similar nature, have a hundred times been denied in Second-Advent periodicals, and proofs have been called for of the truthfulness of these statements. No one has been able to produce the proofs. But still the tongue of slander takes delight in repeating the old threadbare falsehood. Elders Loughborough and Strong met it at Orange, Mich., in January, 1868, and Elder V. Cornell met the same at H. Johnstown, Mich., a few weeks later. In both cases the miserable untruth was declared from the pulpit by professed ministers of Jesus Christ.

"The people, generally, credit the statements of these ministers, and conclude that the story of ascension robes is true. Especially do those who are not favorable to Second-Advent views enjoy this sort of clerical slander. And the fact that our people are not always prepared to meet it, is the reason why I have felt called upon to notice the matter at this time.

"In 1847, while on our passage in a steamboat from [312] Portland, Me., to Boston, Mass., Mrs W. was speaking to those around her in the ladies' cabin, of the fearful storm we encountered in a recent passage between these two cities. She spoke of the importance of being always prepared for the close of our probation, either at death, or at the coming of Christ. A lady near her replied:

"'That is the way the Millerites talk. I mean to have a jolly good time before I become a long-faced Christian. The Millerites are the most deluded set on earth. On the day they were expecting Christ to come, companies in different places put on their ascension robes, and went into graveyards, and upon the tops of houses and high hills, and there remained, praying and singing till the time passed by.'

"Mrs W. then inquired of the lady if she saw any of these persons thus attired. She answered:

"'No, I did not see them myself, but a friend who saw them told me. And the fact is so well understood everywhere, that I believe it as much as though I saw it myself.'

"At this point another lady, feeling that the testimony of the first should not be questioned, stated:

"'It is of no use to deny that the Millerites did put on ascension robes, for they did it in towns all around where I live.'

"Mrs. W. asked this lady if she saw them with their robes on. She replied:

"'No, I did not see them, as they were not in my immediate neighborhood. But it was commonly reported, and generally believed, that they did make ascension robes and put them on.'

"By this time strong feelings were evidently controlling these two ladies, because Mrs. W. did not seem to credit what they said against the Millerites. And the [313] first in the conversation stated with emotions of excitement and passion:

"'I know it was so. I fully believe the testimony of those who have told me these things. I believe what my friends have told me about those fanatical Millerites, the same as though I saw it myself.'

"Mrs. W. then inquired of her for the names of some persons who had figured in this fanatical movement. She stated if the putting on of ascension robes was so very common, certainly she could give the names of some. To this she replied:

"'Certainly I can give you names. There were the twin Harmon girls in Portland. My friends told me that they saw their robes, and saw them going out to the graveyard with them on. Since the time has passed, they have become infidels.

"A school-mate of Mrs. W., who had never been an Adventist, was in that cabin, and had watched the conversation with mirthful interest. She had been acquainted with the Harmon girls during the entire period of their Second-Advent experience. She could no longer restrain her feelings, and broke out in a laughing mood, as she pointed to Mrs. W.:

"'This is one of those twin Harmon girls. I have known them always, and know that this report of their making and wearing ascension robes is all a lie. I never was a Millerite, yet I do not believe that anything of the kind ever took place.'

"The storm that was fast arising in that cabin suddenly abated, and there followed a great calm. Mrs. W. then stated that all the stories about ascension robes were probably as destitute of truth as this one concerning the twin Harmon girls. [314]

"Elder Josiah Litch, lately editor of the *Advent Herald*, Boston, in his history of the rise and progress of Adventism, makes the following statement:

"'Those periods came and passed with no unusual occurrence. As soon as they had gone by, a flood of scoffing, reviling and persecution burst forth, not from the infidel world so much, but from the professed friends of the Saviour; the most idle and foolish stories of ascension robes, and going out into the graveyards to watch, going to the tops of houses, etc., etc. These were repeated again and again, both from pulpit and press, until the public were, many of them, at least, almost persuaded to believe them true.

"'How, or where they originated, except in willful falsehood, we cannot devise. Some of the reports of that character, we happen to know, originated with professed ministers of the gospel, who gave date and place, when there was not a word of truth in the whole story. Others must have originated in a similar way.'"

The foregoing, relative to the ascension robes, was given in the *Review and Herald*, April 14, 1868. The article closed with the following paragraph: "Fifty dollars reward is offered to any person who will present unquestionable proofs of the truthfulness of the statements, that believers in the second advent of Christ, on the day of expectation, did put on ascension robes. Those who can produce such proofs, are requested to forward them immediately to the writer, at Greenville, Montcalm County, Mich., and receive fifty dollars by return mail."

Up to this date, July 13, 1868, no one has responded in the way of furnishing proofs that anything of the kind ever took place. Why this silence on the part of our friends, as well as our enemies, if there be [315] the least semblance of truth in the statement upon this subject, gravely made by ministers in the desk as a part of the gospel they preach? If proofs exist, why can we not have them? The reader should regard these statements about ascension robes, which opposing clergymen have the credit of repeating, more than any other class, as malicious slanders, until he has reliable proofs that something of the kind occurred.

The *Review and Herald*, May 20, 1868, has the following from Eld. J.H. Waggoner, which fairly represents this matter of ascension robes:

"Bro. White's remarks on the falsehoods circulated on the above subject, remind me of an incident that transpired some years since in Wisconsin. A Mr. H., an M.E. preacher, deriding the Adventists, said: 'It is a fact that they prepared and put on ascension robes in 1844.' At the close of his remarks I stated that I was very anxious to learn about the facts on that subject, and asked him to give particulars, as to where, by whom, etc. He said that it was not always convenient to give the evidence on matters which had transpired years in the past, and he could not then comply with the request. I turned to the congregation and said:

"'He has said it is a fact. Now if he does not know it to be a fact, he has made a false statement. If he knows it to be a fact, he can procure the evidence of the fact. As he has an appointment here four weeks from to-day, I give notice that I will be here at that time to get his statement, as that will give him time to get the information. If it occurred *anywhere*, it will be easy to prove it in that locality. I hope the people will all be here to get the facts he may present.'

"Being thus pressed to make good his assertion, and having the expectation of the people raised on it, he saw [316] the necessity of doing something, and promptly confessed that he knew nothing about it, but had heard such a report!

"The way the report ran was well illustrated by the following case: A Bro. T., who had lived and labored in Buffalo, and attended the Advent meetings there, was working in Erie in the fall of 1844. After the set day passed, the report spread in Erie that the Adventists in Buffalo put on ascension robes. He was so grieved over their folly, and troubled in his mind, that he determined to visit his friends in Buffalo and talk with them about it. Landing at Buffalo, he met an acquaintance, not an Adventist, who did not know where he came from. He asked if any of the Adventists in Buffalo had put on ascension robes. 'No,' said his friend, 'but they all did in Erie!' A smile by Bro. T. led to an explanation. And so it was everywhere. Everybody *knew* it was so — the *place* where it occurred could not be found."

The part which the Spirit of God has led Mrs. W. to act in close connection with the cause of present truth, has called forth against her a spirit of persecution. The apostle says, "Let all bitterness, and wrath, and anger, and clamour, and evil speaking, be put away from you, with all malice." Ephesians 4:31. But these have been employed against her by the professed followers of Jesus Christ, with the object to crush her testimony and destroy her influence. In this cruel work, with some the tongue of slander has been "set on fire of hell."

The work of the Lord through her has been to encourage the weak, comfort the desponding, exalt the standard of morality and true piety, and reprove sin in all its forms. And why should not the dragon rage? Why may we not expect to see those who are imbued [317] with the spirit of the father of lies, delighting themselves in the most slanderous falsehoods against one who may be engaged in such a work? Such has ever been the work of Satan in all past time, and ever will be, till he is bound. And he has ever found, and ever will find, willing tools to do his work in opposition to the work of God. And these are more frequently found among ministers than any other class. The following from Eld. M.E. Cornell, which occurred on his route from Battle Creek to Ionia, will illustrate the wicked course of some of those who to be called "Reverend:"

"While on the cars, a circumstance occurred which shows the necessity of Bro. White's article on Clerical Slander. A Presbyterian minister from Gratiot county was making special efforts to attract attention to himself by his endeavors to amuse the passengers. Among other things, he stated that Mrs. White had a vision at St. Louis, Gratiot Co., Mich., that she was to leave her husband and take another man; that a man might have as many wives as he chose. He then made some, not very refined, remarks and witticisms, which excited laughter in some, but disgust in the pure-minded. In the cars were several clergymen, and many intelligent ladies and gentlemen from several different States. Of course we could not let such a base slander pass, and a wrong impression go to so many different places; we therefore watched for a chance to correct the misstatement.

"An intelligent Jew soon entered into conversation with him, and turned the tables on him by relating an old slander against Martin Luther, that he had a child by his own daughter, etc. The minister was aroused. Said he, 'It is a base slander, invented by his enemies. [318] There is not a particle of proof of any such thing.' He then came down upon the Jew with the most cutting reproof for making such a statement from hearsay evidence. Now our time had come. The measure he had meted to others had been immediately measured to him again.

"We then stated to the passengers that we had known Eld. E. White and his wife for sixteen years, and that the statement made by the clergyman was an unmitigated slander. First, Mrs. White never had a vision in Gratiot county; and second, she never had a vision, anywhere, of any such nature as had been stated. We then challenged him to stop at Owasso, with any of his friends as witnesses, and we would secure for him *one thousand dollars*, on the condition that he should make good his statement. We urged him to the task with such eagerness, that all in the car appeared to be convinced that he had uttered a slander. He was embarrassed, and said faintly, 'I heard so!'

"An intelligent Infidel, from Dearborn, Mich., then rose up, and made some very pointed remarks on hearsay evidence and condemning a whole body of people, because of a story about some one of their number. 'Shall I,' said he, 'call the Methodists a set of cut-throats, because several of their preachers are now in our penitentiary? Shall I condemn all ministers, because one in our town ran away with Bro. M's wife, last week?' By this time, the tide was turned completely. Several of the passengers expressed themselves very freely to me, and were anxious to know more about it." — *Advent Review for April* 28, 1868.

I do not believe that all ministers who differ with us in faith and practice are alike guilty with this man. No decent man, in or out of the ministry, would take [319] pleasure in uttering such vile slander before a car full of ladies and gentlemen, however much he might feel opposed to the religious sentiments of Seventh-day Adventists. I believe there are God-fearing ministers in all the churches who would no sooner bear false witness of a slanderous character against those who are devoting their lives to the cause of Christ, than they would have the same done to themselves. But while these may be few and far between, the experience of a quarter of a century in teaching unpopular truth has taught me that, where personal interest is concerned, there are but very few ministers who will not stoop to the repetition of the vilest slanders, to injure the influence of those who get the ears of the people, if they differ with them. But in reference to the statements of Eld. Cornell, I will say:

1. Mrs. W. never was at St. Louis, Gratiot County, Michigan.

2. She never had a vision in Gratiot County.

3. Her standard of morality ever has been the ten commandments.

4. Her views, her public and private labors, her books and oral teachings, have ever been in strict harmony with the law of God, the highest standard of morality on earth.

5. She has ever borne the most decided testimony against any departure from the principles guarded by the ten commandments.

6. She has borne a public testimony for twenty-five years, in the several States of Maine, New Hampshire, Vermont, Massachusetts, Connecticut, Rhode Island, New York, Pennsylvania, Ohio, Michigan, Illinois, Wisconsin, Iowa, and in Canada. She has, during this [320] time, written books amounting to more than twenty-one hundred pages, besides many articles for several periodicals. And all who are acquainted with her teach-

ings know that any statement that they are not in strict harmony with God's standard of morality, is a slanderous untruth. Then let her enemies point to one impure sentence in all her writings, or prove that in her religious teachings she has uttered one unchaste word, or cease their slanderous persecution of a self-sacrificing Christian woman.

But I do not indulge the thought that whatever may be said to show the falsity of statements concerning ascension robes, and the views of Mrs. W., will silence the tongue of slander. No. These ministers know the influence they have over us in this respect. Regardless of justice and truth, they will doubtless continue to do this scandalous work, wherever the glorious doctrine of the coming of Jesus shall be proclaimed. We can only expose their sin in this thing, and disabuse honest minds.

The dragon is wroth with those who keep the commandments of God and have the testimony of Jesus Christ. The Devil will use any willing tool to slander and abuse the followers of Jesus Christ. Scoffers will scoff, and liars will lie, whether they bear the title of Reverend, or be patrons of brothels. And the higher the position, the greater the criminality. But for all these things will God bring them into Judgment. Those who fear God and keep his commandments, and suffer reproach for the sake of Christ and the truth, will have their reward. Those who employ the vile tongue of slander against them, in order to crush their influence and keep others from obeying the commandments [321] that they may live, will perish in all their villainy. They, also, will have their reward. The True Witness has spoken relative to the present controversy and the final destiny of both classes of actors, as recorded by the prophet John.

First Class. "Blessed are they that do his commandments, that they may have right to the tree of life, and may enter in through the gates into the city." Revelation 22:14. These are doing right. Although they suffer for well doing, all the hate and slander that wicked men and demons can invent, their reward is the holy city and the tree of life.

Second Class. "For without are dogs, and sorcerers, and whoremongers, and murderers, and idolaters, and whosoever loveth and maketh a lie." Verse 15. These are commandment-breakers, and commandment-haters, and haters of those who keep the commandments of God. They are also noted for two things in particular, namely, loving and making lies. The application of these two items is so natural to these reports of ascension robes and the like, that no further comment is needed. They make lies, and love to publish them from the pulpit and the religious press. But, thank God, in the Judgment they are without. The happiness of those who love God and keep his commandments is then no more to be marred by their poisonous influence. Would God that they would repent of, and forsake, their wicked course, and live, and finally share the holy city and the tree of life. But as they will not do this work, that they may share that reward, their corrupting influence must be borne with Christian patience and fortitude while the controversy lasts. [322]

Present Position and Work

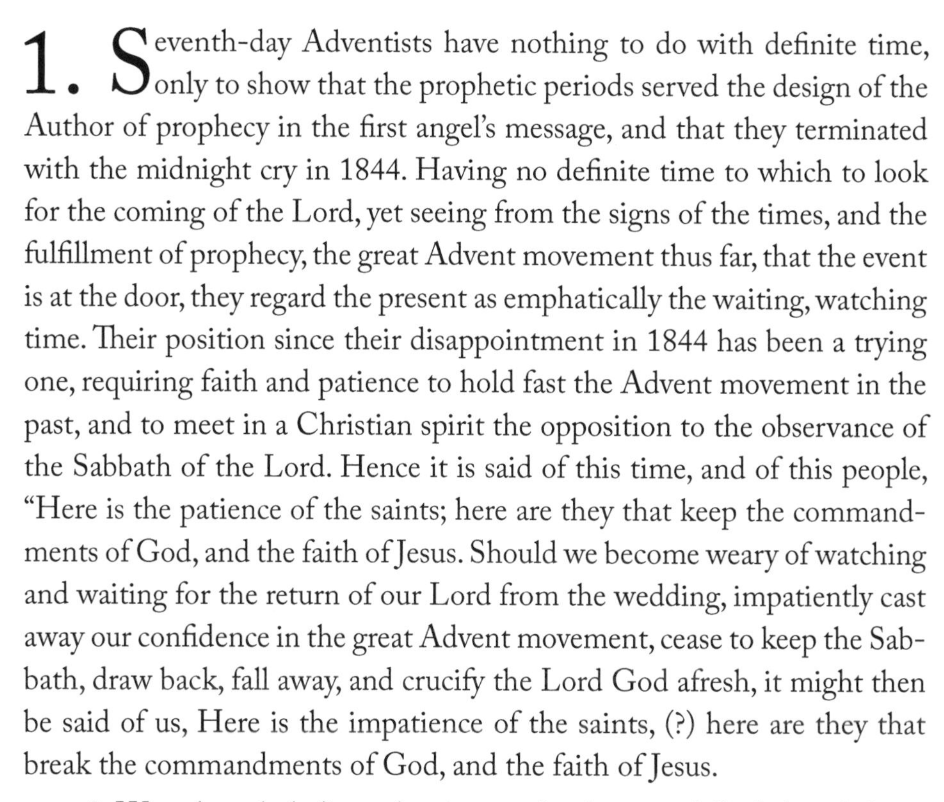

1. Seventh-day Adventists have nothing to do with definite time, only to show that the prophetic periods served the design of the Author of prophecy in the first angel's message, and that they terminated with the midnight cry in 1844. Having no definite time to which to look for the coming of the Lord, yet seeing from the signs of the times, and the fulfillment of prophecy, the great Advent movement thus far, that the event is at the door, they regard the present as emphatically the waiting, watching time. Their position since their disappointment in 1844 has been a trying one, requiring faith and patience to hold fast the Advent movement in the past, and to meet in a Christian spirit the opposition to the observance of the Sabbath of the Lord. Hence it is said of this time, and of this people, "Here is the patience of the saints; here are they that keep the commandments of God, and the faith of Jesus. Should we become weary of watching and waiting for the return of our Lord from the wedding, impatiently cast away our confidence in the great Advent movement, cease to keep the Sabbath, draw back, fall away, and crucify the Lord God afresh, it might then be said of us, Here is the impatience of the saints, (?) here are they that break the commandments of God, and the faith of Jesus.

2. We solemnly believe that it was the design of God that definite time should be proclaimed, and that the 2300 days reached to the Judgment, referred to in the words of the first angel, "Fear God and give glory to him, for the hour of his Judgment is come." In the great Judgment of mankind there are two distinct parts; first, the investigative; second, the executive. [323] The investigative Judgment takes place prior to the second advent, and the resurrection of the just, that it may be known who are worthy of the first resurrection. Those who have part in that resurrection are first ascertained to be "blessed and holy." Revelation 20:6. The executive Judgment, both in the reward of the righteous, and the punishment of the wicked, will be at the close of the great day of Judgment.

The grandeur of the sitting of the great court of heaven in the investigative Judgment is described by the prophet thus: "I beheld till the thrones were cast down, and the Ancient of days did sit, whose garment was white as snow, and the hair of his head like the pure wool; his throne was like the fiery flame, and his wheels as burning fire. A fiery stream issued and came forth from before him; thousand thousands ministered unto him and ten thousand times ten thousand stood before him. The Judgment was set, and the books were opened. I saw in the night visions, and behold, one like the Son of man came with the clouds of heaven, and came to the Ancient of days, and they brought him near before him. And there was given him dominion, and glory, and a kingdom." Daniel 7:9, 10, 13, 14.

The best authorities give the words "cast down" just the opposite meaning. They render them "set up," or "established." Thus, Adam Clarke says: "*The thrones were cast down*] might be translated *erected*; so the Vulgate, *positi sunt*, and so all the versions." Dr. Hales, in his "Sacred Chronology," Vol. 2, p.505, renders Daniel 7:9, thus: "I beheld till the thrones were erected, and the Ancient of days sat," etc. The Douay Version reads, "were placed;" and so Bernard, and Boothroyd and Wintle in the Cottage Bible. Matthew Henry in his Exposition renders it "set [324] up." Of the original Hebrew word, Gesenius, in his Lexicon says, "*R'mah*, (1.) To cast, to throw, Daniel 3:20, 21, 24; 6:17. (2.) To set, to place, *e.g.*, thrones. Daniel 7:9; comp. Revelation 4:2." The term used by the Septuagint is, which literally rendered, according to Liddell and Scott, would be, "the thrones were set." Other authorities might be given. The Judgment scene here introduced opens with,

1st. The Judgment of thrones and the sitting in Judgment of the great God, amid the brightness of that glory, feebly represented by fire and flame, accompanied by the millions of his attendants.

2nd. The opening of the life-records of men, from which they are to be judged.

3rd. The Son of man approaches the Ancient of days, attended by multitudes of angels, here represented by the clouds of heaven, to receive dominion, glory, and a kingdom. This does not represent the second appearing of Christ to this world, unless it can be shown that the Ancient of days is here.

3. Seventh-day Adventists believe in the perpetuity of spiritual gifts. They believe that the spirit of prophecy was designed to be with the people of God in all ages, and that dreams and visions are a medium through which God has spoken to his people in past time, and through which he will speak, till faith is lost in sight. "If there be a prophet among you, I, the Lord, will make myself known unto him in a vision, and will speak unto him in a dream." Numbers 12:6.

They find no prophecy in the Old Testament pointing to the opening of the Christian age as the time for spiritual gifts to be removed from the people of God, and no declaration in the New Testament that the church would not need them, and that therefore they [325] were about to cease. No, nothing of this kind appears upon the sacred page. But we hear the prophet of God say, "And it shall come to pass afterward, that I will pour out my Spirit upon all flesh; and your sons and your daughters shall prophesy, your old men shall dream dreams, your young men shall see visions. And also upon the servants and upon the handmaids in those days will I pour out my Spirit. And I will shew wonders in the heavens and in the earth, blood, and fire, and pillars of smoke. The sun shall be turned into darkness, and the moon into blood, before the great and the terrible day of the Lord come. And it shall come to pass that whosoever shall call on the name of the Lord shall be delivered; for in Mount Zion and in Jerusalem shall be deliverance, as the Lord hath said, and in the remnant whom the Lord shall call." Joel 2:28-32.

Notice, first, that the prophet points to the last days, as quoted by Peter. Acts 2:16-20. There can be no days later than the last, a period in which these things will be removed from the church; and, second, that he also points to signs and wonders in the heavens, and in the earth, in the sun and in the moon, to appear in connection with the manifestation of the spirit of prophecy. Third, he mentions the deliverance of those who call on the name of the Lord. This naturally applies to the deliverance of God's people who will cry to him day and night in the time of trouble. Luke 18; Daniel 12. They will be delivered, according to the words of the prophet. And may not the "remnant" here mentioned be the same spoken of in Revelation 12:17? "And the dragon was wroth with the woman, and went to make war with the remnant of her seed, which keep the commandments [326] of God, and have the testimony of Jesus Christ."

The woman is a symbol of the church, and the remnant of the church represents the Christians of the last generation of men living just prior to the second advent. The dragon makes war on these for keeping the commandments of God, Sabbath and all, and having the testimony of Jesus Christ, which according to the inspired definition of chap. 19:10, "is the spirit of prophecy." Here, then, are the causes of the dragon's warfare upon the remnant. They teach the observance of the ten commandments, and the revival of the gifts, and acknowledge the gift of prophecy among them. When the Devil got one foot upon the fourth commandment, and the other upon the gifts planted in the Christian church by Jesus Christ, then his satanic majesty was filled with revengeful delight. But when the remnant, whom God designs to fit for translation to Heaven without seeing death, "ask for the old paths, where is the good way, and walk therein," then the dragon is wroth, and makes war on them.

The true spirit of the dragonic host, which is already being somewhat developed, is vividly described in Isaiah 30:8-13, as being manifested just prior to the sudden destruction of those who hate the pure testimony, and love smooth and deceitful things.

"Now go, write it before them in a table, and note it in a book, that it may be for the time to come forever and ever [margin, 'the latter day']; that this is a rebellious people, lying children, children that will not hear the law of the Lord; which say to the seers, See not; and to the prophets, Prophesy not unto us right things, speak unto us smooth things, prophesy deceits; get you out of the way, turn aside out of the path, cause [327] the Holy One of Israel to cease from before us. Wherefore thus saith the Holy One of Israel, Because ye despise this word, and trust in oppression and perverseness, and stay thereon: therefore this iniquity shall be to you as a breach ready to fall, swelling out in a high wall whose breaking cometh suddenly at an instant."

Mark this: In "the latter day" men will not hear the law of the Lord, the commandments of God; and they will say to the seers, those who have the spirit of prophecy, See not. They will receive neither. They war against both. See also Mark 16:15-20; Matthew 28:18-20; Ephesians 4:4-13; 1 Corinthians 12:1, 28; 13:8-12; 1:4-8; Revelation 19:10; 1 Thessalonians 5; Matthew 7:15-20; Isaiah 8:19, 20; Jeremiah 14:14; 23:16, 17; 8:10, 11; 5:30, 31. For a full exposition of the subject of the perpetuity of spiritual gifts, as held by Seventh-day Adventists, see their works upon the subject.

But it is objected that since the volume of inspiration was completed, spiritual gifts have not been needed. Who knows this to be the case? The disciples of Jesus had the law and the prophets, yet needed the manifestations of the gifts of the Holy Spirit. We have both Testaments, and who knows that we do not also need the gifts of the Spirit of God?

The great design of the sacred Scriptures was to give man a perfect rule of faith and practice. God purposed that his people should follow this rule and by it develop characters perfect before him. Said Paul to Timothy, "Thou hast known the holy Scriptures which are able to make thee wise unto salvation." There is no fault in the Scriptures that makes it necessary that the gifts of the Holy Spirit should be manifested. The necessities in the case exist in the imperfections of the people of God, in the fact that they do not follow their perfect rule. [328]

We now see the gifts of the Spirit occupying their proper place. They are not manifested to give a rule of faith and practice. We already have a rule that is perfect in the Sacred Writings. But in consequence of the errors of God's people, and their deviations in faith and practice from this perfect rule, God in mercy manifests the gifts to reprove their errors, and lead them to a correct understanding of the holy Scriptures. This is the position of the gifts. They were not designed to take the place of the Scriptures. And they are not given because the Scriptures are an imperfect rule of faith and practice. But in consequence of the errors of God's professed people, in departing from the perfect rule, which he has given them, the gifts are manifested to correct the erring, and point them to the Bible as their lamp and guide.

God designed that his people should be one. This was the burden of the prayer of Jesus. John 17. Hear him as he prays in agony, "That they all may be one, as thou, Father, art in me, and I in thee, that they also may be one in us, that the world may believe that thou hast sent me." Paul exhorted the Corinthians in the name of the Christ to be perfectly joined together in the same mind, and in the same judgment. Read 1 Corinthians 1:10; Romans 15:5; Philippians 2:1, 2; 1 Peter 3:8; 5:5. But do we see this unity in those who profess to take the Bible as their rule, and reject the gifts? We see divisions, and with many, confusion to the utmost. The fault, however, is not in the Bible. It is in those who fail to follow the teachings of the sacred Scriptures. And God in mercy and condescension infinite purposes to help them by the gifts. But many of them refuse to be helped in this way, because that in the Bible they have a perfect rule. If they obeyed the sacred Scriptures, [329] and walked in unity, both among themselves, and with God, they would not need the gifts. But in their confusion, and their distance from Christ, while still rejecting the gifts, there is no help for them in God.

Again, I ask, Who knows that the gifts of the Holy Spirit have not been needed since the completion of the volume of inspiration? It is admitted that when completed it was a more perfect rule then when but a portion of it was given. But how does its completion take the place of the gifts? If they were given because of the imperfections of the people of God, their removal supposes perfection on the part of God's people. Do we find perfection in the church since the days of Paul, to that degree as to need no special manifestations of the Spirit, reproving sin and correcting deviations from God's perfect rule? The history of the church, setting forth her terrible apostasies and corruptions, her endless schisms, divisions and creeds, and her conflicting expositions of the plainest truths of the Bible, testifies too plainly of her imperfections. Her sad history and present wretchedness, show that necessity still remains, since the completion of the Book of God, for the manifestations of the gifts of the Spirit.

The gift of prophecy is by the apostle classed with the callings of the Christian church in Ephesians 4:11-13. He distinctly states their object: "And he gave some, apostles, and some, prophets, and some, evangelists, and some, pastors and teachers, for the perfecting of the saints, for the work of the ministry, for the edifying of the body of Christ, till we all come in the unity of the faith, and of the knowledge of the Son of God, unto a perfect man, unto the measure of the stature of the fullness of

Christ." These were *all* given at the same time, [330] all for the same purpose, *all* to cease at the same time. Do we recognize in the Christian church, evangelists, pastors, and teachers? Why not prophets? Does the church still need them? Why not the gift of prophecy? Will those continue till the church is perfected, ready to meet her descending Lord? So will the gift of prophecy.

Paul, in his letter to the Corinthians, has spoken very definitely upon this subject of spiritual gifts. In 1 Corinthians 12:1, he says: "Now concerning spiritual gifts, brethren, I would not have you ignorant." He regarded this subject as one of the highest importance, and urges an understanding of it. In all he has said relative to it, he has not once intimated that the gifts were to cease before the perfect day of glory should come. But he does clearly point to the time when the gifts will cease. 1 Corinthians 13:8-12: "Charity [*agape* — love,] never faileth: but whether there be prophecies, they shall fail; whether there be tongues, they shall cease; whether there be knowledge, it shall vanish away. For we know in part, and we prophesy in part. But when that which is perfect is come, then that which is in part shall be done away. When I was a child, I spake as a child, I understood as a child, I thought as a child: but when I became a man, I put away childish things. For now we see through a glass darkly, but then face to face; now I know in part, but then shall I know even as also I am known."

The apostle here contrasts the mortal state with the immortal; the present imperfect, with that which will be perfect; the cloudy present while we walk by faith, with the open glory of the life to come. Here, we only know in part, prophesy in part; there, that which is in part, will be done away. Here, we see through a glass darkly; there, face to face. Here, we know in part; [331] there, we shall know, even as we are known. Charity, or love, will never end. Here, it is the highest Christian grace; there, it will be the crowning glory of immortals forever and forever. In this sense love will never fail. But prophecies will fail, tongues will cease, and knowledge will vanish away. The light of Heaven through the dim medium of these, and the other gifts of the Holy Spirit, is represented as being only in part, to be superseded by the perfect day of glory when we may talk face to face with God, Christ, and angels, as our first parents talked with God in Eden before sin entered. But when? This is the vital question. When were the gifts to be done away? Let Paul answer: "But when that which is perfect is come, then that which is in part shall be done away." "And let all the people say, Amen."

4. God has had a truth in every age, by which he has tested the people of that age. This was true in the days of Noah, and at the first advent of Christ. It is especially true at the present time, as God is preparing to visit the wicked with judgments and the righteous with salvation. All revealed, practical, truth ever has been, and ever will be, a test of man's fidelity to God. He will have to give an account to the Author of truth how he treats it. If he obeys, he may be saved; if he rejects it, and violates its claims upon him, he must be lost.

But the law of God, in an eminent sense, is a test to man. It is the highest authority in all earth and Heaven. If God's law is not a test, there is no such thing as a test. Seventh-day Adventists solemnly believe that God is proving and testing the people by his holy law. In point of sacredness and importance, they regard the fourth commandment equal to either of the other nine, and the sin of violating it, when as well understood, [332] equal to that of breaking either of them. They believe that the present time, in the providence of God, during the proclamation of the third angel's message, is the period for the sabbath reform, and that in the last message, the Sabbath of Jehovah is to be the special test in the law of God for the people. The great question to be decided before the wrath of God shall be poured out upon a guilty and ruined world is, Who will be loyal to the God of Heaven? Such, if washed from their sins by the blood of Christ, become heirs to the future inheritance, and receive a crown of unfading glory at the second appearing of Jesus. Says Christ, "If thou wilt enter into life keep the commandments."

Seventh-day Adventists are charged with making the Sabbath a test. And some will have it that we denounce and reject all who do not believe as we do. It is true that we teach that God is testing the people by his law. But we deny the charge that we denounce and reject those who differ from us.

Our course toward all men whom we can reach with our publications, our sermons and our entreaties, proves the charge false. We beseech all men, without respect to profession of religion, color, or rank in society, to turn from their sins, keep God's commandments and live. And we manifest a zeal and earnestness in this matter somewhat in proportion to the importance of the testing message we bear. And because our testimony is pointed and earnest, condemning those who choose to pass along with the popular current, and violate the law of God, some are disturbed, and with feelings of retaliation, falsely charge us. It is not our work to test, condemn, and denounce, the people. It is not in our hearts to unnecessarily injure the feelings of any. But with our present convictions of truth and duty, we should do great violence to our [333] own consciences, and sin against God, should we cease to declare to the people the purpose of God in testing the world by his law, just before the day of wrath.

And God has greatly blessed such testimony. As a people, Seventh-day Adventists were heard of, as it were, but yesterday. As a people, they do not claim to be more than a score of years old. And yet in point of numbers and efficiency they have a little strength. And why? Because, when they have borne a pointed and earnest testimony, God has been with them, and added to their numbers and strength.

But if the Sabbath is not a test, it is not worth our while to be to the trouble of teaching and observing it in the face of decided opposition. If we can be as good Christians while breaking the fourth commandment, as while keeping it, should we not at once seek to be in harmony with the rest of the Christian world? Why be so odd as to obey the commandment of God, if one can be as good a Christian while living in violation of it? And there are frequent inconveniences, and pecuniary sacrifices, to be suffered by those who are so particular concerning the observance of the fourth commandment. If the Sabbath is of so little importance as not to be a test of Christian fellowship and eternal salvation; if men who break the Sabbath should be embraced in our fellowship the same as if they observed it; and if they can reach heaven as surely in violating the fourth commandment as in keeping it; why not abandon is at once, and cease to agitate the public mind with a question of no real importance which is so unpleasant and annoying.

Seventh-day Adventists believe that in the restoration of the Bible Sabbath, under the last message of mercy, God designs to make it a test to the people. [334] Hence many of them labor with earnestness to teach it, and are ready to make any sacrifices in order to observe it, and do their duty in teaching it to others. Convince them that it is not a test, and they will not trouble the people nor themselves longer with it. But should they give the people to understand that they regard the Sabbath of so little importance as not to be a test, "the sword of the Spirit'" on that subject at least, would become in their hands as powerless as a straw. They could not then convict the people upon this subject. Indeed their position before the people, in earnestly calling their attention to a subject that is of so little importance as not to constitute a test of Christian character, and which would subject them to a heavy cross, much inconvenience, sacrifice, and reproach, would be but little less than solemn mockery. With our present view of the importance of the subject, we have a sufficient reason for earnestly urging the claims of the fourth commandment upon our fellow-men.

The remarks of Elder J. N. Andrews in reference to the Sabbatarians of England in the seventeenth century, have so direct a bearing upon this subject that I give the following from his *History of the Sabbath*, pp. 335, 336:

"The laws of England during that century were very oppressive to all dissenters from the established church, and bore exceedingly hard upon the Sabbath-keepers. Yet fine, imprisonment, and even capital punishment, would not have proved sufficient to suppress the Sabbath. It was in the house of its own friends that the Sabbath was wounded. In the seventeenth century eleven churches of Sabbatarians flourished in England, while many scattered Sabbath-keepers were to be found in various parts of that kingdom. Now but three of those churches are in existence. It was not the lack of [335] able men among the Sabbath-keepers to defend the truth, nor the fierce assaults of their persecutors, that has thus reduced them to a handful. The fault is their own, not indeed for any disgraceful conduct on their part, but simply because they made the Sabbath of no practical importance, and lowered the standard of divine truth in this thing to the dust. The Sabbath-keeping ministers assumed the pastoral care of first-day churches, in some cases as their sole charge, in others they did this in connection with the oversight of Sabbatarian churches. The result need surprise no one; as both ministers and people said to all men, in thus acting, that the fourth commandment might be broken with impunity, the people took them at their word. Mr. Crosby, a first-day historian, sets this matter in a clear light:

"'If the seventh day ought to be observed as the Christian Sabbath, then all congregations that observe the first day as such must be Sabbath-breakers... I must leave those gentlemen on the contrary side to their own sentiments; and to vindicate the practice of becoming pastors to a people whom in their conscience they must believe to be breakers of the Sabbath.'"

The Seventh-day Baptists of America have done a good work in teaching the Sabbath. We should respect them, and regard them with peculiar interest for this. But had they been faithful to the sacred trust committed to them, their numbers and strength might have been a hundred-fold greater than they now are. They have had the reproach, the cross, and the inconvenience of the Sabbath, without that strength and force which teaching it as a test gives. For nearly two centuries, in their feebleness, they have been holding up the Sabbath, while, if they had been faithful in teaching it, in observing it, and urging it upon the consciences of the [336] people, the Sabbath would have held them up, and been the strength of that people.

Seventh-day Adventists have nothing to boast of. God has often reproved and chastised us for unfaithfulness. And when we have returned to him, and humbly and faithfully battled for the truth, amid reproaches and persecutions, he has greatly blessed us. Nothing is so much to be dreaded as that calm which is the result of tempering unpopular, testing truth to the ears of the people so as not to offend. Rather let the reproach come, and the storm rage, if it be the result of speaking the truth of God in love.

As a people we have had our difficulties to surmount, our trials to bear, and our victories to gain. We are gathered from Methodists, Regular Baptists, Freewill Baptists, Seventh-day Baptists, Presbyterians, Congregationalists, Episcopalians, Dutch Reform, Disciples, Christians, Lutherans, United Brethren, Catholics, Universalists, Worldlings, and Infidels. We are composed of native Americans, English, Welsh, Scotch, Irish,

French, Germans, Norwegians, Danes, Swedes, Poles, and others. To bring together a body composed of such material, affected more or less by the religious sentiments and forms of the several denominations, with all their national peculiarities, has called for much patient, and persevering toil. And it is by the grace of God that we are what we are. And let his name be praised that in our darkest hours, when we have humbled ourselves, he has ever come to our aid.

From their past brief history Seventh-day Adventists may learn much as to their present work and future prospects. When in humility they have borne a decided testimony in the fear of God, their labors have been signally blessed. When they have been willing [337] to bear the cross of present truth, and sacrifice time, convenience and means to advance the work, they have shared the approving smiles of Heaven. They have seen that nothing can keep the body in a healthy condition but the plain and pointed testimony. This will do the work of purification, either by purging their sins, or separating from them the unconsecrated and rebellious. Let the result be what it may, such testimony must be borne, or this people will fall as others have fallen. And terrible would be their fall, after having so clear light, and having had committed to them so sacred a trust as the last message of mercy to sinners.

From the past we may also learn what to expect in the future, in the line of persecution. Satan has been angry because this people have been seeking for the "old paths," that they might walk therein. He has been especially disturbed as they have plead for the restoration of the Sabbath, and the gifts of the Holy Spirit. If the people be taught that God is testing them upon the Sabbath, and that they should listen to the testimony of Jesus, in the spirit of prophecy, which reproves their sins, and calls on them to consecrate themselves and what they possess to the Lord, we may depend upon it, the ire of the dragon will be stirred. This we have witnessed and suffered in proportion to our faithfulness in the work. When we have borne a pointed testimony, we have been the especial objects of the wrath of the dragon; but with it have also shared largely the blessing of God. When we have been unfaithful, the dragon has been comparatively quiet, but we have suffered leanness of soul. And thus we may expect it will be for time to come.

The position of suspense is not the most happy one. Those who wait for the return of the Lord in uncertainty [338] as to the definite period of his second advent, are in danger of becoming restless. Hence the application of certain texts to this time, and to the people who are waiting for their Lord. "Ye have need of patience, that, after ye have done the will of God, ye might receive the promise." Hebrews 10:36. "Be ye also patient, stablish your hearts; for the coming of the Lord draweth nigh." James 5:8. "Here is the patience of the saints, here are they that keep the commandments of God, and the faith of Jesus." Revelation 14:12.

In such a position, how natural the often-repeated inquiry, "How long before the Lord will come?" But no definite answer can be given to this inquiry. And it is best that this question cannot be definitely answered. Definite time has answered the purpose of God. It brought the Advent people to the waiting time, requiring great patience. Throughout this entire period of the patience of the saints, the only safe position is to keep the coming of Christ ever before us, and to regulate all our acts in full view of the terrible realities of the Judgment. To put off the coming of the Lord, and view that event in the distance, and enter into the spirit of the world, would be dangerous in the extreme. It is true that there are prophecies to be fulfilled, just prior to the coming of the Lord; but their fulfillment is of such a nature that it can be realized in a short time. Unbelief may suggest that as the time has continued longer than the waiting ones expected, it may still continue many years. But saving faith takes the safe position, and views the event at the door. This fact should ever be borne in mind, that while we have no means of showing that the Lord will come at an immediate definite point, no one can prove that he may not very soon come. And while it cannot be proved that the Lord will not very [339] soon come, I call attention to the following facts which show that the second advent cannot be a distant event.

1. The three messages constitute a solemn warning to the world to prepare for the coming of Christ. The closing division of this great warning is a test to the world and ripens the harvest of the earth. Those who

receive the warning and prepare for the coming of the Lord, are ripened by it for immortality. Those who reject it, are ripened for the day of slaughter.

2. The warning given by Noah, the manner his message was treated, and the wrath of God in a flood of water, illustrate the closing events of the present state of things. "As the days of Noah were, so also shall the coming of the Son of man be." God did not call this preacher of righteousness to warn the next to the last generation before the flood, but the very last. The very generation which drank the waters of the flood, saw Noah build the ark, and heard his warning voice. How absurd the supposition that Noah built the ark, and gave his warning message in the time of next to the last generation, so that those who heard his message and saw his work, passed into the grave, and the ark went to decay, and their children came upon the stage of action to witness unwarned the terrors of the flood.

3. The last great warning was to be given to the last generation of men. The very ones who hear it, receive it, obey it, and are waiting for the Lord, will exclaim, as the Son of man shall return with his angels down the blazing vault of heaven, "Lo! this is our God, we have waited for him, and he will save us." And the very men who reject the warning, and justly merit the wrath of God, will also witness the second advent in flaming fire with terror and anguish. This warning is not given to next to the last generation, but to the very last. Then, [340] as certain as the great warning, illustrated by the three messages of Revelation 14, has been, and is being given in our day, just so certain the generation that has heard the warning will witness the day of wrath, and the revelation of the Son of God from Heaven. One of two things is certain; either Seventh-day Adventists are wrong in the application of the messages, or Christ is very soon coming. If they are correct in their application of the great warning, then the very men who hear it will witness its terrible realities.

"Verily I say unto you," says Christ, "this generation shall not pass away, till all these things be fulfilled. Heaven and earth shall pass away, but my words shall not pass away." Matthew 24:34, 35. We do not believe that the word generation marks any definite number of years. The Lord designed to teach that the people who should live at the time of the fulfillment of the last sign mentioned, (falling stars of 1833,) and should hear the proclamation of the coming of Christ, based partly upon the fulfilled signs, should witness the scenes connected with his coming. God has raised up men to give the solemn warning to the world at the right time. The signs were fulfilled at the right time to give force to the warning. And the very generation of men that live after the three great signs are fulfilled, and who hear and reject the warning message, will drink the unmingled cup of the wrath of God. And those of this very generation who receive the message, suffer disappointment and endure the trials of the waiting position, will witness the coming of Christ, and exclaim, "Lo! this is our God, we have waited for him."

Dear reader, if watchful and faithful to duty, we shall very soon enter the harbor of eternal rest. Keep a good look-out. Oh, be not deceived, and overcome by [341] the world, the flesh, and the Devil. True faith forbids your looking into the future, and laying plans for the benefit of the next generation. It shuts you up to the present. But it is to be feared that those who are employing their physical and mental forces to accumulate wealth for their children, while they are neglecting their duty to the cause of present truth, and do not give themselves and families time to seek and serve God, are making a terrible mistake. They not only fail to help the cause, and fail to walk with God, and fail to exert the best influence in their own families, but their influence in professing so solemn and definite a position as that the present is the period for the third and last solemn warning, while in works they deny their faith, is decidedly against the cause.

The world exhibits madness in grasping for wealth. A spirit of insanity has taken hold of men upon the subject of worldly gain; and many who profess present truth are more or less imbued with it. With those who do not fear God and keep his commandments, and are not looking for the soon coming of his Son, this is what might be expected. But with Seventh-day Adventists there is no excuse. With them it is insanity and madness. Why should they accumulate wealth for their children? Should the Lord remain away a hundred years, wealth handed down to them would be their almost certain ruin. Look to the history of truly good and great men. Have they sprung up amid wealth? Or have they come from families trained in the school of poverty and want? Read the histories of the early lives of Martin Luther and Abraham Lincoln. Both were poor boys. But they both became great men, by facing want, grappling with poverty, and overcoming those obstacles ever lying in the path of want. Such a [342] struggle in early life gave them experience, and was the safeguard of their purity. While the names of these good men are embalmed in the memory and affection of the people, those of hundreds, who received riches from their parents, have rotted, because money was in the way of their doing what they should have done, and being what they might have been. Setting aside the coming of the Lord, there is no more certain ruin to the children than for them to look to, and lean upon, their parents' wealth.

But what can be said of the influence of those brethren who profess to believe that the last great warning to the world is being given, yet devote their entire energies to accumulating wealth for their children? What can be the influence upon their children? Is it not to lead them to love this world? to put off the coming of the Lord? to neglect the necessary preparation? Are they not taking a course directly to shut them out of the kingdom of Heaven? And is there any hope of the salvation of either parents or children while pursuing such an inconsistent course? Without the faith of the soon coming of the Lord, they are pursuing a course to deny it in work, they are making that ruin certain.

The short period of probation remaining should be improved in laying up treasure in Heaven, and seeking that preparation necessary to its enjoyment in the next life. Parents, I entreat of you, live out the precious Advent faith before your children. Lead them to Jesus, and teach them by your faith and works to secure a preparation for his coming. Let your influence in favor of truth and holiness extend to all around, that it may be said to you, "Well done, good and faithful servant, enter thou into the joy of thy Lord. [343]

The Law and the Gospel

"I and my Father are one." John 10:30

The Father and the Son were one in man's creation, and in his redemption. Said the Father to the Son, "Let us make man in our image." And the triumphant song of jubilee in which the redeemed take part, is unto "Him that sitteth upon the throne, and unto the Lamb, forever and ever."

Jesus prayed that his disciples might be one as he was one with his Father. This prayer did not contemplate one disciple with twelve heads, but twelve disciples, made one in object and effort in the cause of their master. Neither are the Father and the Son parts of the "three-one God." They are two distinct beings, yet one in the design and accomplishment of redemption. The redeemed, from the first who shares in the great redemption, to the last, all ascribe the honor, and glory, and praise, of their salvation, to both God and the Lamb.

But if it be true that the law of the Father and the gospel of the Son are opposed to each other, that one was to take the place of the other, then it follows that those saved in the former dispensation are saved by the Father and the law, while those of the present dispensation are saved by Christ and the gospel. And in this case, when the redeemed shall reach Heaven, at last, and their redemption shall be sung, two songs will be heard, one ascribing praise to God and the law, the other singing the praises of Christ and the gospel.

This will not be. There will be harmony in that song of redemption. All the redeemed will sing the facts as they have existed during the period of man's probation. All will ascribe the praise of their salvation [344] to God and the Lamb. Adam, Abel, Enoch, Noah, Abraham, and Moses, will join with the disciples of Jesus in singing of the redeeming power of the blood of the Son, while those who have lived since the crucifixion of Christ, saved by his blood, will join the patriarchs and prophets in the song of praise to the Father, the creator and lawgiver. Therefore the law and the gospel run parallel throughout the entire period of man's probation. The gospel is not confined to some eighteen centuries. The dispensation of the gospel is not less than about six thousand years.

The word gospel signifies good news. The gospel of the Son of God is the good news of salvation through Christ. When man fell, angels wept. Heaven was bathed in tears. The Father and the Son took counsel, and Jesus offered to undertake the cause of fallen man. he offered to die that man might have life. The Father consented to give his only Beloved, and the good news ran through heaven, and resounded on earth, that a way was opened for man's redemption. In the first promise made to man that the seed of the woman should bruise the serpent's head, was the gospel of Jesus Christ, as verily as in the song the angels sung over the plains of Bethlehem, to the shepherds as they watched their flocks by night, "Glory to God in the highest, peace on earth and good will to men."

Immediately after the fall, hope of a future life hung upon Christ as verily as we can hang our hopes on Christ. And when the first sons of Adam brought their offerings to the Lord, Cain in his unbelief brought the first fruits of the ground, which were not acceptable. Abel brought a firstling of the flock, in faith of Christ, the great sacrifice for sin. God accepted his offering. Through the blood of that firstling, Abel [345] saw the blood of Jesus Christ. He looked forward to Christ, and made his offering in the faith and hope of the gospel, and through it saw the great sacrifice for sin, as verily as we see the bleeding Lamb as we look back to Calvary, through the broken bread and the fruit of the vine. Through these emblems we see Christ crucified. Abel saw the same through the lamb which he offered. Do we hang our hopes in faith upon Christ? So did Abel. Are we Christians by virtue of living faith in Christ? So was Abel.

Abraham had the gospel of the Son of God. The apostle says that the scripture, foreseeing that God would justify the heathen, preached before the gospel unto Abraham. Galatians 3:8.

Paul testifies of the Israelites in the wilderness, that they "were all baptized unto Moses in the cloud and in the sea; and did all eat the same spiritual meat; and did all drink the same spiritual drink; for they drank of that spiritual Rock that followed them; and that Rock was Christ." 1

Corinthians 10:2-4. The gospel was preached to the children of Israel in the wilderness. The apostle says, "Unto us was the gospel preached, as well as unto them; but the word preached did not profit them, not being mixed with faith in them that heard it." Hebrews 4:2.

Moses and the believing Jews had the faith and hope of the gospel. Through the blood of the sacrificial offerings, they saw Christ, and by faith embraced him. Their hopes of the future life were not in the law, but in Christ.

"The law," says Paul, "having a shadow of good things to come." The typical system is but the shadow. The good things, of which Christ as a sacrifice and mediator is the center, are the body that casts its shadow [346] back into the Jewish age. The bleeding sacrifices of the legal system were but the shadow; Christ, bleeding on the cross, was the great reality. Every bleeding sacrifice offered by the Jews, understandingly and in faith, was as acceptable in the sight of heaven as what Christians may do in showing their faith in the sufferings, death, and resurrection of Christ, in baptism and the Lord's supper. The one was done in the faith and hope of redemption through the blood of the Son of God, as verily as the other may be. The gospel dispensation, which is the dispensation of the good news of redemption through Christ, has been six thousand years long.

The dispensation of the law of God is longer than that of the gospel. It commenced before the fall, or there could not have been in the justice of God any such thing as the fall. It existed as early as there were created intelligences subject to the government of the Creator. It covers all time, and extends to the future, running parallel with the eternity of God's moral government. Angels fell, therefore were on probation. They, being on probation, were consequently amenable to law. In the absence of law, they could not be on probation, therefore, could not fall. The same may be said of Adam and Eve in Eden.

The ten commandments are adapted to fallen beings. As worded in the sacred Scriptures given to man in his fallen state, they were not adapted to the condition of holy angels, nor to man in his holy estate in Eden. But the two grand principles of God's moral government did exist before the fall, in the form of law. These are given in the Old Testament, and are quoted by Christ in the New, as the two great commandments: "Thou shalt love the Lord thy God with all thy heart, and with all thy soul, and with all thy mind. This is [347] the first and great commandment. And the second is like unto it, Thou shalt love thy neighbor as thyself. On these two commandments hang all the law and the prophets." Matthew 22:37-40. Compare Deuteronomy 6:5; Leviticus 19:18.

These two commandments require supreme love to the Creator, and love to fellow-creatures equal to that bestowed upon one's self. Angels could do no more than these require. Adam could do no more. We can do no more. The two great commandments embrace all that is required by the ten precepts of the decalogue. They are the grand circle inside of which is the will of God to man. No precept, and no principle, of the Book of God, extends beyond this circle.

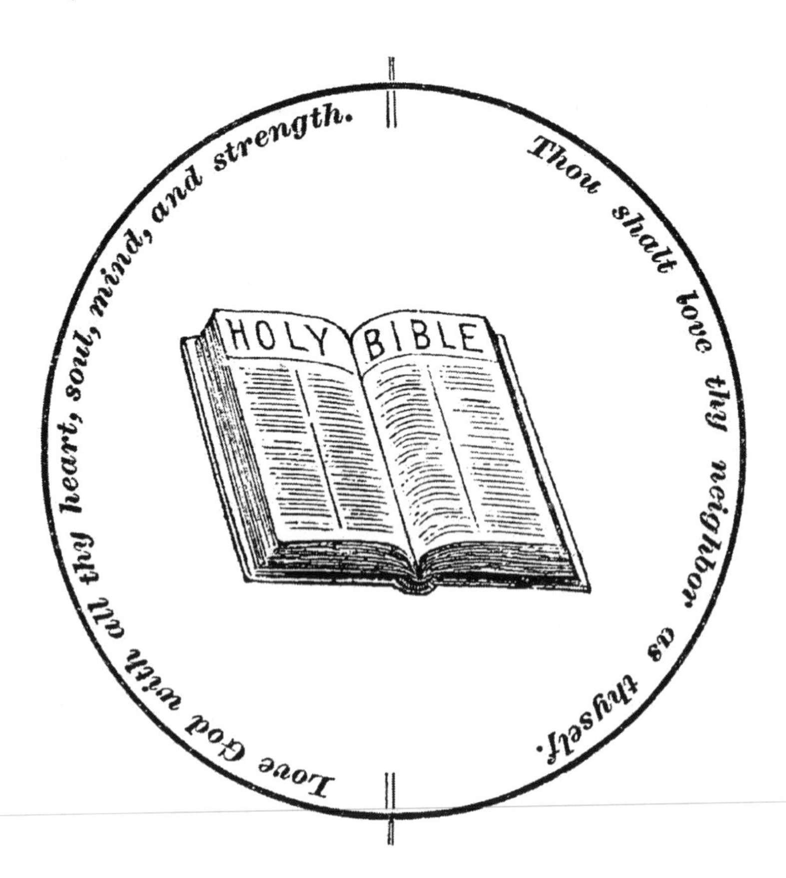

Soon after the fall, we see this circle in ten parts. The two principles of God's moral government are seen in ten precepts, worded to meet man's fallen condition. [348] Love to God is taught in the first four commandments, and love to our fellow-man is taught in the last six. The prophets of the Lord, the Son of God, and the apostles of Jesus, have all spoken in harmony with the ten precepts of the law of Jehovah. The whole duty of man, says Solomon, is to fear God and keep his commandments.

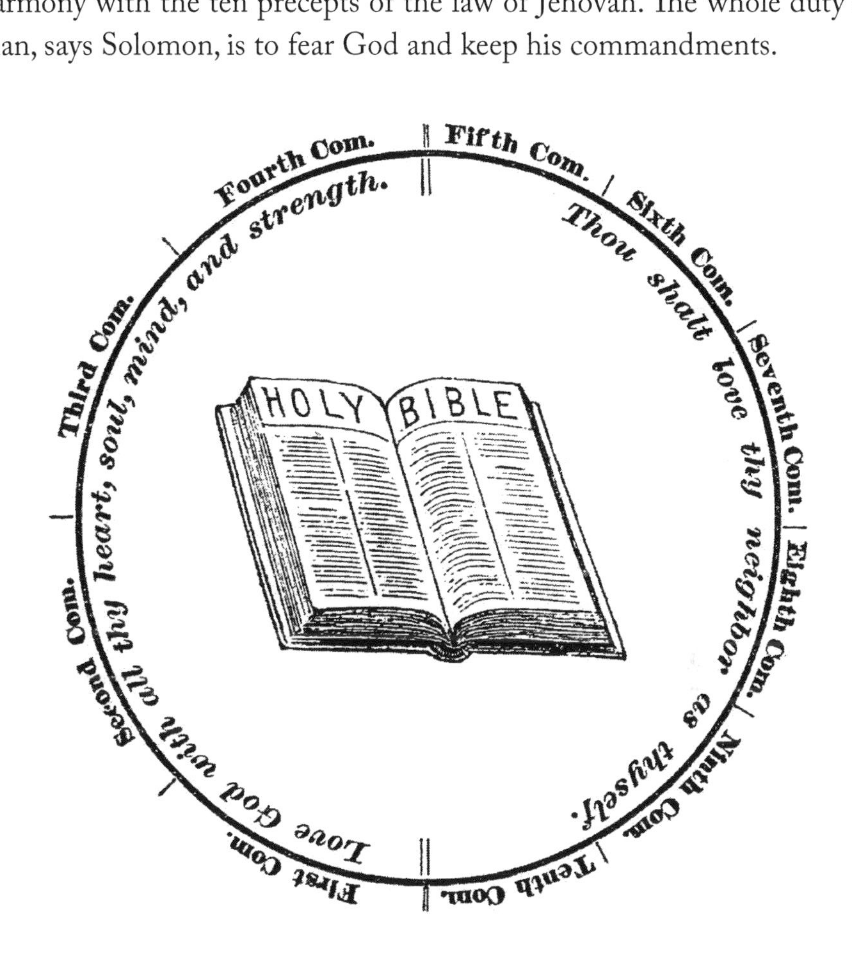

The ten precepts of the decalogue, adapted to man's fallen condition, were enforced as early as the circumstances demanded them. The first three were applicable to Adam immediately after the fall. And although the Sabbath of the fourth precept was instituted at the close of the first week of time, before the fall, and we have evidence that Adam was directed to observe it as a memorial of creation, yet that portion of the precept adapted to the fallen state, relative to the man-servant, the maid-servant, and the stranger, could not exist till a later period when such relations existed. The fifth [349] commandment could not be enforced, until applicable to Adam's children. The sixth, seventh, eighth, ninth, and tenth, were enforced as early as the parties existed to whom they could properly apply.

There is nothing in the moral condition of man in his fallen state, not in the nature of the ten commandments themselves, to restrict them to any one dispensation more than another. Man's moral wretchedness is the same, only more deplorable as he advances from the gates of Paradise toward the close of probation. And the law of God, adapted to his fallen state, is applicable and necessary throughout the entire period of his fallen condition, from Paradise lost to Paradise regained.

The reign of sins runs parallel with the reign of death, from Adam until sin and sinners shall cease to be. And parallel with these, stretching through all dispensations, there has been the knowledge of the principles of the ten commandments, consequently a knowledge of sin.

The means of this knowledge has been the law of God. "By the law," says the apostle, "is the knowledge of sin." Romans 3:20. "I had not known sin but by the law." Chap. 7:7. As proof that this knowledge did exist immediately after the fall, see Genesis 4:7, 23, 24; 6:5, 11, 12. Also, Noah was righteous before God. Chap. 7:1. He was a preacher of righteousness. 2 Peter 2:5. By his preaching right-doing, reproving the sins of the people of his time, he condemned the world. Hebrews 11:7. The men of Sodom and Gomorrah were great sinners, excepting one man. Abraham interceded, saying, Wilt thou destroy the righteous with the wicked? Genesis 13:13; 18:20, 23, 25; 19:7. The blessing of God came upon Abraham, because he obeyed his voice and kept his commandments. Genesis 26:5. Those who refused obedience, experienced [350] his wrath for their transgressions. The cities of the plain were condemned for their unlawful deeds. 2 Peter 2:6-8.

As an illustration of this subject, I will briefly notice the murder of righteous Abel. Cain killed his brother, and, as a sinner, received the mark of God's displeasure. Sin, says the apostle, is the transgression of the law. 1 John 3:4. Cain broke the sixth commandment; hence that precept existed in the time of Cain. Otherwise he did not sin; for where no law is, there is no transgression. Romans 4:15.

The foregoing positions relative to the law of God would meet with but little opposition were it not for the Sabbath of the fourth commandment. The proper observance of the Bible Sabbath is not only crossing, but with many inconvenient, and not favorable to the successful prosecution of their worldly plans. The fearful and unbelieving shun its claims, brand it as a Jewish institution, and frequently assert that it was unknown to men until the Sabbath law was proclaimed from Sinai. Sacred history, however, proves this statement to be false. It is true that Sabbath-keeping is not mentioned in the book of Genesis. But this does not prove that it did not exist during the long period covered by that brief record. The facts connected with the giving of the manna show that the Israelites understood the obligations of the Sabbath, that some of the people violated them, and were reproved by Jehovah, thirty days before they saw Mount Sinai. See Exodus 16-19.

I come to the New Testament. The first four chapters of Matthew are devoted to a sketch of the genealogy of Christ, Joseph and Mary, the birth of Jesus, Herod slaying the children of Bethlehem, John [351] the Baptist, the temptation of Christ, and his entering upon his public ministry. The fifth chapter opens with the first record of his public instructions. In that memorable sermon upon the mount, Christ warns his disciples against a terrible heresy that would soon press its way into the church.

The Jews boasted of God, of Abraham, and of the law, but despised and rejected Jesus. The great facts connected with his resurrection were soon to be so convincing that many would believe. And as the Jews were to reject and crucify the Son, while boasting in the law, Christians would run to the opposite and equally-fatal heresy of trampling upon the authority of the Father, and despising his law, while receiving Christ and glorying in the gospel. It has ever been Satan's object to separate, in the faith of the church, the Father and the Son. With the Jews was the cry, The Father, Abraham, the law; but away with Jesus and his gospel. With Christians the cry was to arise, Christ, the cross, the gospel; but away with the law of the Father. To meet this heresy, ere long to arise in the Christian church, the Master, in his first-recorded sermon, spoke pointedly. Listen to his appeal to his disciples in the presence of the assembled multitudes:

"Think not that I am come to destroy the law, or the prophets: I am not come to destroy, but to fulfill. For verily I say unto you, Till heaven and earth pass, one jot or one tittle shall in no wise pass from the law, till all be fulfilled. Whosoever, therefore, shall break one of these least commandments, and teach men so, he shall be called least in the kingdom of Heaven; but whosoever shall do and teach them, the same shall be called great in the kingdom of Heaven."

These words of warning from our Lord fully meet the [352] case. They need no comment. The history of the church, showing how loosely, great and apparently good men have held the law of God, and the present, closing controversy respecting it, gave them especial force.

Jesus did not come to legislate. In no case did he intimate that he would give a new law to take the place of that of his Father. Speaking of the Son, the Father says, "He shall speak unto them all that I shall command him." Deuteronomy 18:18. Jesus answered them and said, "My doctrine is not mine, but his that sent me." John 7:16. "I do nothing of myself, but as my Father hath taught me, I speak these things." Chap. 8:28. "The word which ye hear, is not mine, but the Father's which sent me." Chap. 14:24.

Let us consider the grave question of the great apostle to the Gentiles, relative to the law of God and the faith of Jesus: "Do we then make void the law through faith?" Romans 3:31. This question points directly to the true issue between us, and the men of this day who teach that the gospel of the Son makes void the law of the Father. Paul decides the question in these emphatic words: "God forbid: yea, we establish the law."

The gospel is a necessity in consequence of law transgressed. Where there is no law, there is no transgression, no sin, no need of the blood of Christ, no need of the gospel. But the gospel teaches that Christ died for sinners, on account of their sins. Sin is the transgression of the law. He came, therefore, as the great sacrifice for those who transgress the law. The gospel holds him up as the bleeding sacrifice for the sins of those who transgress the law. This fact establishes the existence of the law of God. Remove the law, and we have no further need of Christ and his gospel.

In the gospel arrangement for the salvation of man, [353] there are three parties concerned; the Lawgiver, the Advocate, and the sinner. The words of the apostle are to the point: "If any man sin, we have an advocate with the Father, Jesus Christ the righteous." 1 John 2:1. Sin is the transgression of the law of the Father; hence the sinner offends the Father, is in trouble with the Father, and needs Jesus to plead his cause with the Father. But if the Father's law has been abolished, and Christ sustains to the sinner the relation of lawgiver, who is his advocate? "Mother Mary," or "father Joseph," or some other one of the multitude of canonized saints will answer for the Papist; but what will the Protestant do in this case? If he urges that Christ, and not the Father, is the lawgiver, and that in the present dispensation, sin is the transgression of the law of Jesus Christ, then I press him to tell me who the sinner's advocate is. And I ask him to harmonize his position with the words of the beloved John, "If any man sin, we have an advocate with the Father, Jesus Christ the righteous."

Paul addresses the elders of the church at Miletus, relative to the fundamental principles of the plan of salvation, thus: "I kept back nothing that was profitable unto you, but have showed you, and have taught you publicly, and from house to house, testifying both to the Jews and also to the Greeks, repentance toward God, and faith toward our Lord Jesus Christ." Acts 20:20, 21. The apostle has here set before the men of the present dispensation two distinct duties. First, the exercise of repentance toward God, for his law is binding upon them, and it is his law that they have transgressed. Second, the exercise of faith toward Christ as the great sacrifice for their sins, and their advocate with the Father. These are both indispensable. Paul presented [354] both. He kept back nothing pertaining to the plan of salvation, that was profitable.

The closing words of the third angel point directly to a body of Christian commandment-keepers. "Here are they that keep the commandments of God and the faith of Jesus." Revelation 14:12. The Jew takes no stock in this text, because he sees in it the despised Jesus of Nazareth. Many professed Christians find it as objectionable as the Jew, for the reason that they find in it the equally-despised commandments of God. But said the adorable Jesus, "I and my Father are one." So the law of the Father and the gospel of the Son pass through all dispensations of man's fallen state, in perfect harmony. Oh! that both the blind Jew and the blind Christian might see this, and embracing the whole truth, instead of each a part, might keep the commandments of God and the faith of Jesus, and be saved.

But here let it be distinctly understood that there is no salvation in the law, that is, there is no redeeming quality in law. Redemption is through the blood of Christ. The sinner may cease to break the commandments of God, and strive with all his powers to keep them, but this will not atone for his sins, and redeem him from his present condition in consequence of past transgression. Notwithstanding all his efforts to keep the law of God, he must be lost without faith in the atoning blood of Jesus. And this was as true in the time of Adam, of Abel, Enoch, Noah, Abraham, Moses, and the Jews, as since Jesus died upon the cross. No man can be saved without Christ.

On the other hand, faith in Jesus Christ, while refusing obedience to the law of the Father, is presumption. An effort to obtain friendship with the Son, while living in rebellion against the Father, is Heaven-daring. [355] No greater insult can be offered to either the Father or the Son. What! Separate the Father and the Son, by trampling on the authority of the one, and making a friend of the other? "I and my Father are one." The Jew insults the Father, in his rejection of the Son; and the Christian flings in the face of Heaven equal insult, in all his acts of worship in which he vainly thinks to make Jesus his friend while, with light upon the subject, he breaks the commandments of God.

The oneness of the Father and the Son is seen at the transfiguration. That voice which is the highest authority in the universe, is there heard saying, "This is my beloved Son; hear him." It is also seen in the closing benediction of the Son, in the last chapter of the Bible, which presents before those who are loyal, the glories of the reward in reserve for the obedient. "Blessed are they that do His commandments, that they may have right to the tree of life, and may enter in through the gates into the city."

I briefly call attention to three grand events, which have taken place in connection with the sad history of fallen man, either one of which is sufficient to establish the perpetuity of the law of God.

First, the fall, with all its terrible consequences. If the law of God was of such a nature that it could, in any particular, be changed at any time, it would have been thus changed when there were but two fallen beings, Adam and Eve, just before leaving Eden. If the plan of God's moral government could be changed, it would then have been changed, so as to set them free, and save the tide of human wretchedness and agony, which has followed. But, no; it could not be changed. The curse must fall on man, and upon the earth for man's sake; and the blight and mildew of sin must follow [356] everywhere, and hang upon creation like a pall of death. Why? Because God's law that had been transgressed, could not be changed — could not be abolished. Every fading flower and falling leaf, since man left Eden, has proclaimed the law of God changeless. This has been the result of sin. It is the result of the terrible fall. And this has all come about because of the transgression of that law which is as changeless as the throne of Heaven. If that law could ever be changed in any particular, it would have been changed when there were but two fallen beings, in such a way as to free them from the sentence of death, and raise them from their degradation, and the race from continued sin, crime, and woe.

Think of the recent American war, with all its terrible agony. But this is only an item in the vast catalogue. For six thousand years, the tide has been swelling, and creation has been adding groan to groan. Oh! the sorrow, the wretchedness, the agony! Who can compute it? The fall, then, with all its accumulated wretchedness, proclaims God's law changeless. I hasten to notice the next great event which proclaims this truth.

Second, the announcement of the ten commandments from Sinai with imposing display. It was not left for Moses to proclaim this law. It was not left for an angel to assemble the tribes of Israel, and utter these ten holy precepts in their hearing. It was not even left to the Son of God to do this. But the Father, the great Eternal, descends in awful grandeur, and proclaims these precepts in the hearing of all the people.

Do you say that that was the origin of the law of God? Do you say that God descended on Sinai, and [357] there legislated? And do you say that he has since abolished that code, or changed it? When did he do this? Where did he do it? Has any prophet foretold that such an event should take place? And has any apostle recorded that such a work was ever done? Never.

The commonwealth of Michigan sends her legislators to Lansing to enact laws. These laws are published throughout the commonwealth. The people understand them. Some of these laws are repealed or changed. It is done in secret, and the people permitted to know nothing about it? No. The same body that enacts laws, also changes, amends, or abolishes them, and the people are apprized of the fact. This is made as public as the enactment of the law. And has not the all-wise and merciful God manifested as much wisdom in managing affairs in which man has so great an interest, affairs which effect his eternal welfare? He came down upon Sinai, and proclaimed his law under such circumstances as to impress the people with its grandeur, dignity, and perpetuity. Who can suppose that he would abolish, or alter it, and say nothing about it?

Third, the Crucifixion establishes the law of God. If that law was of such a nature that it could be abolished, or any of its precepts changed, why not have this done, and set man free, instead of the Son of God laying aside his glory, taking our nature, living the sad life he lived here upon the earth, suffering in Gethsemane, and finally expiring upon the cross? Oh! why should the divine Son of God do all this to save man, if that law which held him as a sinner could be changed, so that he could be set free? But no; nothing could be done in that direction. Man had sinned, had fallen, and was shut up in the prison-house of sin. His sins [358] were of such a nature that no sacrifice was adequate but the sacrifice of Him to whom the Father had said, "Let us make man." The death of an angel was not sufficient. He only who engaged with the Father in the formation of man, constitutes a sufficient sacrifice to open the door of hope by which he might find pardon, and be saved. In the language of the hymn we sing, "Come, O my soul, to Calvary," and there behold love and agony mingled in the death of the Son of God.

Behold him groaning in Gethsemane. His divine soul was in agony as the sins of man were rolled upon him. "My soul," said he, "is exceeding sorrowful, even unto death." The weight of man's sin in transgressing God's immutable law was such as to press from his pores as it were drops of blood.

He then bears his cross to Calvary. The nails are driven into his hands and feet. The cross is erected. There the bleeding Lamb hangs six terrible hours. The death of the cross was most agonizing. But there was in his case the additional weight of the sins of the whole world. In his last expiring agonies he cries, "My God, my God, why hast thou forsaken me?" and bows his head in death.

The sun, the brightest luminary of heaven, can no longer view the scene, and is vailed as with sackcloth. The vail of the temple, the noblest work of man, is rent in twain. Christ, the noblest being in the universe save One, is dying in agony. Creation feels the shock, and groaning and heaving, throws open the graves of many of the saints, who come out of their graves after his resurrection. This great event transpired because it was the only way by which sinners could be saved. The law must stand as firm as the throne of Heaven, [359] although the earth shake, and the whole creation tremble, as the Son of God dies in agony.

The law of God was given to man as his saviour. He broke it. Could it then redeem him? It is not in the nature of law, either human or divine, to redeem the transgressor. Those who transgress the law of this commonwealth, must suffer the full penalty, unless the Governor shall pardon the transgressor. This is his only hope of escaping the full sentence of the law. It is said by those who do not fully understand our position, that we trust in the law, and the keeping of the Sabbath for salvation. No, friends, you may observe all these precepts, to the best of your ability, conscientiously; but if you look no further than the law for salvation, you can never be saved. The hope of eternal salvation hangs upon Christ. Adam hung his hope there. Abel, Enoch, Noah, Abraham, and the believing Jews, hung theirs there. We can do no more. The hope of the next life depends upon Jesus Christ. Faith in his blood can alone free us from our transgressions. And a life of obedience to the commandments of God and the faith of Jesus will be a sufficient passport through the golden gates of the city of God. [360]

God's Memorial

The Sabbath is a memorial of what the Creator did during the first week of time. He wrought six days. He rested on the seventh day. Here is the origin of the week. The weekly cycle is not derived from anything in nature. Months are suggested by the phases of the moon; years, by the returning seasons; but the week can be traced only to the six days of creation, and the seventh of rest. The patriarchs reckoned time by weeks and sevens of days. Genesis 29:27, 28; 8:10, 12.

The Sabbath was instituted in Eden, at the close of the first week, by three acts on the part of the Creator. First, God rested on the seventh day. Second, he placed his blessing upon the day. Third, he sanctified the day of his rest. He rested on the seventh day, and in this set an example for man. He next blessed the day upon which he had rested. He then sanctified, or "set apart to a sacred use," the day of his rest. He gave the first six days of the week to man, in which to obtain a livelihood, and reserved the seventh day to himself, to be used sacredly by man.

The great God was not wearied with the six days of creation. His rest upon the seventh day means simply that on that day he ceased to create. Nor did man in Eden need rest from toil, as since the fall. In fact, rest from labor is not a leading feature of the Sabbatic institution. The fourth commandment makes no reference to man's physical wants of a day of rest. Neither does it speak of his spiritual necessities of a day of public worship. [361]

It gives quite another reason for the Sabbath. Here it is: "For in six days the Lord made heaven and earth, the sea, and all that in them is, and rested the seventh day; wherefore the Lord blessed the Sabbath day and hallowed it." Exodus 20:11. This reason relates to what God did in the first week of time. He has given no other. It is as old as the world, and will continue to be the reason why man should revere Jehovah's rest-day as long as the world shall continue. Man rests upon the day of the Sabbath in honor of the Creator. And wherever he may turn his eye, whether to the heavens, the earth, or the sea, there he beholds the Creator's work. As he rests upon the seventh day, he sees in the countless varieties of nature the wisdom and power of him who created all in six days, and thus is led from nature up to nature's God. The Sabbath now becomes the cord that binds created man to the infinite Creator. It is the golden chain that links earth to heaven, and man to God. Had he always observed the Sabbath, there could not have been an idolater nor an atheist. The Sabbath, as a memorial of what the Creator did during the first week of time, is now seen in its dignity and importance. It is the memorial of the living God. Man is to rest on the day of the week on which the Creator ceased to create.

But those who belittle the grand Sabbatic institution to only serve man's physical wants of a day of rest, and to provide for him a day of public worship, and see no higher design in it, are satisfied with a change of the day of the Sabbath. They think that a day on which the Creator did not rest, will do quite as well as the day on which he did rest. With this limited view of the subject, why may they not be content with the [362] change? If a day of rest from toil, and a day for the public worship of God, are all the blessings secured to man by the Sabbath, the one-day-in-seven and no-day-in-particular theory looks quite plausible. For, certainly, man can rest his weary limbs, or weary brain, on one day of the week as well as on another. And if only a season of divine worship is to be secured, Sunday may answer for this purpose. In fact, one day in six might do as well for rest and worship as one day in seven, if rest and a day of public worship are the sum total of the reasons for the Sabbath. There is nothing in man's physical or spiritual wants to mark the number seven.

The original design of the Sabbath was for a perpetual memorial of the Creator. Yet it secures the seventh day of the week to man in his fallen condition, not only as a day of rest, but a day for public worship, in which to draw nigh to God and share his pardoning love. But these blessings, of comparative importance, can be obtained on either of the other six days of the week, and do not constitute the grand reason for the Sabbatic institution. That reason given in the law of the Sabbath is, in its importance, as much above the simple idea of repose from weary toil, and a day for public worship, as the heavens are higher than the earth. With this agree the words of the prophet: "If thou turn away thy foot from the Sabbath, from doing thy pleasure on my holy day, and call the Sabbath a delight, the holy of the Lord, honorable, and shalt honor him, not doing thine own ways, nor finding thine own pleasure, nor speaking thine own words, then shalt thou delight thyself in the Lord." Isaiah 57:13, 14.

Here the great object of the Sabbath is set forth. It is to honor God. Man is required to turn away his feet from the Sabbath, and refrain from seeking his [363] own ways, words, and pleasure, on that day, not because he needs a day of rest, but because by so doing he can honor the great God. Those who keep the Sabbath with this object in view, will call it a delight, the holy of the Lord, and honorable.

The fourth commandment points back to what God did during the first week of time. The creation and rest occupied the first week. Immediately following, Jehovah sanctified and blessed the day on which he had rested. In this way the seventh day became the holy Sabbath of the Lord for Adam and his posterity. It was ever to be observed by the race as the memorial of the living God.

Those who locate the institution of the Sabbath at Sinai, urge that no mention is made of Sabbath-keeping in the brief record of the book of Genesis, as proof that the Sabbath was made for the Jews alone. As evidence of the unsoundness of this position, please notice the following facts:

1. The sacred record nowhere intimates that the Sabbath was instituted at Sinai, while it distinctly locates its institution at creation.

2. The Sabbath being made for man, Mark 2:27, as a memorial of creation, there are no reasons why the Jews alone should enjoy its blessings. All men have need of it as much as they.

3. The facts connected with the giving of the manna show that the Israelites understood the obligations of the Sabbath, that some of the people violated these sacred obligations, and were reproved by Jehovah, thirty days before they saw Mount Sinai. See Exodus 16-19. They came to the wilderness of Sin, where the manna was first given, on the fifteenth day of their second month. On the sixth day they gathered a [364] double portion of the manna, sufficient for that day and for the Sabbath which

followed. Moses said to the people, "This is that which the Lord hath said, Tomorrow is the rest of the holy Sabbath unto the Lord." On the seventh day, Moses said, "Eat that to-day; for to-day is a Sabbath unto the Lord. To-day ye shall not find it in the field. Six days ye shall gather it; but on the seventh day, which is the Sabbath, in it there shall be none. And it came to pass, that there went out some of the people on the seventh day for to gather, and they found none. And the Lord said unto Moses, How long refuse ye to keep my commandments and my laws? See, for that the Lord hath given you the Sabbath."

Here we see that the Sabbath was understood, and its violation was rebuked by Jehovah. But the Israelites had not yet seen Sinai. Indeed they did not come to the mount from which the ten commandments were proclaimed, until thirty days from the time the manna was first given. See chap. 19. Here is a nail driven in a sure place, and ministers and men should cease to assert that the Sabbath was first given at Sinai, till they have searched the sacred narrative with greater care.

The original plan of the Sabbath contemplated its perpetual observance as long as God, the creator, and created man should exist. It does not point forward to redemption. It looks back to creation. It was made for man before the fall; but, in consequence of the fall, it is of tenfold more importance to him throughout the entire period of his fallen condition. And it will exist during man's future life upon the new earth, in all its original significance and glory. We have seen the Sabbath based upon the great facts of [365] the creation in six days, Jehovah's rest upon the seventh day, and his sanctifying and blessing the day of his rest. As long as these continue to be facts, so long will the Sabbath continue. Redemption does not propose the creation of a new world as the inheritance of the redeemed. "Behold I make all things new," says the Redeemer. This world, redeemed from the curse and all its results, will be the eternal possession of the righteous. And notwithstanding the work of redemption, the great facts connected with the creation week will ever be vividly impressed upon the immortal minds of the redeemed. Thus saith the prophet: "For as the new heavens and the new earth which I will make shall remain before me, saith the Lord, so shall your seed and your name remain. And it shall come to pass, that from one new moon to another, and from one Sabbath to another, shall all flesh come to worship before me, saith the Lord." Isaiah 66:22, 23. There is no point of time in the past when all flesh have come to worship before the God of Heaven on the Sabbath; and this can never be while the wheat and tares, the children of the kingdom and the children of the wicked one, grow together; and these will not be separated until the harvest, which is the end of the world. This unity in reference to the memorial of the great God will be seen only in the immortal state, when from one Sabbath to another, and from one new moon to another, all flesh shall come to worship before the Lord. "What! the moon in Heaven?" No, not in such a Heaven as that of which the poet sings,

> "Beyond the bounds of time and space,
> Look forward to that heavenly place,
> The saint's secure abode." [366]

Beyond space there would be no room for the moon, nor for the sun; neither would there be room for the resurrected saints, possessing bodies like their Lord's resurrected, glorious body; and beyond the bounds of time, there would be no need of the sun and the moon which are God's great time-keepers. We are not looking for a general smash-up in the universe, and then the creation of all new things, for immortal saints beyond the bounds of time and space. It is this planet that has revolted. And the Redeemer, who is coming to bring it back into allegiance to the government of God, says, "Behold I make all things new." The revolt did not affect the sun, moon, and the other planets. Redemption will not affect these heavenly bodies. When the Restorer shall have established the immortal saints in the new earth, it will continue its revolutions, and the sun and moon will measure off days, and months, and years, as long as eternal ages shall roll. The redeemed will have right to the tree of life, which Adam lost through disobedience. That tree yields twelve manner of fruits each month. And why may not the words of the prophet in reference to all flesh appearing before the Lord from one new moon to another, be fulfilled when the entire family of the redeemed shall come each month to partake of the new fruit of the tree of life?

But to return to God's memorial: The position taken in these pages presents the one-day-in-seven-and-no-day-in-particular, or one-seventh-part-of-time, theory, in its true light. If the Sabbath was made for man, for the simple reason that he needed rest from physical toil, and a day of worship, one day may answer as well as another. But if it be a memorial of Jehovah's rest, the seventh, and no other day of the week, is the day of the Sabbath. [367] Sabbatarians are charged with being great sticklers for the day. And so they are. Sabbath signifies rest. Man is required by the fourth commandment to celebrate the rest-day of the Lord, or the day on which the Lord rested. God rested on the seventh day. He hallowed the seventh day. Hence, the seventh day, and no other, is the day of the Sabbath. Change the day of the Sabbath, and you cease to celebrate the rest of the Lord. If God rested on one day in seven and no day in particular, man may do the same; but if God rested on the seventh day of the first week, acceptable Sabbath-keeping is the celebration of the seventh day of each succeeding week.

The passover was a memorial of an event that occurred on the fourteenth day of the first Jewish month. The celebration of the day of the passover became a statute in Israel from Moses to Christ. Remove this observance to a day on which the event commemorated did not take place, and the celebration would lose its significance. It would cease to be the passover.

The American people celebrate their national independence on the fourth day of July. And why? Because July 4, 1776, patriotic men signed the Declaration of Independence. The men of this nation are great sticklers for the day; and well they may be. Should they change our national celebration from the day on which the Declaration of Independence was signed, to a day on which it was not signed, it would lose its significance. It would cease to be a celebration of our independence. Let the people of this country celebrate their independence on the twenty-fifth day of December, and let the Declaration of Independence be read from every orator's stand on that day, as is customary on the [368] fourth of July, and the American people would be regarded as a nation of fools.

And what Jew ever thought of observing one three-hundred-and-sixty-fifth part of time, or one day in three hundred and sixty-five and no day in particular, and calling that the passover? And we might as well talk of celebrating our national independence on one day in three hundred and sixty-five and no day in particular, as to talk of celebrating the rest-day of Jehovah upon one day in seven and no day in particular. The veriest American idiot that can recollect of ever hearing about George Washington or the Declaration of Independence, might well laugh at the folly of changing the day of our national celebration. Verily, as our Lord has said, the men of this world are wiser in their generation than the children of light. It is only in matters of religion that people seem to be satisfied with that which, in regard to any other subject, would be considered consummate folly.

And do these men who use the one-day-in-seven-and-no-day-in-particular theory, advocate a change of the Sabbath from the rest-day of the Father, to the resurrection-day of the Son? Then I inquire of them, Who ever thought of celebrating the resurrection of Christ on one day in seven and no day in particular? If they say that this can be done, then I inquire again, Where is the change of the Sabbath? Was it a change from one day in seven and no day in particular of the former dispensation, to one day in seven and no day in particular of the present dispensation? This would be "confusion worse confounded."

And to those who assert that redemption, as a greater work, is to be celebrated on the first day of the week, [369] as creation was anciently to be celebrated on the seventh day of the week, I would say, We only have your word for that. Please notice these facts:

1. The Bible is silent relative to redemption's being greater than creation. Who knows that it is?

2. The Bible is silent as to the observance of a day to commemorate redemption. Who knows that a day should be kept for that purpose?

3. We have in the Lord's supper, and baptism, memorials of the two great events in the history of the Redeemer's work for man. These are appropriate.

4. There is no fitness in keeping a day of weekly repose to commemorate the agonies of the crucifixion of Christ, or the activities of the morning of his resurrection.

5. But if a day of the week should be kept, to celebrate man's redemption, which should it be? the day on which he shed his blood for our sins? the day on which he rose for our justification/ or the day on which he ascended to the Father, to intercede for sinners? The day of the crucifixion, when the greatest event for man's redemption occurred, has the first claim. The apostle does not say that we have redemption through the resurrection; but he does say, "We have redemption through his blood." Ephesians 1:7. Now if a day should be kept to celebrate redemption, should it not be the day on which he shed his blood? Redemption is not completed; but in the Lord's supper and baptism are two memorials of the greatest events that have occurred in connection with this work for man. Neither of these are weekly memorials. Baptism may be received by the believer on any day of the week; and it is said of the emblems of the broken body and shed blood of the Son of God, without reference to any particular [370] day, "As often as ye eat this bread and drink this cup, ye do show the Lord's death till he come." 1 Corinthians 11:26. These memorials point back to the death, burial, and resurrection, of Jesus Christ. God's great memorial points back to the day of his rest. And why not let all these remain, answering the purpose for which they were instituted? Why should the work of creation be lost sight of in the work of redemption? Why not celebrate both here? Both are equally remembered hereafter. It is said of the redeemed:

"And they sung a new song, saying, Thou art worthy to take the book, and to open the seals thereof; for thou wast slain, and hast redeemed us to God by thy blood out every kindred, and tongue, and people, and nation." Revelation 5:9. The same also "cast their crowns before the throne, saying, Thou art worthy, O Lord, to receive glory, and honor, and power; for thou hast *created* all things, and for thy pleasure they are and were created."

Revelation 4:10, 11. Here the redeemed are represented as ascribing praise to both the Creator and the Redeemer. And again, every created intelligence in the universe, in joyful sympathy with man in view of his redemption, is represented in chap. 5:13, as ascribing "blessing, and honor, and glory, and power, unto Him that sitteth upon the throne [the Creator], and unto the Lamb [the Redeemer], forever and ever."

We here see that the redeemed, with all the enrapturing facts of redemption completed before them, do not lose sight of the creation. The Creator shares their adoration equally with the Redeemer. How, then, must Adam have felt, when, in the garden of Eden, he first awoke to all the glories of this creation which the redeemed so joyfully remember! Fresh from the hand of his Creator, he springs to life in all the vigor of perfect [371] manhood. With an intellect capable of appreciating the glories of Eden, and comprehending the grandeur and dignity of his position, and with a heart unsullied by sin, how must he have turned in gratitude and adoration toward the mighty Maker of himself and all these glories! If the redeemed could cast their crowns before Jehovah in reverent worship, in view of a creation accomplished over six thousand years before their song of praise was uttered, how must every fiber of Adam's being have thrilled with emotions of thanksgiving and adoration to the beneficent Author of his creation, as he stood there in Eden, enraptured with the strange delight of a new existence! And how could he best express the emotions of his heart? Would it not be by celebrating, amid all the surrounding glories of his Eden home, a day of rest in honor of his God? Say not that Adam had no occasion for the Sabbath in Eden. It was the very means by which he would rise into communion with his Maker, and offer the service of a grateful heart to him from whom he had just received the gift of life and all its blessings.

And if the Sabbath was thus appropriate, thus necessary, in Eden, what shall we say of it since the fall? With sin came man's estrangement from God, and his proneness to forget his Maker, and wander away from him. How much more needful the Sabbath, then, that he might not entirely break away from the moorings which held him to the heavenly world. The flood of sin and crime has rolled broader and deeper with each succeeding year; and the further we come from Paradise, the weaker and more prone to sin do we find the race, and hence more in need of God's great memorial.

Did Adam, while yet unfallen in Eden, surrounded with all its heavenly influences, and in free and open [372] converse with his Maker, need the Sabbath? How much more, when, with the gates of Paradise forever closed against him, he could no longer speak face to face with his Creator, but must henceforth grapple with the sinful promptings of his own heart, and grope his way amid the moral darkness that began to settle upon the world when the glorious light of Eden was obscured by sin! And if needed then by Adam, how much more still by Abel, whose eyes had never looked upon the beautiful garden, and who had never personally experienced the nearness to Heaven which Adam there enjoyed! And it was still more essential to the spiritual wants of the race in the days of Enoch and the more degenerate age of Noah, when the influence of Eden, like the last rays of twilight from the setting sun, were fading from the hearts of men. Abraham needed it still more to save him from the idolatry of his father's house; and Moses and the Jewish nation, yet more, to keep them from the open apostasy of the heathen nations around them. But more than to Abraham, to Moses, or to the Jews, was the holy Sabbath a necessity to the church in the gospel dispensation, when the Man of Sin was to arise, and oppose, and exalt himself above all that is called God; when there should be a tendency to multiply feasts and festivals, uncalled for by the Scriptures, in honor of Christ, and to rank the Sabbath of Jehovah with Jewish ceremonies, and sweep it away with them.

And now we have come down nearly six thousand years from the gates of Paradise. Through all this time, has sin reigned, and iniquity abounded, and the hearts of men grown less and less susceptible of divine impressions, and in the same proportion more prone to forget the Creator. And can we dispense with the Sabbath [373] now? True, the dawn of Eden restored, is visibly approaching; but the world is farther from God than ever before. Infidelity and atheism run riot, and seemingly the race would fain banish all thoughts and love of God from mind and heart. More than ever, then, is the Sabbath now needed, to save men from utter apostasy. With all the original reasons for the institution, the accumulated necessities of six thousand years of sin, now call upon us to throw all possible safeguards around this sacred institution. If ever a memorial of the great God and a golden link to bind man to Heaven, was needed, it is needed now. And the necessity of this institution will even yet increase through the few remaining days of peril. Can we dispense with it? Never. More and more sacredly should we cherish it, while with earnest hearts we breathe the prayer,

> "Let earth, O Lord, again be thine,
> As ere with vengeance cursed;
> And let the holy Sabbath shine
> As glorious as at first."

Adventist Pioneer Library

Made in the USA
Middletown, DE
26 July 2019